Advanced Praise

"I don't think there is a single top management team that we serve globally that isn't talking about collaboration internally, with suppliers, and other strategic allies. For those of us who witnessed historic strategic alliances that fail to produce value, Enabling Collaboration is a refreshing look at the key components that must be managed for success. It's one of the best guides to both collaboration and strategic alliances that I've found for consultants, facilitators, and executive coaches who work with leaders. Business schools who teach strategic alliances will find this book a useful text. Anyone who wants more collaborative partnerships or needs to work closely with strategic partners should have a copy of this book."

Barbara Singer Cheng
CEO Executive Core
www.executivecore.com

"If you desire to consciously create powerful, productive strategic alliances and partnerships, this book shows you how to prepare, invite, negotiate, create, and launch successful partnership initiatives. Echavarria clearly lays out the steps that need to be taken, along with the mind-set and approaches required for success. Had I been able to apply the 5 Territories of Alliance Development when I was an executive, our firm would have achieved far greater success with our strategic partnerships. "

Dorianne Cotter-Lockard, *PhD*
Former Fortune 100 Company executive and collaboration expert

"Enabling Collaboration is a heroic effort to provide a grand buffet of research and approaches towards learning, development and collaboration. Echavarria has assembled vast resources, provocative insights and questions in service of coherence and integration. Once you like what you have tasted, dig deeper in the delectable and potent bibliography. You will not be disappointed!"

Sarita Chawla, *MCC,*
Senior New Ventures West Faculty
Coach & OD Consultant

"Martin Echavarria's *Enabling Collaboration* is a rare and important gift to leadership, in that it not only discusses the importance of collaboration within alliances and partnerships, but carefully lays out the critical "how-tos" of this work. It is an invaluable guide to increasing effectiveness in an ever more globally connected world of business and relationships. Mr. Echavarria offers wisdom from his real-world experience as a leader, coach and master "connector" of people and organizations."

Ruben Rodriguez
Executive Coach at Integral Impact

"Enabling Collaboration presents us with the missing link why businesses alliances and partnership fail ...the lack of understanding and focus on "group leadership" instead of customary "individual leadership" focus. This is a must-read for leaders in all focus areas, it provides several insightful guidelines to help organizations re-think what will catapult them into future success while guaranteeing their current achievements."

CB Bowman, *MBA, CMC, BCC, MCEC*
CEO Association of Corporate Executive Coaches

ENABLING
COLLABORATION

ACHIEVING SUCCESS THROUGH
STRATEGIC ALLIANCES AND **PARTNERSHIPS**

MARTIN ECHAVARRIA

Published by
LID Publishing Inc.
31 West 34th Street, Suite 7004,
New York, NY 10001, US

One Adam Street
London. WC2N 6LE

info@lidpublishing.com
www.lidpublishing.com

A member of:

www.businesspublishersroundtable.com

Printed in the United States
ISBN: 978-0-9860793-3-7

Cover and page design: Caroline Li

ENABLING
COLLABORATION

ACHIEVING SUCCESS THROUGH
STRATEGIC ALLIANCES AND **PARTNERSHIPS**

MARTIN ECHAVARRIA

LONDON   MONTERREY
MADRID   SHANGHAI
MEXICO CITY   BOGOTA
NEW YORK   BUENOS AIRES
BARCELONA   SAN FRANCISCO

Dedicated to...

My Mom and Dad,
and my sons Adrian and Kiran

Table of Contents

Acknowledgments

I first want to thank Monica Agostino for her mentorship, support and dedication to my work and this book. She introduced me to the work of Enrique Pichon-Rivière and many other thought leaders in social psychology and spent many hours editing and reviewing. I also appreciate very much the help of Kristen McLean who read through the manuscript and provided valuable feedback. Thanks to Jon Freeman, for his support and guidance with the work of Clare Graves, and Clara Castillo who spent many hours organizing all the articles, books and resources that went into the book.

The insights and methods described in the book would not have been possible if it were not for Scotiabank, where the methodologies and processes were optimized. Thank you to Peter Kastanis of Scotiabank, who had the foresight to see partnerships as critical to building their business. His persistence and dedication allowed us to produce some very successful alliances that continue today. Of course there is equal appreciation to the executives and their teams of alliance partners we worked with over the years. Through their honest engagement, I was able to learn for myself how to support groups to be productive. To Luce Veilleux and Jeff Hindle who supported alliances at Scotiabank. I also want to thank the people I worked with at MasterCard and American Express where I was able to learn some valuable lessons in how to establish longer-term partnerships. They include Paulo Claussen, Dan Austin and others.

I would like to also express my appreciation of Noah Rabinowitz, who introduced me to Lore International and then Korn/Ferry, which helped me to deepen my own coaching work and broaden my professional experience in collaborative leadership. Thank you to Barb Cheng of Executive Core for her support of my work and Bill Isaacs for his excellent work in group dialogue. I'd also like to thank the people of New Ventures West, where I received my coaching certification. Special thanks to Ruben Rodriguez, Sarita Chawla and the work of James Flaherty. Their compassion and capacity to stay in relationship and in human connection has informed much of what I do today.

Finally, I am thankful for and awed by the amazing work of the many thought leaders, researchers and contributors to the fields of partnerships and alliances, social psychology, systems thinking, collective collaboration, human development, and integral thought from which I have learned and drawn out the methodology of this book. My work rests on their insights. And finally to my good friend Andrei Savchenko, who had to endure my rants over the course of two years writing the book.

Introduction

We are living in the most challenging interdependent times in human history, which is also one of the most promising. Products are designed in one part of the world, using resources made in another, while they are manufactured in a different continent altogether. Global shipping brings these goods to everyone's doorstep. People living in the most isolated part of the planet produce and interact with others across oceans and continents. Even young companies, run by small teams, forge international collaborations to bring products to market that can change and disrupt current business models on a significant scale.

Today, companies, non-profits and public agencies work together across all elements of their supply and value chains to bring products and services consistently to market. They collaborate through partnerships and alliances on every level: from creating the next new technical device to working on environmental issues.

Clearly the age of global interdependence socially, economically and environmentally is indeed here, and the opportunity it brings will profoundly change the way companies and organizations do their work. Because of today's global complexity, we can no longer expect to form successful organizations on the backs of individuals alone but also on group collaboration. Individual leadership alone will not get us there. We must learn to grow our collaborative leadership capability, while applying ourselves individually to contribute to its emergence. It is only then through group collaboration, that we can be successful in developing organizational partnerships and alliances to meet the challenges and opportunities of today.

Surely, by their sheer size and ability to mobilize, corporations are at the center of realizing the true potential of global partnership collaboration. Out of the largest world economies, many companies overtake entire countries when comparing Gross Domestic Product figures to corporate revenues. According to the 2014 Fortune 500 list, Wal-Mart is the world's largest public company employing 2 million people and generating top-line revenues of US$479 billion. This makes Wal-Mart about the 30th largest "economy" on the planet, ahead of whole countries like Venezuela and the Philippines, whose populations are 30 to 100 times greater than Wal-Mart's employee base. Companies like Wal-Mart employ people across the globe, transferring physical and economic value seamlessly, a capability that no nation state can match. They do this by organizing and coordinating a network of activities that bring products and services to market.

Partnerships and alliances are a key component of these supply and value chains. From product design to the sourcing of raw materials, and across channel relationships, partnerships and alliances are interwoven throughout all supply and demand elements of corporate value creation. That is one piece of the potential of collaboration: the efficient and effective management of supply and value chains that leverage the interconnected nature of world markets. The other important element is the ability to address the social and environmental challenges faced on a worldwide basis by interweaving the way they create value through a network of partnerships.

A case in point is Unilever, a large global consumer products firm which operates in over 190 countries and sells to more than 2 billion people globally. In 2009, the company launched The Compass business plan, and in 2012, the *Unilever Sustainable Living Plan.* By completely reshaping Unilever's supply chain through strategic partnerships, these ambitious directives are meant to decouple Unilever's future growth from any negative environmental and social impact. Since the project's inception, Unilever has launched several multi-year strategic alliances with companies, non-governmental organizations (NGOs), small- and medium-size enterprises and R&D experts and academics. In 2010, for example, Unilever signed a multi-year partnership with Jacobs Engineering Group Inc., an international technical professional services firm, to reduce its carbon, water and waste footprint across manufacturing sites. By the end of 2014, over 50% of Unilever's factories were part of their *World Class Manufacturing* program (Unilever, 2013, p. 20). By 2015, because of a unique value chain partnership with the NGO Rainforest Alliance, Unilever will source all tea for its Lipton and PG Tips products from certified growers and by 2020, 100% of tea will be sustainably sourced. These goals will also be applied to other natural resources used in Unilever products across their supply chain. In addition, Unilever has partnered with competitors such as Nestle, Danone, and The Coca-Cola Company to form a plant-based bioplastics alliance to look for alternatives to petroleum-based packaging. These strategic collaborations make Unilever's supply chain more sustainable and, as a result, more resilient to the uncertainties and ambiguities of a complex and interconnected global economy.

Unilever is just one example of a growing trend in making strategic collaboration the key competency for sustained competitive advantage. In 1980, only 2% of corporate value worldwide was tied into some kind of collaborative venture. Today, as much as 25% of corporate revenues and value are tied to alliances. This amounts to trillions of dollars that depends on business collaboration. Additionally, the total number of alliances that started over the last decade continues to grow significantly. International alliances in emerging markets in the form of joint ventures grew from US$5.2 billion in 2000 to US$12.1 billion in 2012, doubling even after the recession of 2009, mirroring Foreign Direct Investment (FDI) growth trends that continue to expand (Yuk, 2012). From international go-to-market partnerships to R&D alliances that reduce costs to operational collaborations that combine back-office processes, today's companies are partnering more deeply and broadly across all parts of their supply and value chains. They do so to access new markets, reduce costs and become more nimble, competitive and innovative, thus increasing their resilience as they face the complexities of the international marketplace.

Nike, headquartered in Beaverton, Oregon, is the largest producer of athletic footwear and athletic gear worldwide. Yet Nike does not manufacture a single shoe or athletic shirt. Rather, they produce with strategic suppliers in China, Indonesia, Vietnam and the Philippines to reduce costs and maintain flexibility. Boeing, the world's largest aircraft company, manufactures its planes by purchasing 95% of its parts through a network of partner suppliers (Elmuti & Kathawala, 2001, p. 205). Apple and IBM are now partnering to integrate their capabilities for shared customers. For Apple, a partnership with IBM opens an opportunity to enter the corporate market to sustain growth. For IBM, leveraging business software expertise and big-data applications with a product like the iPad makes its products and services more accessible and easier to use. In the biotechnology and pharmaceutical industries, biotech-pharma alliances have grown since the early 1990s as smaller firms with competencies in scientific research partner with larger firms who have strength in drug development. In 2011 alone, strategic alliances amounting to nearly US$2 billion were launched between Samsung and Quintiles, Merck & Co. and Hanwha Chemical (South Korea), to name a few (IMAP, 2012, p. 8). All over the globe, firms operating in a variety of industries are establishing partnerships and alliances to bring products and services to market more efficiently and sustainably, developing opportunities and capabilities that generate more value than any company could accrue alone.

The opportunities to form collaborative alliances are not lost to not-for-profit organizations. NGOs and public entities turn to partnerships and alliances as a strategic tool to grow and lower costs. Many non-profits have combined back-office processes and others conducted joint programing activities. Ten years ago, Big Brothers Big Sisters of America and Boys & Girls Clubs of America began a joint programing alliance that continues to operate today. At a local level, they work together with schools, community organizations and businesses. Promoting local partnerships between mentor charities and clubs seems to make particular sense. NGOs are no different. Many of them create long-term strategic relationships with private-sector companies that advance their causes and support companies to build better business practices.

However, it is abundantly clear that delivering on the promise of collaborative partnerships is challenging. Studies from the Association of Strategic Alliance Professionals (ASAP) dating as far back as 2000 have consistently pointed to a real gap between the potential of these alliances and their actual success rate. According to ASAP, even in this recent 15 year period of growth, 50% to 60% of alliances fail, and 50% of those that survive do not meet expectations. This means that only one in four alliances are successful, a poor result for such a critical business strategy. These failures are costing global companies not only billions of dollars in wasted resources, effort and revenue, but also lost opportunities to grow and excel.

Much of the literature points to the underlying relationship dynamics as the main cause of alliance failure. ASAP proposes that alliance culture is the next major stumbling block after good alliance design and tools are put in place (De Man, Duysters, Krijnen, & Luvison, 2012, p. 9). According to alliances academic Ard Pieter De Man, professor at VU University Amsterdam, failure to resolve the trust and control dilemma is another major reason for such high failure rates and one of the key challenges in developing partnerships (De Man, 2014, pp. 1–20). Additionally, experts agree that building a collaboration mind-set and establishing collaboration behaviors is the solution. They also cite the importance of investing time to build relationships with internal stakeholders and partners (Hughes & Weiss, 2007, p. 7). It is clear that to increase success rates, the intersubjective capacities of individuals and groups to create a culture of collaboration, as well as the application of effective alliance processes, practices and tools need to be in place (Vanpoucke & Vereecke, 2009, pp. 20-21).

The focus of *Enabling Collaboration* is to describe a new framework and provide a methodology, a map, practices and tools in order to achieve a successful rate of partnerships and alliances. It is as much a question of learning to collaborate internally within a company, as it is about collaborating with other companies, nationally as well as internationally. The methodology presented can be applied to all kinds of groups. From building cross cultural, interorganizational or multi-disciplinary strategic alliances to working with internal teams and members of the board, the methodology enables group collaboration to be developed. The goal is improved Collaborative Advantage, a skill and capability needed to succeed and remain relevant in today's economy.

The framework is centered on a methodology for coaching and facilitating group operability, as well as a business process for building strategic alliances and partnerships. As such, it draws from years of research on groups from social and group theorists (Beck, 1996; Graves, 2005; Isaacs, 1999; Lewin, 1948; Maturana, 1996; Moreno, 2008; Pichon-Rivière, 1985; Senge, 1990; Wilber, 2000). At the same time, the work incorporates thinking on business strategy, theory and practice in strategic alliances as well as in the fields of systems thinking, communications theory, collaborative economics, and organizational development (De Man, 2013; Griffin, 2003; Lewis, 1990; Littlejohn & Foss, 2011; Schein, 1999; Schelling, 1980; von Bertalanffy, 1968).

Of particular importance to the methodology is Enrique Pichon-Rivière, a world-renowned Argentine psychoanalyst and social and group theorist recognized in Europe and Latin America for his applied research in operative group processes. *Enabling Collaboration* introduces Pichon-Rivière's methodology on "small groups" to strategic alliances and partnerships. His applied theoretical framework uses tools that map the intersubjective journey of groups and provides methods and approaches that support group cohesion and collaboration.

Working together productively, small groups discover shared goals and opportunities through communication and cooperation. This enables the group to become operative, promoting learning through productive engagement. Pichon-Rivière's approach provides important insights which help to address the subjective challenges of trust and culture that lead to alliances' success. The ***Operative Partnership Methodology*** presented in Section Two provides a rich foundation for supporting groups to collaborate effectively, thus producing successful partnerships that lead toward successful outcomes. While this book is centered on the topic of alliances and partnership, it is also an applied methodology for enabling *Collaborative Leadership*; that is, the capacity of groups to productively work together.

The thinking behind the framework is simple: successful partnerships and alliances are possible if the human dynamics of relationships—clear communication, group cohesion, complementarity of ideas, intentions, emotions and goals—are given the same importance as the financial models, marketing and PR strategies, operating contracts, governance processes, and negotiations: elements that are at times considered more important in business practice.

Collaborative Leadership, a posteriori to any sustainable alliance, conceives group leadership irrespective of individual leadership capabilities. It is a phenomenon that comes from the moment-by-moment reflective inquiry at the group level. It emerges with the support of the ***Partnership Coach*** who employs the *Operative Partnership Methodology* described later in Section Two.

The *Operative Partnership Methodology* coincides with the **5-*Territories of Alliance Development*** presented in Section Three. This is an alliances business process that employs tools and facilitative interventions to produce the best possible partnership. The territories are:

> **Territory One: *Align & Prepare*** aligning the alliance strategy to the corporate development plan and preparing the organization with the right tools, and teams for developing strategic relationships.

> **Territory Two: *Invite & Commit*** the process, tools and activities by which a company invites another company to form a partnership and from which they commit to developing an alliance.

> **Territory Three: *Create & Consolidate*** the work by which the group creates the roadmap of the alliance and consolidates the key structural elements into an Alliances Term Sheet.

> **Territory Four: *Negotiate & Launch*** involves the negotiation of key contractual elements into a workable contract and the launching of the alliance in the marketplace.

> **Territory Five: *Sustain & Deepen*** the continued work of the group to sustain the alliance and partnership after launch and the activities to deepen the business relationship in new potential areas of collaboration.

This framework incorporates over 15 years of developing alliances and partnerships in the field and integrates the work of strategic alliances academics, such as Ard-Pieter De Man (2013) and Jordan D. Lewis (1999), among other thinkers in the fields of negotiations, strategy and business practice. Integrating the understanding of such diverse sources provides valuable insights into creating successful group and organizational collaboration that can be applied across industries, organizations and cultures. Together, they form a framework that can be applied simultaneously as practice for Collaborative Leadership and as a process for developing organizational alliances of all forms and types.

The *Operative Partnership Methodology* and the *5-Territories of Alliance Development* are built upon five key concepts.

1. Group *Collaborative Leadership* is foundational for any collective activity to be successful, an alliance or any endeavor that requires a group of people working together toward complementary or supplementary objectives. Focusing on groups, this is leadership beyond the individual but not instead of the individual. Individuality remains important to group collaboration by the contribution made to its emergence.

2. *Collaborative Leadership* and the capacity and capability to move into co-creationship are fundamentally an emotional group process of relatedness, belonging and mutuality. It occurs and emerges only at the group level and can be practiced only by groups when they come together to work. It cannot be practiced at the individual level.

3. Collaboration in alliances and partnerships can and will move beyond problem solving into a collective orientation to co-create a desired future.

4. The journey toward group collaboration goes beyond learning into the experience of actually doing.

5. It is essential to have an objective third-party *Partnership Coach* working as an internal resource or an external support to build perspective by illuminating collective blind spots and navigating the inherent challenges when groups come together to work.

The goal of *Enabling Collaboration* is to help bring *Collaborative Leadership* capability to corporations and organizations providing groups and teams a way to perform better together in their partnerships and alliances, so that today's complexity can become tomorrow's shared coherent productivity. *Enabling Collaboration* provides a practical approach to address productively the challenges that occur when individuals meet together to form alliances and partnerships. The methodology is founded on applicable theories and practices that support groups as they traverse the challenges of collaboration. The method articulates a process that can be followed, business practices that support success, specific tools to use and a clear understanding of the professional roles and skills needed.

Section One
The Collaborative Enterprise

The *Collaborative Enterprise* is an organization that consistently demonstrates the collective capabilities to collaborate internally as individuals and as groups and teams. It recognizes and works coherently and productively with all its shareholders and stakeholders. It engages with its community, within and outside their industry as part of an ecosystem of inputs, outputs, suppliers, customers, vendors and partners. It does so to face, in a productive and meaningful way, the complexities of the modern international, interconnected and interdependent marketplace.

Most certainly, there are companies that operate at higher levels of collaboration than others. Some are on the path to system-wide collaboration and others may be less operative but, nonetheless, are on the same journey. All companies operate with some level of collaboration and great majority of today's executives view collaboration as a key strategic capability. In a PricewaterhouseCoopers' annual Global CEO Survey from 2009, 75% of respondents rated partnerships as 'important' or 'critical' to their business. In a 2012 study by IBM, *Leading through Connections*, 63% of CEOs noted a collaborative environment as a key focus for their firms. Collaboration in all its forms, either internally between organizational teams or through strategic alliances and partnerships is the capability that leaders believe will drive corporate success in this new era. However, there is no clear understanding of what it really is to be a *Collaborative Enterprise* and even less of an understanding on how to become more collaborative.

The Collaborative Enterprise is more than a Learning Organization. Through group relating, it can metabolize learning effectively to catalyze group operability into productive action. This kind of enterprise practices the disciplines of the *Learning Organization*, originally coined by Peter Senge (1990) in his book *The Fifth Discipline*. He described five disciplines that together help companies to learn and respond to competition and the wider business environment. The first two include *Systems Thinking*, which considers wholes and interrelationships rather than static snapshots (1990, p. 68), and *Personal Mastery*, which refers to personal growth and learning (Ibid., p. 141). The third and fourth disciplines include *Mental Models*, the images, assumptions and stories that individuals carry about the world and which determine how they make sense of it and take action (Ibid, pp. 174–75). *Shared Vision* involves the articulation of a common potential that unites organizations toward excellence and includes the personal visions of individuals. The final discipline, Team Learning, involves a commonality of purpose, a shared vision and an understanding of the way each individual complements another's efforts (Ibid, p. 234).

The *Collaborative Enterprise* takes Team Learning into the next stage of organizational excellence by channeling the capabilities and capacities of Small Groups, which are the unit of collaborative productivity. Small Groups as defined by Pichon-Rivière are made up of people who meet in a temporal space and, through their internalized models of each other, operate together as a unit. In this sense, *Small Groups* learn to manage the explicit activities they engage in while, facing the implicit relational–emotional obstacles they experience. *Small Groups* of 3 to 20 people are either a team or a collective group of people that come together to perform a task and then disperse. In this case, they can include intact teams working jointly, e.g. marketing and finance groups collaborating or one company looking to develop a strategic partnership and alliance with another.

Consequently, based on Pichon-Rivière's (1985) model of group operability, learning is not only based on exploring fixed assumptions and shared mental models (Senge, Ibid), which certainly contribute to operability, but also includes the group's journey toward relationship. Group learning incorporates the psycho-social and emotional needs of the group, including the different roles the group members take on as they become a productive operating unit.

The *Collaborative Enterprise* operates from a conception that is quite different from that of the atomized company, a company that is only interested in its own growth. Unlike the atomized companies that are slowed and politicized by the complaints of marketing not working well with finance, finance having difficulty with operations and so on, for the *Collaborative Enterprise* there are practices and processes employed to support teams and groups to work together effectively, consistently and productively. Here, a culture of collaboration is in place. It can be associated with the entire organization or it can be treated as a subsystem, such as an alliance development unit that functions to extend inter-organizational alliances across an industry (Kożuch, 2009, p. 21) to advance collaboration and improve competitiveness.

Whatever the case, the *Collaborative Enterprise* is not meant to become a panacea of the perfect work environment, but rather a place where the difficulties of group relating are leveraged. In this respect, conflict between people and groups exists, yet it is used in a productive way to help groups work through the challenges of learning and decision taking.

It is common knowledge that meetings at the highest levels of global firms can be rife with politics. People are afraid of saying something that is not perfectly articulated and scientifically accurate, stifling innovation, creativity and capability to learn and address the realities of global complexity. However, for the *Collaborative Enterprise*, the politics may not go away fully, but the team's capabilities to deal with the difficulties are enhanced. A *Collaborative Enterprise* does not have to be a major Fortune 100 company or a global networked firm. It could be a local restaurant in which there exists a high level of collaboration and cohesion where people work together productively. All the staff members earn a good living wage, help each other through productive disagreement, challenging and jointly creating to produce an optimal experience for clients. Customers with special dietary needs are given options, and suppliers deliver freshness and quality. Thus, the restaurant functions as a successful and coherent enterprise of relatedness and collaboration. In doing so, the *Collaborative Enterprise* creates an internal capability unique to itself. *Collaborative Advantage* is built upon the expanding capacity to partner internally as well as externally with other firms (Kożuch, 2009, p.23-26).

Expanding *Circles of Influence* and *Circles of Concern*

The concepts of *Circles of Influence* and *Circles of Concern* originated from the work of Steven Covey (1993). In *First things First*, Covey distinguished between *Circles of Influence*—places where individuals can make a difference—and *Circles of Concern*—areas of interest where an individual's subjective thoughts and worries lie (such as work, children, marriage and other areas of life). Covey determined that, for individuals to be highly effective, they should focus efforts where their *Circles of Influence* and *Circles of Concern* converge. These same concepts can be extrapolated to the *Collaborative Enterprise*. Greater collaboration can occur across a company's supply and value chains where there exists expanded convergence of *Circles of Concern* and *Circles of Influence*. For a company, *Circles of Concern* relate to the collective thoughts and areas of interests that guide corporate commitments and promises. These are expressed through a company's vision, core values, ideology and purpose related to employees, customers, clients, suppliers and others. *Circles of Influence*, stemming from *Circles of Concern*, are where resources and activities are placed (Figure 1).

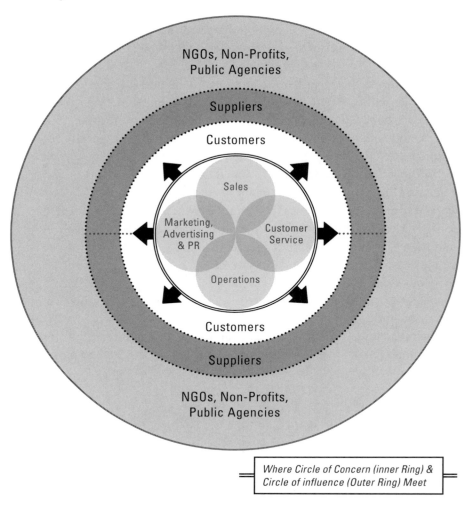

NGOs, Non-Profits,
Public Agencies

Suppliers

Customers

Sales

Marketing,
Advertising
& PR

Customer
Service

Operations

Customers

Suppliers

NGOs, Non-Profits,
Public Agencies

*Where Circle of Concern (inner Ring) &
Circle of influence (Outer Ring) Meet*

Figure 1 – Expanding Circles of Concern and Circles of Influence

Take, for instance, a company that produces men's shaving products in the metropolitan area of New York. The company operates its business in a specific geographic market. It employs a handful of staff to sell the product through a few high-end boutique stores. Here the company's area of concern could be simply to maintain a high-end market segment that only caters to the local market. The concern is for its localized customers, employees and the manufacturer that produces its products. However, should the company want to expand its *circle of concern* and engage in different activities, such as marketing its product as environmentally and animal-friendly or perhaps becoming interested in workers' rights, it must then shift its *circle of influence* to work with other vendors, who are perhaps so specialized that they become strategic partners. For instance, to build its brand and because it believes strongly in animal rights, the company may invest a percentage of its profits in the preservation of a particular species or decide not to produce any products tested on animals. It may also partner with nonprofit companies, expanding its *circle of influence* as a result of its *circle of concern*.

As the *Circles of Influence and Concern* expand, the *Collaborative Enterprise* begins to function from a new perspective, which can improve its ability to react to market changes and oftentimes respond to market opportunities. It sets in place perpetually interlocking feedback loops of relatedness within all its *Circles of Influence* (customer service, sales, marketing, etc.) that weave a tightly knit canvas of optimal learning and practice with outside customers, suppliers, strategic collaborators, partners, government and nonprofit social groups across all areas of its business.

Collaborative Leadership

The *Collaborative Enterprise* thrives from a particular capability to tap into the potential of groups to partner and create opportunities and address challenges together. Through internal firm activities, as well as by collaborating productively with other companies across the supply and value chains as interdependent actors of a system, the *Collaborative Enterprise* becomes more resilient and successful. Regardless of whether the partnering occurs between the marketing and finance teams within a company or on a global scale between Nissan and Renault, the foundations are the same. They involve groups working together based on shared context, interests and affiliations where learning and co-creation is enabled. The only real difference is size and scope, but the essence is the same: *Collaborative Leadership*.

Partnerships and Alliances Framework

Through enabling *Collaborative Leadership*, the *Collaborative Enterprise* builds partnerships and alliances that extend into the outer rings (Figure 1). The *Partnership and Alliances Framework* is made up of two interdependent elements, the relational and the structural, embedded in a shared context applied to help companies develop their business collaboration (Figure 2). In this context the term *Partnership* refers to the human dynamics of connecting in order to create a functional and operative business relationship. The term *Alliance* refers to the objective components of the business structure that is eventually created through collaboration as a result of the operative relationships established.

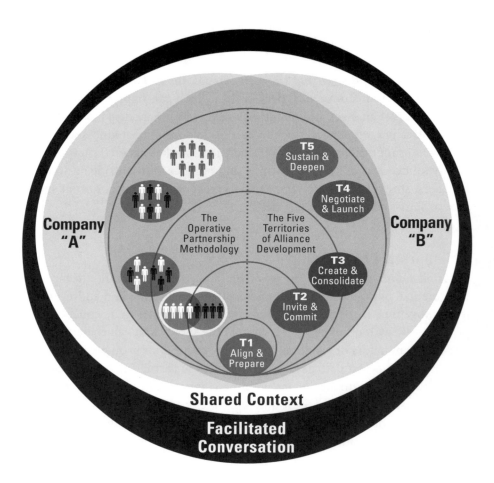

Figure 2 – Partnerships and Alliances Framework

The *Partnership Coach* supports the groups by facilitating conversations, creating the atmosphere of success, supporting decision-making and promoting shared learning (pp. 29-32). He does this by employing the *Operative Partnership Methodology* and using the *5-Territories of Alliance Development* described in sections two and three respectively.

Section Two
Operative Partnership Methodology

Chapter 1
Collaborative Leadership through Group Coaching

People that choose to partner, either within their own company or in a corporate alliance made up of different teams, operate in particular industries and cultures and do things in particular ways. Through the alliance development process, individuals from each company join to become one united group. It is the group leadership practices and how the groups come together—including the ways they communicate, cooperate and traverse challenges—that determine how successful they are in creating an alliance. Partnership development is all about group leadership. Yet group leadership is often left out of the focus of mainstream leadership literature and business practice.

The literature about leadership is heavily weighted toward the importance of the individual in the corporate world, as well as in government and non-profits. At the time of writing, only one of Amazon's top ten leadership books focuses on teams, still with the individual leader of a team being the unit of focus. In partnerships, alliances and other team collaborations, the group is the true leader, but there is not much written on group leadership as a dynamic of study in and of itself. In much of the literature, group leadership is seen as a result of individual leadership, and not as a separate creation. Additionally, many of these books go directly from individuals to an organizational perspective, skipping groups altogether. The idea that an organization can truly grow and consistently meet the challenges of the modern economic system if groups are completely left out of the equation seems incongruous.

Successful group leadership emerges from something altogether different and not simply as the result of individual leadership driving group success. Understanding the difference between group leadership vs. individual leadership is a critical component of successful alliance building and collaboration.

The Leadership Summation Fallacy

The *Leadership* Summation Fallacy results from the false idea that adding up driven, perfect, conscious individual leaders results in strong collective leadership. It assumes that when individuals work on their own leadership and come together with others, they will all work effectively as a group. The business metaphor *"a team is only as strong as its weakest link"* underlines the *Summation Fallacy* suggesting that all links are somehow added together in some linear fashion.

Additionally, there are "dream teams" made up of strong leaders that ultimately fail despite expectations that they would succeed. Major corporations formed by the "best and brightest" of business school graduates, such as Enron, WorldCom and Tyco, ended in disaster. Enron and WorldCom went into bankruptcy due to accounting fraud and pervasive corruption, and Tyco due to outright theft, all occurring at the highest levels of management. Although individuals do come together regularly in "group configurations", that does not mean they are truly operative. How they function together, their capacity to communicate, dialogue, and discuss important issues directly and authentically as a group is critical. At the individual level, alliances and partnership leaders do have to work on themselves, through leadership coaching and other means. Yet the individual leadership development necessary for successful alliances and business collaboration is in itself insufficient for partnership development.

As an individual subject, a person enters a group with a system of unconscious interpretations, fears, fixed ideas and relational qualities that interact and interrelate with other subjects. The chemistry of this interrelationship only becomes apparent when people begin to work together. Then, the individuals begin to discover their relationship challenges within the group and have to work through them. Partnership development requires *Collaborative Leader-ship* for success to happen and not individual leadership to be operative.

This approach considers the team as a whole, a body of interrelated capacities and capabilities that form, conform, conjoin and evolve to become the *Operative Partnership Group*. In partnership development, group members work through a process of conforming to and creating the team's reason for being together, its culture of communication and coalescence. Like individual rivers flowing into and creating an *in nasciente* body of water. The group that results is a systemic living and breathing entity that encompasses all members and transcends them not as a summation of 2+2 = 4, but instead as an emergence of something altogether new and distinct. It is this emergence through the partnership process that leads to a successful and productive group structure.

From Group Theory to Partnership Development

The study of groups in social psychology and as a scientific discipline in the social sciences started a little more than 100 years ago. As early as 1908, a few texts were published on the topic of social psychology depicting two different approaches to the science of groups (Franzoi, 2007). The work of William McDougall in *An Introduction to Social Psychology* (1908) focused on the individual as the key source of analysis for groups. In contrast, Edward Ross in *Social Psychology: An Outline and Source Book* (1908) is considered by many as a social psychologist focused on groups themselves and not considering individuals as relevant (Franzoi, 2007). Sigmund Freud in *Group Psychology and the Analysis of the Ego* (1922) depicted social psychological development as being part and parcel of all individual psychology. In this respect, he did not prioritize one level of analysis over another, but rather combined both. It was not for another 20 years that group theory and the study of groups truly began taking shape in North America, Europe and Latin America.

Important contributions to the study of groups began to emerge around the world in the 1940s, with many prominent thinkers escaping World War II and immigrating to North America. The US saw the work of Kurt Lewin, instrumental in using a scientific approach to the study of groups and how individuals are shaped by the world around them. His work provides understanding of the many contextual elements that act upon groups and individuals. In his

Field Theory in Social Science (1951), Lewin asserts that individuals can and should be studied in relation to the life-space in which they operate. Understanding this idea helps social change agents devise interventions that affect the social system and the groups that operate in them. Lewin defined the distinction between objective sociological problems and how they intersect with the subjective psychological and cultural problems of groups. In so doing, Lewin adopted the concept of T-groups, or training groups. Essentially T-groups were meetings of 3 to 20 people that studied and reflected upon the reactions of each member to the others. The aim was to discover and dissect group norms and dynamics including group emotional interactions. The T-group process assisted the group members to improve interaction by becoming more aware of how they affected each other emotionally. This helped Lewin to discover "sociologically characterized places, like gates in social channels, where attitudes count most for certain social processes and where individual or group decisions have a particularly great social affect" (1947, p. 147). Lewin discovered that emotions and the ways people relate become the conduits from which a group is able to work together as a whole. Another major contribution of Lewin's includes the development of action research influential in organizational development work, organizational leadership and group systems theory.

Jacob L. Moreno, a well-known contributor to the study of groups and a pioneer of group psychotherapy, is recognized for his development of sociometry, a quantitative method for measuring social relationships, and credited for his work in social network analysis. His work focused on helping groups become more alive and awake so that they could be more productive, innovative and creative.

In Great Britain, contemporaries of Lewin and Moreno, S.H. Foulks (1964) and Wilfred Bion (1961) developed important theories. Foulks was known for group therapy work "based on the recognition of man's social nature and of the basic need to relate to others" (Maglo, 2002, p. 31). He is known for identifying and articulating the problems and emotional states of groups conceived through his methods of the work group and the basic assumptions group. According to Bion, these processes are occurring simultaneously when groups interact. The work group refers to the activities and reasons why groups come together, while the basic assumptions group refers to the underlining dynamics operating below the surface that interferes with the group task (Bion, 1961, p. 63-64).

Having grown up in Argentina, Enrique Pichon-Rivière is a world renowned psychoanalyst, social and group psychology theorist, recognized for his groundbreaking work and applied research in operative group processes. He is studied in Europe and Latin America, but is not well known in the US. Combining the theoretical frameworks of Lewin, Moreno, and Bion, Pichon-Rivière developed an approach and methodology that can be applied in all manner of group interactions. Like Foulkes, Pichon-Rivière embarked on serious experimental research on how groups interact and through his studies conceived a "theoretical, methodological and technical" (Adamson, 2013, p.4) framework applicable to all kinds of business collaborations including alliances and partnerships. His methodology helps partnership developers map the inter-subjective journey that groups must undertake to build successful alliances. It also helps them to understand the challenges that groups face while providing a method to quantify group operability toward true collaboration. Coupled with group coaching and group facilitative support, Pichon-Rivière's framework becomes a tool for enabling successful strategic alliances to be created.

Applying Group Theory to Partnerships & Alliances

Business collaboration in the form of strategic alliances and partnerships involves two or more people collaborating together. In fact, often times, it involves several groups working concurrently. Since business collaboration occurs fundamentally at the group level, it is most consistent that group theory and practice be applied to establish successful strategic alliances and partnerships. Although people as individuals do take a part in becoming group members, collaboration occurs when they enter the group and coalesce into an operating process.

In this sense, *Collaborative Leadership* can only occur when participants come together to form a group with a distinct and separate identity from its individual members. Group leadership cannot be developed by individuals working on their own leadership development; group leadership is practiced by the group only at the group level. Even in the case of the team making the initial invitation to partner, the alliances business unit must also build their own collaborative leadership capabilities. As the partnership is being developed between the two companies and two alliances business teams, the leadership capabilities of both as a new alliance group must be fostered throughout the *5-Territories of Alliance Development*.

Therefore, a sensible path to partnership development is constructed through a group approach which requires group learning and the collective contributions of people from varied backgrounds. Focusing on the entire group's capabilities to communicate, collaborate, learn and face challenges as a whole allows the group to become collectively responsible for its results. If individuals are singled out in partnership development it causes fractures in the group that may lead to misunderstandings in the future and, worse, partnership derailment. Rather, a group approach helps the team to confront their interactions as a whole and produce united activities that surmount individualized challenges by taking them to the collective level. The collective is where partnerships and alliances are created. Such an approach supports the development of a successful consolidated partnership.

Facilitating Partnership Development

Collaborative Leadership is critical for alliance development but it is the group phenomenon that occurs at the group level that poses a clear challenge for alliances teams. When individuals communicate and engage in group partnership development, they become contributors as well as receivers of inter-subjective and intra-subjective relational experience. Consequently, individuals lose perspective of what is happening in the group from a third person point of view. They become immersed in experience as they contribute to the group's formation while a third-person perspective can discern the group progress in their task. The *Partnership Coach,* whose task is to observe, reflect and provide feedback from this third-person perspective, can discern the group's progress (Figure 3). When individuals are immersed in relating, they cannot see what is happening in the group, they only experience what is happening through their reactions and contributions. Only an outside perspective can see the group as a whole operating unit and help it be successful in its task.

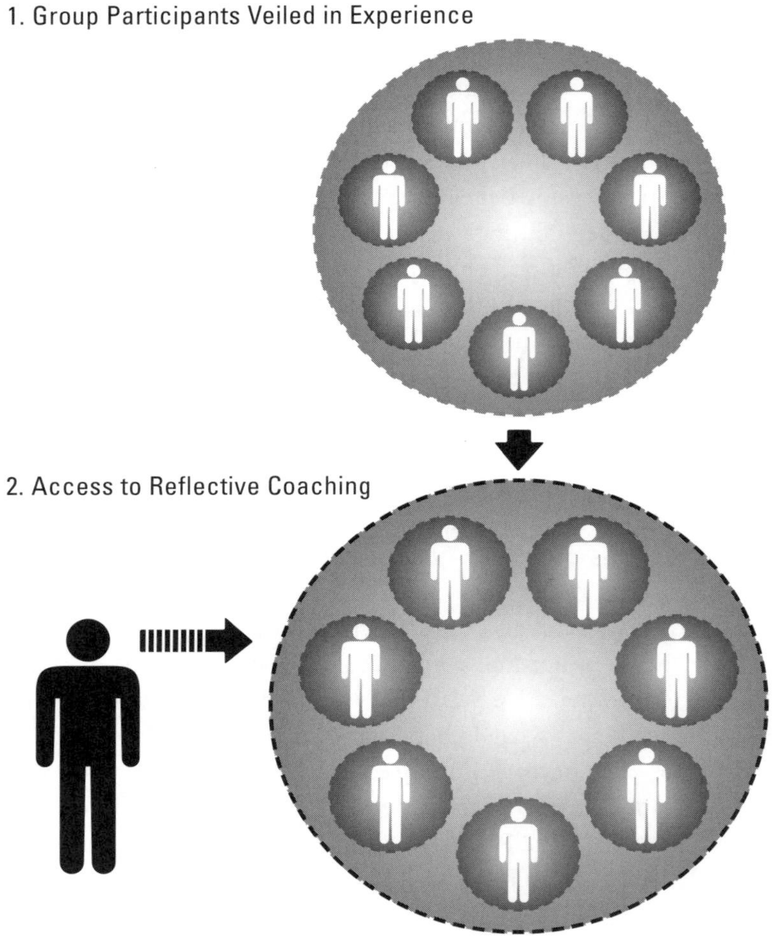

1. Group Participants Veiled in Experience

2. Access to Reflective Coaching

Figure 3 – Partnership Coach's Third Person Perspective

The *Partnership Coach,* being both part of and separate from the group, can take this third-person perspective. From this role new insights and new opportunities for action can be discerned and reflected back to the group to elaborate.

Partnership coaching involves the process of discerning patterns of communication, interaction and relationship occurring within the group. From this point of view, the group's overall functioning can be mapped and experienced as an emergent quality created by the relational field developed through and between the individuals of a group. In this respect, it is a new corpus that is formed, where no single individual—weak or strong—dominates this emergence. Like an orchestra playing, each individual plays his or her part and the music that arises becomes an entirely new phenomenon generated by group process. Just as this new music is much more than a summation of individual capacities or identities, so too is the successful group partnership made up of entirely new biological and socio-cultural phenomenon generated by the group which the coach helps to consolidate.

Partnership Creation Through Effective Partnership Coaching

Much as in individual leadership coaching, *Collaborative Leadership* development has tools and methods that help groups operate well together. Individual leadership development would require coaching to support personalized development. The same process applies to group leadership development. For groups to lead successfully as a unit, they require a methodology that includes coaching, tools, practices and support to traverse the partnership journey and overcome the challenges that emerge within the group process.

All group collaborations, including alliances and partnerships, are in fact an objective process that is taken by companies interested in creating an alliance, as well as a subjective leadership journey experienced by the groups to establish the partnership. Based on a trained understanding of operative group practices, methods and tools, the *Partnership Coach* supports both the business and the interpersonal aspects of this important work.

The Role of the Partnership Coach

The role of the *Partnership Coach* is to support the optimal functioning of the groups as it journeys through the subjective challenges inherent in forming an *Operative Partnership Group*, i.e., a group that functions at an optimal level on the tasks it sets for itself. To do this, the coach employs a specific method of practice described in the following chapters to support group collaboration throughout the alliance development process.

The role of the *Partnership Coach* can be taken by either an experienced member of an organization's alliances team or by an outside consultant. Both options have challenges and benefits (Table 1).

Coaching Role	Challenges	Benefits
As an internal alliance team function	Coach must maintain and demonstrate objectivity in the interaction between the groups. Coach must be granted a certain amount of leeway from the internal team to do his work. His social role of an authority figure vs. his likely functional role as team member must be respected.	Coach can help the alliances business unit team to become more aware of the patterns that are being generated, help them build awareness and increase overall performance. Can provide insights that can be used to move the process forward from a purely business perspective.
As an outside consultant	If the facilitation services are being paid by one firm, it is possible that there may be an implied favoritism. If the facilitation is paid by both firms, there is less belief in favoritism and perceived lack of objectivity.	Provides objective and unbiased support for the entire process.

Table 1 – Challenges and Benefits of Internal and External Partnership Coaches

Regardless of the approach taken, the coach must ensure that the relational challenges outlined above are made explicit to the group to ensure there are no misunderstandings and misconceptions. In either case, the methods adapted, techniques applied and tools used by the coach are the same. Both approaches require praxis—a process of understanding and of developing oneself to embody the role.

Chapter 2
Foundations
of Partnership
Coaching

Developing partnerships through coaching and facilitation of group inter-action is a complex process where the coach organizes and supports the team through the approach and methodology presented in Section Two. Unlike the *5-Territories of Alliance Development* (described in Section Three), which is more linear and operational, focusing on gates, signed agreements, business processes and strategies, group partnership development through facilitation is not linear, but rather cyclical and therefore more complex.

At its core, it is a living process that emerges from shared psycho-social interactions which coalesce together to form an *Operative Partnership Group*. Because of this complexity, it is important to frame the practice of partnership facilitation by first reviewing some core and foundational con-cepts. These concepts are the building blocks of partnership coaching and facilitation that ground the methodology and the strategies used throughout alliance formation.

Everything and Everyone Functions in Relationship

For the purposes of partnership development, the concept of "relationship" is taken in its broadest sense used to orient facilitation as the baseline: everything and everyone functions in the relationship. Everything is inter-connected and interdependent to everything else.

This describes a dynamic interplay between and through individuals, the organizations they are a part of and the industries in which they function. This dynamic relationship is present in companies and industries. A company has inputs and outputs made up of suppliers, partners and customers functioning in relationship. No individual is an island; neither is any group or company. Companies are embedded in the entire economic ecosystem, participating in relationships with a greater whole. In the same way, individuals and groups through their social, emotional and connectedness are also embedded in the social and cultural human ecosystem of living. All companies, groups and individuals function in relationship with each other, participating in greater and greater fields of relationship with norms and boundaries that involve distinct types of interaction.

From this point of view, the coach interprets all forms of communications that occur in the field. They are not isolated events coming from one person but inter-related causal activities that flow through the relationship field. This inter-relationship could be the flow of communication between teams demonstrating shared mental models and shared emotional messaging. It may also be interpreted as coming from outside sources that reflect the cultural challenges and assumptions from other participants or groups that are not even present in the room. For example, a team that works closely with an operations team will be influenced by that relationship, even if the operations team is not physically present.

Since individuals and groups are all in relationship and, in many respects, these relationships are created by and through the people that are in them, the coach can take this knowledge to help the group build their own field of relationship. The ongoing goal of partnership development is the creation of this field of relationship which has norms, rules and procedures that help the group consolidate an understanding of itself. Here, the coach focuses attention on establishing the field of relationship where the group will work (Chapter 3 pp. 41-51). Over time, the group establishes this field as it becomes comfortable in expressing more and more openly what it is thinking and feeling. This group understanding fosters the operating conditions to interact, face challenges and find innovative solutions that maintain relationship and cohesion.

Patterns of Relationship

As was pointed out, these fields of relationship have norms, boundaries, human emotions, language and intra-psychic processes that move through and between people. As in any symphony, there is communication between the instruments, tonality of play and vibrancy that emerges as a patterned set of activities. The patterns refer to how it all emerges together through the playing of a score, what people say, how they relate together and the cultural rules they establish for themselves. All these fields are ever expanding and ever-more complex entities created through conversation, connection, and human relating. "In a circular way, these contexts affect and shape the interactions that are a part of them" enveloping and emerging simultaneously through human relation (Littlejohn, 2011, p. 229). These interactions are what are referred to here as *Patterns of Relationship* that occur in the field.

In the context of partnerships, patterns of relationship are repeating interactions of tonality, emotionality and communication that occur within the groups and which the coach can discern. For example, you may have a group of five people and for some reason they each take a certain role. One may express the emotionality of the group, becoming the depository of the emotions that occur among its members. Another member may take on the role of being the knowledgeable strategic participant. That person is considered by the group as the one who directs its progress. Others in the group take on supportive or obtrusive roles that pattern out based on the groups willingness to produce. Over time the group creates certain patterns and norms that solidify and at times help productivity and at other times curtail it. The group may also have recurring language or expressions that it understands and jointly develops. It is the role of the coach to discern these interactions and support the processes of reinforcing the productive ones and bringing awareness to those that limit and undermine performance. Through facilitation, the group begins to learn and create the appropriate actions to focus on the tasks at hand.

These *Patterns of Relationship* will occur throughout the process, at every meeting and at different intervals. Relational repetition will occur from altitudinal (pp. 58-66) and directional (p. 37) perspectives. From an altitudinal point of view, in every meeting the group will be confronted with certain patterns that repeat themselves in similar ways. Although different people may take on different relational roles, the patterns may be the same (pp. 63-66). Over time, the group will reach greater and greater depths of relatedness as it recognizes and adjusts these patterns. These greater depths of related-ness equip the group to meet the increasing challenges of alliance making and bring it closer and closer to operability. Over time, from a perspective of directionality, they will progress across the 5-Territories that will support the alliances group to arrive at its goals: to build the alliance structure and over time negotiate the details.

In addition to these altitudinal and directional patterns, there are other relational patterns which relate to dimensions of emotional quality, depth and amplitude, sequence, pace, rhythm, and atmosphere. They occur across the journey and also at moments in time as the group engages together. Patterns of quality of relatedness refer to the emotional patterns that are being expressed throughout the group. These can be opposite pairs of vic-tim/aggressor, power/powerless, knower/ignoramus, control/fear, sadness/apathy, excitement/lethargy, exuberance/depression and others that are subjectively experienced by the coach and the group. Emotional patterns can be experienced as self-balancing elements that support or curtail the work of the team. Dimensions of depth and amplitude relate to the strength of feelings and/or behaviors of a group (Littlejohn, 2011 p. 247). Sequence patterns relate to how long patterns last over time within the group. Patterns of pace and rhythm refers to the rapidity of events and the intervals of move-ment, silence and general feel of communication and activity. The final one, atmosphere, relates to the conglomeration of space-time and feeling that is felt and actively created. This dimension is made up of place, space, time and includes all the others discussed.

Furthermore, these patterns that occur in the field of relationship may be stage- or state-related patterns. Stage-related patterns stem from the stage of development of a group and the meaning making systems in which the group resides (Chapter 5, pp. 82-89). These are more rigid patterns of interaction that occur at deeper levels and require longer exploration and facilitation by the coach. State patterns refer to experiences that are transitory and repeated every time teams get together, e.g., the state of lower energy and lethargic mood that occurs right after lunch during a workshop or meeting. This is a temporal state of tiredness and low energy that will eventually change. Pichon-Rivière identified three states that teams encounter every time they meet, pre-task, task and *project moments*, each with discernable qualities and ways of relating and activities that groups demonstrate (Pichon-Rivière, 1985, p.33). They do not reside deeply in the groups operating dynamics, like stage patterns, but occur more on the surface every time groups meet. (This is discussed in greater detail in Chapters 4 and 5.)

Partnership Coaching & Facilitation as a Living Process & Practice

The final element that frames partnership facilitation and coaching practice is that all partnerships are created through groups where operative and subjective relationships are established. Partnerships, like all relationships, are living entities. They are always in creation and are never fully formed. They go through ebbs and flows, ups and downs, and sometimes seem as though they are at a complete standstill or just about to fully break down.

Consequently, relational patterns are experienced by the group and discerned by the coach as internal and external dialectic tensions that surface. Dialectic tensions are the opposing forces that need to be resolved through conversations, cooperation and learning in order for group productivity to emerge. It is this living dialectic tension that must be worked through coaching and facilitation as groups learn to operationalize and collaborate. Dialectic tensions are present in all fields of relationship. They can include the normal tensions between judgment vs. acceptance, independence vs. connectedness, inclusion vs. seclusion, revelation vs. concealment, openness vs. closeness. Through the partner process, contradictions emerge as a dynamic interplay between unified oppositional forces that are interdependent and mutually negate each other, yet remain present (Griffin, 2003, p. 158). These contradictions can be related to individual responsibilities and the fact that the group is responsible for the project's success. There exists a tension between what one partner is responsible for doing as part of the alliance and how this fits into the whole of the alliance's activities. These tensions are worked through and organized by the alliances group, by finding resolutions and accommodations through the social-relating fabric of the group and the resulting negotiated structure of the alliance.

Understanding these dynamics, the coach helps the team become conscious of the tensions it is experiencing and make it more aware of the polarities it must traverse, from moment to moment, and across the journey. It is the members in the group who are creating the group as they act within it. They are responsible for the communication, the interactions and the structures that result from their interactions. During the process, the coach points out the social-relating patterns that are curtailing productive activity, so that the group can become more aware of the structures it is creating and can take greater control (Griffin, 2003, p. 245). These social patterns relate to the implicit, less-obvious elements of group dynamics that must be made explicit by the coach, so that the team can actively work through their resolution and/or accommodation.

Additionally, as new entrants become part of the group, they change it in a short period of time. New group members introduce new patterns, new opportunities and challenges for the alliance as well as new implicit relationship patterns. As such, the process throughout the journey is not only of change from within the original group that meets in **Territory Two (T2)**, (**Invite & Commit**, Chapter 9, pp. 166-184) but also as new entrants join and leave the group in **Territory Three (T3)**, (**Create & Consolidate**, Chapter 10, pp. 187-224) as the fields of relationship expand to allow the alliance to launch and grow thereafter (p. 123, Figure 18).

Because there is a living process occurring, there are actions that the coach puts into practice to bring continuity to group activities in support of its eventual coalescence. This relational field is ongoing and emergent, expanding and shifting throughout the alliance development process as individuals enter and leave the group. The role of the coach is to frame the interactions and the structural elements of the group to support the goals of alliance making and to help establish the social contracts that eventually lead to successful ongoing business collaboration. This is not to say that the coalescence is static. Instead, it is a culture of cooperation, a social contract of sorts that allows for increasing fields of relationship to be established and the alliance to grow over time. Yet, in certain respects, when launched, the alliance has in place boundaries, rules, governing contracts and arrangements which remain as fixed living entities. The intention is that this alliance and partnership once formed remain able to self-sustain and self-generate opportunities in the marketplace.

Chapter 3
Framing the Partnership Field of Relationship

The *Partnership Field of Relationship* has norms, boundaries, rules of engagement and routines that help the group to co-operate and become operative. It is consciously architected and at the same time fostered throughout the alliance development process by the methods, tactics and ways of being of the *Partnership Coach*. The work of the coach is to support the development of this field by establishing consistent practices and applying specific techniques that help to weave the field of relationship. These framing activities involve how meetings begin and end, the place and space where they occur, practices to consolidate thinking around key topics and other activities to support the group. In addition to the *Operative Partnership Methodology* (Chapter 4), the active practice of framing the field of relationship occurs throughout partnership development.

Framing the Field Throughout the Journey

Because the partnership journey is emergent and involves teams choosing to take the journey in the initial phases and then working together to build the alliance, the framing of the field of relationship will also be emergent and unimposed, facilitated but never forced. As such, in the beginning territories, the coach will only employ certain practices to slowly build the frame, adding others over time as the field grows. It is a living process, consciously constructed, woven and supported at the same time.

For instance, in the initial gatherings of **T2**, there will likely be a different structure for the meetings than later as the teams become more familiar with one another and as the role of the coach becomes clearer. For instance, choosing together the place and kind of space where meetings are to be held may not happen in **T2**, but over time place and space will certainly be agreed to by the group, based on how appropriate they are to specific work tasks. As commitment is solidified toward the end of **T2** and beginning of **T3** (Phase 1: Create), principles and cultural norms will begin to be identified and put into practice. Breakout sessions may be used more often as work-teams are established after the initial innovation session in Phase 1 of **T3**. As the convergence of alliance structure occurs toward the end of **T3**, a more directive approach may be employed to ground critical negotiations.

The tools and approaches described below are meant to share the kind of coaching activities that help establish the frame. However, it is the process of walking the journey and the awareness to know what to use, and when, that allows for effective partnership coaching and facilitation.

Setting the Beginnings and Endings of Meetings

All partnership meetings are started with a *check-in* and *check-out*. The check-in is the technique of requesting every person in the room to communicate where they are at in that very moment, what is present for them, concerns, ideas and desires, why they are there and what they want to accomplish. For individuals that are new to each other, they can also introduce their functional role to the team. The coach begins the session by voicing his/her own interests and aspirations of the group as well as making clear his/her role. They do this through emoting what is real and present for them at that moment, as both the coach and active individual wholeheartedly interested in the goals of the group.

As a matter of good practice, the inviting team (the team that is making the invitation to partner in **T2**) should sit within rather than across the table of the invited team. This practice, while simple, is an important beginning step to developing the cultural norms of the partnerships group. Additionally, it is the role of the coach to set in place the reasons why the group is meeting, what is being asked of the group and what outcomes or tasks the group is setting out to achieve. At the end of the meetings, in the *check-out*, the coach requests that each person voice where they are, what they consider was accomplished and what questions and concerns still remain. The group then reviews action items and next steps.

The process of beginning the session with the *check-in* and ending it with a *check-out* provides the coach with valuable information as to where the group is and what is occurring in the field (discussed at more depth in Chapter 4). Over time, the *check-in* and *check-out* practice also provides the group a moment where it can express itself openly. These practices help the group to expand the capacity of the field to express how it is feeling and what it is thinking so that over time it can productively address collective challenges.

The *check-in* and *check-out* moments also provide the coach with valuable information on the group's progression toward greater levels of operability. The *check-in* gives an indication of the group's emotionality, concerns, possible resistance to the task and their aspirations. The check-out gives the coach an understanding of where the group is once the meeting is over and what unconscious desires or obstacles exist. Comparing the *check-in* with the *check-out* the coach can then discern if the group has progressed in its task and if there are additional obstacles. This information helps the coach to plan follow-up meetings.

Setting Intentions, Principles & Priorities

Intentions, principles and priorities are elements that help the coach consistently set the *Partnership Field of Relationship* from meeting to meeting. The intentions relate to both the goals of the meeting and the reason why it is being held. The principles relate to the operating social rules of action that the group slowly weaves into its work. The priorities refer specifically to the activities that the group chooses to do first, second and third. At every meeting and after every *check-in*, the coach works with the group to establish intentions, priorities and operating/engagement principles for that particular reunion. The term intention here is used to encompass both the "what" and the "why" of having a meeting. The term can have a threefold sense. These include first the intentions the coach has for him or herself directed toward the kind of interaction that will be fostered through conscious intervention and facilitation. The intentions of the coach are internal to how he or she facilitates each meeting. The other two senses encompass the goals that the group sets for itself and the reasons why those goals are important. The reasons why something is important relate specifically to the needs that have brought the group to come together and what they hope to achieve at the end of the session. Oftentimes the intentions are set prior to the meeting. However, it is always best practice to review and, when appropriate, make changes that coincide with the clearly expressed purposes and wants of the moment.

Additionally, the intentions articulated by the group generate questions of how: "*How* will we execute against those intentions?" The setting of principles helps the group agree how they would like to be together as they work together. Oftentimes the coach will provide some principles and will work with the group to round out others.. These principles should fall in line with the intentions of the group as well as where they are in the partnership journey. For example, toward the beginning of the journey in **T2** groups may have principles such as "look for comparative excellence" and "share concerns openly". In contrast, in **T3** groups these may have developed into principles such as "explore questions that matter" and "say what you mean". These principles come from a variety of dialogic approaches that the coach may employ depending on where the group is in the journey toward collaboration and partnership.

Over time, there will be principles that are maintained throughout the alliance development process that become the cultural glue which helps the teams to operationalize its longer-term intentions. These principles are referred to as Alliance Operating Principles that slowly emerge through the territories and become further solidified toward launch. These *Alliance Operating Principles* are discussed in **T3**, Phase 3 of the alliance development process (pp. 217-218). They build the alliance's continuity into the future as it is sustained and deepened.

Working with Time and Rhythm & Pace

Time, rhythm and pace are the underlining structure of a meeting and emerge from the step by step, moment by moment activities of the group and facilitation by the coach. As the meetings begin, the coach has to take into consideration the use of time, and how communication and interaction emerge. Time is related to how strictly the group sticks to a precise agenda. The use of a strict agenda where every conversation is measured in minutes and seconds produces the illusion that activities will require less time than really expected and that in completing the activities the group is actually progressing.

Oftentimes, however, an overly strict use of time leaves important discussions by the wayside and does not allow for the surfacing of grievances and opposition, which are ingredients of a productive field of relationship and collaboration. Time, therefore, needs to be used lightly by the coach, with some structure based, of course, on how the group operates. Agenda setting needs to take into consideration sufficient time for discussion in order to allow for real conversation to emerge and for the group to self-organize its activities. Here, time is not imposed on the group, but rather the group unfolds its work into time (Bojer et al., 2006, p. 17). It is the work of the *Partnership Coach* to discern how to use time when the group needs more discipline for action or more space for reflection and dialogue.

When time is inappropriately imposed on the group, the action items and the "doing-ness" are made more important than the "being-ness" of the group. The relating and the field that is being created are as important as the action items that are being checked off. Group collaborative leadership is paramount in this respect. More often than not, the relating and productive connecting is more important than checking off activities. Good dialogue often allows the teams to work through the decisions of what actually needs to get done rather than what is simply busy work imposed by unproductive patterns of relating and the authority of a few participants.

Consequently, through the conscientious use of time, rhythm and pace, the coach addresses issues that emerge. At moments in the conversations, the group may be moving too quickly, not letting things settle and not pursuing issues in the needed depth. Individuals may not be contributing and something may simply be missing. At times the tendency to want to speed things up can happen in the entry point of the meeting or at moments of high tension and emotion. Helping the team to stay with the process and pace the interaction allows them to establish a working rhythm that is productive, thus creating a field of trust and solidity that fosters good collaboration. At other times, the pace may be slowed because the group is getting tired or a break is called for. There may also be times of silence. Not the silence of inactivity, but instead the silence of thinking together, of those illuminating moments of clarity experienced by the group where there is simply nothing to say.

Working with Tone

Tone, according to the Oxford Dictionary, is the modulation of the voice expressing a particular feeling or mood. The dictionary also refers to it as the prevailing character of the morals and sentiments in a group. In partnership development, tone relates to the level and degree of emotionality occurring in the field. The more the field can handle in terms of emotionality, the greater the level of cohesion of the group and the greater the level of operability. Introducing emotions such as frustration, excitement, anger, empathy, vigilance, commitment and others, shifts the general mood of the field and allows for new structures within the group to emerge. For instance, in "deep democracy" (Bojer et al., 2006, p. 36) dialogue, the coach can turn up the volume in a conversation. When participants speak in a way that is indirect and ineffective, the coach intervenes and speaks from that person's emotionality, amplifying what they are saying, making it more direct and taking out the politeness (Bojer et al., 2006, p. 37). These acts of working with tone are in essence part of the art of facilitation. Working with tone requires the coach to understand and know what living elements of the group are being stifled and how to allow them to come to the surface. Based on the *Operative Partnership Methodology,* it is the process of making explicit what is implicit (pp. 66-70).

Choosing Place and Space

Place and Space refers to where meetings are held and how tables, chairs, whiteboards and other tools are arranged. It includes the room location and the space that is created in that particular setting. While decisions of *Place and Space* may seem trite, certain places enable connection and communication while other places do not. The use of Place and Space is one important tactic that can be consciously used throughout the partnership development process to help foster the goals of a particular territory and support the groups in their work. Are meetings to be held at the invited company offices, off-site or within the inviting party's place of business? Should meetings be held in a conference room, at a nearby hotel, or perhaps a country club with access to nature? What tools should be in place to support group work?

While earlier in the alliance process **T2** the coach may not be able to suggest a meeting venue, as the groups move toward commitment, suggesting the right *Place and Space* based on goals should be taken into consideration by the group. Meeting places in a natural setting allow for certain outcomes while enclosed office conference rooms in the city allow for others. Place always has a role to play in creating the *Partnership Field of Relationship*.

At times, the teams decide to work together in a neutral space away from the office where there are potentially fewer interruptions and the group can focus on establishing the alliance. This is particularly true in **T3** where teams need the space for creative collaboration and where a larger group of people may be involved. Space considers the amount of available room between people without crowding, the tables that they use to work, the walls etc. Does the room where meetings are to be held provide enough room for individuals to have space for themselves while also being part of the team? Is the room too big; does it take over the groups? All these elements enable collaboration, or challenge its emergence. Best practice is a room that is just the right size, has good natural light with a view into nature, and walls where work group product can be posted.

Room Set-up

Various room set-ups work for different goals, intentions and times during the process. At some points, the intention is to deliver information and advocate a certain way of approaching an issue, while at others the goal is to work together to address critical questions important to the group. In the beginning of the journey, the process involves, more often than not, a meeting room structure of delivering information and inquiring if there is indeed an opportunity to partner. This requires a simple conference room setup with a long rectangular table, and a projector screen for presentations and videos etc.

However, by the time the alliance group reaches **T3**, the goal is to begin to build a culture of collaboration, exploration and opportunity. Here there is both a presentation-style setup and breakout work-tables arranged in a circle or, if a larger group is involved, various circles. Note that circles relate to a certain type of relationship while rectangles relate to another. In circles, all participants are equally important and connection and collaboration is primary. Rectangles show power structure, people on the ends hold power, while those on the sides in certain respects respond and follow. Those on the corners can act as bridges or sabotagers.

When real connection is needed and there are issues of transparency and challenges to authentic engagement, a circle format can be used. Removing the tables and exposing the group to itself, while unsettling in the beginning, can be quite effective in overcoming group obstacles. For instance, during the consolidate phase 3 of **T3**, where change and difficulty can be the most acute and the teams need to tackle challenges, a circle set-up can be quite helpful. In such a set-up the group must face themselves and work toward finding the best and common solutions based on consensus and compromise.

Continuing toward **Territory Four (T4), (Negotiate & Launch, pp. 222-241)**, when negotiations are taking place, the room set-up is also quite different. In fact, it can be more intimate with a small conference room at a small circular table. In **Territory Five (T5)**, where expanding the *Partnership Field of Relationship* takes place, several room set-up activities conjoined with presentations take place. In all these instances, Place and Space still play an important role. Room set-up requires the coach to think through what the goals and intentions are, what type of interaction is needed and how the chairs, flip-charts, table and such are arranged. The coach must also take note of what is happening in the group's relationship so that the right room set-up is put in place to support the explicit goals, while addressing the implicit challenges the team is facing in its relating.

Using Materials & Media

While it may seem pointless to consider materials and media as useful in framing the field of relationship, it is important to consider that physical tools, much like *Space and Place*, can be a good way to build group collaboration. For example, ensuring that there are whiteboards and large flip-charts for working sessions allows groups of people to focus and physically work on the same things. This is particularly true for times when group thinking and group coordination are needed. As such, the coach needs to always have note-pads, white-boards, flip-charts and other materials to support group work, although the meeting may not specifically call for them. These can also include voting dots, larger Post-it notes, pads, different color pens and dry erase markers.

Varied use of media in meetings is also an excellent tool for fostering the field of relationship and establishing a productive atmosphere. For innovation sessions, background music helps to build the atmosphere of cooperation, while using TED-Talks, and other video clips helps spur critical thinking and conversation.

For specific situations, other tools may be used to enhance group collaboration and learning and/or help groups to work through specific challenges they are experiencing. These may include the use of Lego pieces and other such objects that can be physically used by the group to help bring forth differences and establish shared understanding of the business. Such tools are excellent for dealing with change in the mid part of **T3** where alliance consolidation takes place and the alliance structure is being established by the group.

Creating Atmosphere

Although creating the right atmosphere does include the use of *Place and Space*, and the other physical tools described, *atmosphere* is fundamentally an experience that is felt by the participants interacting together. The coach may not have the luxury of providing all the physical elements due to lack of budget or other constrains, but he has the ability to affect atmosphere in the sense of the kind of relatedness needed to establish the field. This can be done with the uses of *check-ins* and *check-outs*, setting intentions, priorities and principles, and working with *time, rhythm and pace*, and *tone* with the intention of supporting the group along the journey.

Additionally, creating the right atmosphere at the right time is about the appropriateness of what is happening with the group, aligned to where the group is along the alliance development process. For instance, **T2** requires an atmosphere of an open invitation of opportunity and possibility. Here, the atmosphere is of potential; there is excitement tinged with a level of uncertainty.

Through the mid-point of **T2** a more serious atmosphere is introduced to evaluate in detail the opportunity and ground the process toward real commitment with less uncertainty. As commitment is in place, more questions are introduced, and greater urgency and increased uncertainty return. Teams may push to negotiate every aspect rather than remain open to building a greater sense of the shared opportunity. All this requires the coach to know where they are on the journey to enable the right communication to emerge given the constraints in the relating and the activities that need to be addressed at each point in the process.

Essential Qualities of the Partnership Field of Relationship

Overall, the goal of establishing the *Partnership Field of Relationship* is to create the conditions that support the groups' work together so they can become productive. As such, the coach facilitates the establishment of the relational space where the group can access all its capacities for collaboration and approach challenges productively by addressing the collective problems encountered. The *Partnership Field of Relationship* is a place where connection, authentic emotions and diverse points of view are allowed. This gives the group an opportunity to produce the best possible solutions for the alliance. The *Partnership Field of Relationship* contains qualities of honesty, directness, openness, thoughtfulness, perspective, respect, commitment, fairness and a capacity for change. It helps to foster real engagement and thoughtful interaction, but it does not itself cause authentic collaboration and cooperation of an *Operative Partnership Group*. Framing the *Partnership Field of Relationship* simply sets the field where the group must learn to play and work well together.

Chapter 4
Operative Partnership Methodology

These groups come together through a specific process where one team invites another to form a partnership and structure an alliance. Based on a shared context and potential opportunities, these teams become an *operative group* as they collaborate and traverse the journey from the initial invitation and commitment phase to the final contract negotiation and launch phases. The term *operative group* refers to a technique and methodology proposed by Enrique Pichon-Rivière a Swiss-born Argentine psychiatrist. His work on operative groups focused first on therapeutic purposes. He then extended its application to all groups interested in achieving an outcome based on their working together regardless of the domain of activity e.g. business, government or social services. His approach is employed through a particular facilitative method and stance taken by the *Partnership Coach* to unravel patterns that block learning and communication which obstacle cooperation, change and collaboration.

The **Operative Partnership Methodology** describes walking the 5-Territories of the alliances process, using the methods and techniques of Pichon-Rivière for addressing the implicit and unconscious challenges faced by groups. The *Partnership Coach* employs this praxis for the group to identify, understand and overcome the obstacles, relationship traps and challenges that arise dez de Tubert, 2004, pp. 37-38). This methodology, employed throughout the alliance development process, can be applied well after the alliance has launched, when executing, sustaining and deepening it. The *Operative Partnership Methodology* is therefore applicable for all *Partnership and Alliances Development Activities* and all areas where business collaboration and groups play a part.

Pichon-Rivière used the term, *Conceptual Referential Operative Schema* (CROS) (*Esquema Conceptual Referencial Operativo*, ECRO) to frame the use of his methodology. The concept of a CROS refers to the entire system of knowledge and attitudes of groups. It is both an individual and a shared phenomenon. However, used within the context of the methodology, it is mainly referred to as a precondition of group operability which exists when a group understands itself well and can manage productively the complexities of collaboration. In this sense, it is also a process that groups undergo to arrive at place of operability.

Peter Senge uses the "ladder of inference" (1994, pp. 242-246) developed by Chris Argyris to demonstrate how the minds of individuals work in breaking up experiences into parts and then move up the ladder, creating inferences and conclusions based on small slivers of experience. These slivers are broken down by individuals as they interact with reality and are used to make decisions and act in the environment. James Flaherty uses the term "Structure of Interpretation" (2010, p. 8) to define a related phenomenon as it concerns integral coaching and the concepts and ideas that individuals make about the world around them. The structure of interpretation is that which moves individuals up the ladder of inference and organizes what they choose to pay attention to. Pichon-Rivière would attribute the pattern and process of moving up the ladder of inference and the structure of interpretation as the CROS. The patterns of concepts and references that support our human operating "system" are made up of what the group perceives, thinks, feels and does and constitute a fabric of human functioning. All these are similar concepts, although Pichon-Rivière's methodology considers the CROS working at the individual level and also at the group level. When groups come together they must create and contain a common *Group-CROS* in order to become operative in the tasks they set for themselves. The coach uses both the concept of a CROS in the application of the *Operative Partnership Methodology* as well as the *Group-CROS* that is woven throughout the journey.

The *Alliances Conceptual Referential Operative Schema (Alliance-CROS)* is the methodological framework or schema (Tubert-Oklander & Hernández de Tubert, 2004, p. 48) for establishing partnerships and alliances used by the *Partnership Coach*. Using Pichon-Rivière's original concept of the CROS with reference to alliance making, the *Alliance-CROS* is made up of the following interrelated ideas:

> The first term, *Conceptual*, is concerned with the definitions or relations of the concepts of some field of enquiry rather than items of fact and allows for the wide generalization of ideas that occur in a particular industry or field applied to understand reality. Here the conceptual relates to fields of partnership and alliances development as understood by the coach. In this case and from the broadest point of view we are talking about relationships and the shared context in which groups collaborate through their affiliation between separate organizations that also have a shared context. Individuals, groups and companies collaborate through alliances based on specific strategic objectives and based on their embeddedness within greater and greater fields of relationship. Conceptually, these different fields of relationship make up interdependence between companies in similar or even different industries; through their interdependence they have an opportunity to collaborate. This refers to the super-structural aspects of partnership and alliance development and the concepts the coach uses in his/her application of the methodology. In addition, because the *Alliance-CROS* is a way of guiding facilitation and coaching, it is also made up of infra-structural aspects. These relate to the experiences and modes of approaching reality of the coach and of the group as they take on the process (Tubert-Oklander & Hernández de Tubert, 2004, pp. 50-51).
>
> The second term, *Referential*, relates to the act of referring to something, a certain part of reality. In partnership development, this means the act of referring to the activities pertaining to the field of business and alliances making, i.e. to the alliance process in general and the activities and goals of each of the 5-Territories as well as the methodologies and structures of human collaboration that make them possible. In this respect, the *Alliance-CROS* is always referring to concrete experience which is being used as a guide for action. This means that it is always being tested with the group and modified based on

its concrete experience and learning as it builds the alliance. When the learning concords with the referential aspects of the *Alliance-CROS*, the group and coach ratify the results and continue working and, in instances where learning discords, they rectify and shift their approach. In this sense, it is a process of theorizing experience and letting experience correct the theory, in a continued cycle of perception-reflection-action-new perception–praxis (Tubert-Oklander & Hernández de Tubert, 2004, pp. 5-52).

The third term, *Operative,* involves the acts of ensuring that the concepts and references made are actually applicable to what is taking place with the group throughout the partnership development process. Here, operative refers to the acts of checking with reality that what is made explicit is supporting the group to become successful in meeting its objectives effectively in each territory of the alliance development process. What makes the process operative is the methodology and the tools used at specific times across the alliance development process.

Finally the term *Schema*, according to the Oxford Dictionary, is a conception of what is common to all members of a class; in this case alliances development professionals and coaches.

The *Alliances-CROS* is a shared understanding and operative structure that the *Partnership Coach* uses to support groups through the partnership and alliance process. In this sense, it is a body or system of related doctrines, theories, etc. that serve to orient perception, thinking and action in the formation of strategic business relationships (Tubert-Oklander & Hernández de Tubert, 2004, p. 48). The *Alliance-CROS* is a reflective process of adaptation to the real world as the concepts and ideas are tested by the alliances group and supported through facilitation. This involves testing within each organization the kind of alliance that would work, as well as testing the products and services being contemplated. This includes aligning concepts for the eventual partnership relationship (operating/engagement principles, action-reflection practices) and alliances structure (collaboration and governance, roles and responsibilities, contact terms etc.) being developed. The right focus is toward a common understanding of approach with the goal of developing an *Operative Partnership Group.* This is a group that is able to work operatively and productively in partnership to establish a self-sustaining and self-generating Strategic Alliance. As such the *Alliance-CROS* is also a referential inquiry for the coach to help guide his/her own thoughts on how to support the group through specific facilitative interventions.

On beginning the work of facilitation and coaching, the coach enters the work with his/her personal CROS, how the *Partnerships Coach* understands and approaches groups. Over time, the coach's own CROS is reflected upon and continuously re-evaluated so that the acts of facilitation support the continual emergence of the particular *Group-CROS (Chapter 4, p. 73)* that is critical for the alliances group to become an *Operative Partnership Group*. By critically reviewing and reflecting on meetings and employing the methodology, the coach works with his/her original CROS, but also modifies it as he learns throughout the process. It is a reflective and inclusive process where the facilitation work is part of the groups' development as well as being separate from it (pp. 107-121).

Operative Partnership Methodology

The *Operative Partnership Methodology* is a praxis built around a technique that in itself is reflected upon during the process of building alliances (Chapter 6). An *Operative Partnership Group* is essentially a living entity with the capacities to co-learn, react actively to the challenges of reality and enter a state of productive functioning. The technique that supports groups to adapt to reality and change accordingly through the partnership journey is employed as "know-how" to build operative partnership groups, not as "know what," and requires specialized training and development on the part of the coach.

As such, this know-how involves understanding and discerning the moment-to-moment challenges that teams experience as they walk throughout the partnership journey. According to Pichon-Rivière, when groups are formed, the participants desire to be both part of the group, while simultaneously they want to maintain their individuality. They want to be part of and contributing to the group, but not engulfed by it. These internal and unrecognized desires play a role in the ability of the group to come together. For participants to work successfully as an *Operative Partnership Group* they must share their personal as well as organizational interests and needs, so that they may be able to support each other and the group to be successful in building the alliance. The process of coupling individual needs and wants into the work allows the teams coming together as a group to further motivate and mobilize together. The needs considered here are the desire to be heard, to be respected and included as important contributing members. The wants relate to the career and professional aspirations members hold for themselves as the alliance is created.

Consequently, as the teams from each company become a consolidated group, the change that they experience and in many respects co-create, supports them to grow as a group and individually as well. As such, the group exists concretely as a result of its relationships and capacities for greater levels of relatedness. *Operative groups* according to Pichon-Rivière are groups that work on the activities they assign themselves, while also proactively traversing inter-relational challenges inherent beneath the surface. These challenges are inter-subjective relationship obstacles that are experienced as anxieties shared by the group. In order for the group to become operative the group must accommodate its members to each other and grow internally for tasks to be completed.

Yet, for alliances in particular, the process of arriving at an *Operative Partnership Group* has additional challenges. For instance, in **T2** the teams that meet in the initial invitation to partner may not know each other or represent the same company and, as such, may not have a clear reason for working together. At that moment in the journey, they need to identify as a group the business interests and needs of each company, and focus on the task of determining in broad brushstrokes if there exists an opportunity to partner. Over time, they will work to establish an ongoing business relationship across the 5-Territories. This process is one of accommodation and dynamic creative acculturation as the group develops its own norms and forms of cooperating and working together. It becomes a group that will result in an alliance that will eventually become self-correcting and self-generating. Additional challenges also involve the fact that the group itself can be in a state of flux. On the one hand, the group represents the interests of each company while also slowly becoming part of a unique alliance group that itself needs to function. It is therefore the work of the teams to be able to openly address the inherent challenges of facing potentially competing interests of their respective companies. The group also needs to be able to address them productively together, thus becoming an *Operative Partnership Group*. In seeing challenges as something shared rather than concrete obstacles that split the teams, the group can learn to tackle them effectively. However, resistance to change and the emotionality experienced as the group comes together never truly goes away. By becoming better at dealing with change and accommodating to the continued challenges faced as a group, the alliance over time becomes a self-correcting and self-generating entity.

Basic Concepts of the Methodology

To apply the methodology, there are basic concepts that the coach needs to consider: the *interactions* between participants in the group, the *learning* they must engage together in, the *relating* that occurs as the group interacts and learns, the *cohesion* that begins to happen as teams produce and what finally *emerges* as a result.

Interactions are the behavioral *communication* that occurs in the group, both verbal and non-verbal. Non-verbal communication may include rolling the eyes, looking angry, using posture, etc. In verbal communication, the words, concepts and tone are taken into consideration. Interactions involve a patterned set of communication and even silence that may occur from time to time. Many times, needs are not communicated through verbal exchange but through non-verbal means in either conscious interactions or unconscious exchanges, all of which provide valuable insights into what is actually occurring in the relational field.

Learning is a process elaborated throughout the journey. According to Pichon-Rivière, learning involves an internal integration that occurs in the group over time. The learning either occurs within each person and/or within the group as they confront the real challenges in building the partnership and learning what can and cannot be done through the alliance. Communication is the road to learning. In certain respects it is the rails that allow the partnership to travel forward through learning. The process of learning also relies heavily on the contact that is made in the group to ask relevant questions and elaborate together on possible solutions based on collective learning. Particularly in **T3**, where learning and change can become the most intense, it is up to the group to be able to catalyze the experiences and build the right structure for the business alliance. Through relating, the group is able, as a whole, to find creative and innovative solutions to opportunities in the marketplace where collaboration is needed.

Relating refers to the bond established in the group through the repeated interactions and deepening relationships created as the group learns to work together. It is a much stronger connection than the simple interactions that occur from time to time. This deeper relating involves a real commitment to each other and the group, directed toward a common goal to build something together. In the relating, each participant's individuality is not lost in the group; instead, the personal strengths and attributes of each individual remain theirs and are leveraged toward a unique and shared process of co-learning and co-creation.

Cohesion happens when individuals shift their focus from themselves to others, decentering their focus toward the group, recognizing the subjectivity of others' perspectives and their respective needs. The capacities to recognize people as legitimate others allows for greater levels of relatedness to develop and, as a result, greater abilities of the group to work productively together. Through cohesion, it can shift interpretations of reality and as such mobilize capacities to create more innovative solutions.

Emergence refers to what is happening in the moment, arising from the group, based on interactions from moment to moment. Emergence relates to both what is going on and what is just about to happen. The coach supports the group process to move from one state of relatedness to another, considering what emerges in the group's interactions. What emerges provides the coach with input into what is occurring in the relational field and which interventions may be appropriate.

The Operative Partnerships Methodology applies techniques that allow the coach to discern the emergent elements when groups interact. What is emergent is analyzed through the *Alliance-CROS* where specific tools are applied to help the coach understand the conditions of resistance that groups undergo throughout the journey and in every meeting thus, supporting the group's cohesion over time. The technique is employed with the understanding of oscillating living systems. Progress is not always discernable but the coach knows that something is always happening. What is occurring provides insights for facilitation to support the positive and reinforce elements that allow for successful collaboration. To do this the coach first orients the work toward the moments of relatedness that occur in every meeting throughout the journey.

Pre-Task, Task & Project Phases of Group Relatedness

Social scientists have tried over the years to map the evolving pattern of relatedness that teams undergo in order to better understand how to support teams to be successful when they tackle tasks set before them. These patterns in certain respects are discernable and yet unpredictable in that they can change from moment to moment. Several thinkers (Bruce Tuckman, 1965; Bill Isaacs, 1999; Kurt Lewin, 1947) and others have used a variety of tools and approaches to help situate themselves during group meetings and discern the patterned progression of social movements that teams go through at every meeting. For our purposes, we will adopt Pichon-Rivière's conception of *pre-task phase, task phase* and *project phase*. Each has particular discernable activities and communications patterns that emerge in a dynamic way every time a group meets, and in fact every time individuals meet for any purpose.

The beginning *pre-task* phase involves a kind of splitting of thinking, acting and sensing. Culturally conditioned, in the US it can be perceived as speaking about the weather or other such topic. Bill Isaacs refers to this as politeness and shared monologues and will include what he also refers to as conflict (1999, p. 261). For our purposes, these monologues are perceived as talking about something, pontificating about strategies and testing who has more power and control, but not really getting to work on the task at hand. In its productive form, this can be experienced as arriving and joining, taking time to connect through the facilitated *check-in* process and establishing a clear understanding of the challenges and goals of the meeting. In its less productive aspects, it can last forever, where no work is accomplished and no efforts are made to consider the purpose and goals of meeting. From a group perspective, no risk is taken to authentically engage. Systemically, the conversation seems as if it is disjointed, not flowing, with little to no give-and-take of ideas and even less relating. Cognitively, it is characterized by an atmosphere of "not knowing what will happen" and emotionally it reflects the unease that results from not-knowing.

Pichon-Rivière stated that the unease shows itself in two basic forms, fear of losing something, particularly a social and relational structure, and fear of being attacked, for whatever reason, perhaps by others in the group. Additionally, for groups that enter the *pre-task* phase and do not know each other, as in the invitation phase of **T2**, the resistance to the task and to connecting in the *pre-task phase* contains a higher level of anxiety and may also show itself as patterned conversations of fear and control (which is perceived as the "perfect" remedy to relieve the basic unease felt by the group, but, in fact, is yet another obstacle to overcome). These anxieties may be experienced in **T2** but can continue well into **T3** and beyond.

These patterned conversations of fear and control produce the sensation of things being tied into a knot. Oftentimes this knot is created by the emotional and systemic interplay between the group's challenge to deal with its fears and insecurities in having to reveal business interests and intentions, and the perceived challenges that may result from doing so. Here there is a tension between the desire to build a partnership and the fears of approaching another person whom you do not fully know or understand, knowing still that they are fundamental to the deal. Due to these challenges many groups resort to various defense routines which restrict the team from entering the actual task phase. For the coach, these stereotypical fears of the *pre-task phase* are simply defensive routines of the group which need facilitative support through the application of several possible interventions. They occur in all groups and throughout the partnership development process, yet become most acute in the middle **T3**.

When the group enters the *task phase*, participants confront the realities of working together and begin to operationalize as a group in order to achieve the goals of the meeting and approach the work at hand. In the *task phase* they begin to bond. Conversations develop where positions and ideas emerge simultaneously, at times creating constructive and non-constructive conflict. From a relational point of view the "others" in the group become real people and the group begins to integrate ideas and have shared conversations. Still, there exists a kind of rehearsal of roles and conditions that can be limited and which results in low levels of real productivity vis-a-vis the challenges of building a successful alliance. No longer are there shared monologues where there is essentially no subjective other, but instead a give and take of information sharing, the beginnings of collaboration between individuals who are actively working together.

The final stage is the *project phase*. Here the "new" emerges. This is where change is produced by the group through its abilities to learn together. Change can come in the way the group conceptualizes the challenges at hand, produces new approaches and new ideas that help resolve the pressures of relating, and actually create together. Here, without losing the individualities of each member it comes into relationship as a cohesive unit. Learning takes place in a dynamic interplay of communication and creation. It is not that there is no conflict of ideas in the field, but rather there exists greater capability to tackle such challenges, inquire into them and find solutions together. The *project phase* implies a kind of break from past relational norms and patterns, which can still become stuck and stereotyped. The reason for this is the production and collaboration implicit in the *project phase* which requires that individuals contribute with their full selves. This implies that they engage authentically and contribute to the group their knowledge, experiences and expertise. Through the collective contributions of each member, in the *project phase* they have the potential to really make a qualitative leap in terms of productive change and relational depth. Whatever potential there is here is founded on the group's ability to access all their capacities as well as play the roles assigned to them as participants.

Assigned Roles of the Methodology

There exist three roles in the application of the methodology, the *Partnership Coach*, the *Observer* and the *Participants*. The first two roles work to employ the *Operative Partnership Methodology*, and help the coach reflect on the *Alliance-CROS*. The *Partnership Coach* role is to assist the group to become operative through facilitation and coaching. The coach works on the group to set the conditions for successful relating and helps the group establish appropriate boundaries of interaction. By working on the group, the coach guides the conversation and interaction by applying the methodology and tools. The second support role is that of a non-participant. The *Observer* works with the coach by chronicling the interactions and conversations of the group and reporting at the end of the partnership development meeting. This information is used by the coach as well as by the group to examine and reflect on interactions and operability. The *Observer* typically begins to work with the groups in **T3**. The coach uses the information derived from the meeting chronicles taken by the *Observer* to build future facilitated interactions that help the group face relational and business challenges it could be avoiding.

The third role is that of the *Participants*. Their role is to actively work within the frame established by the facilitation and to focus on the tasks at hand. From a functional business perspective, in certain meetings you may have financial and marketing experts, while in other meetings operational and sales people. Their functional roles are of course important but only in as far as the need to have particular expertise in order to do the work set out for the meeting exists. The focus of the *Operative Partnerships Methodology* is that the group works well together and becomes able to catalyze the contributions of everyone, regardless of function. In fact, titles and even functional roles if overly emphasized in the relating can have a negative effect because they presuppose patterns of communication and even decision making that may not help the team to enter the *task* and *project phases*.

Nevertheless, there will be moments in the alliance development process where functional roles are needed, titles are respected and reporting structures are taken into consideration. These ultimately help to structure the business elements of the alliance, such as the governance structure, negotiating details and running financial models etc. This is all necessary. Yet again, in as far as the *Operative Partnership Methodology* is concerned, the focus of the facilitation is to support the optimal functioning of the whole group from a social-relational perspective. This is not to say that work activities are discounted, but that the teams are functioning effectively as they tackle challenges and find solutions to obstacles. In this respect, effective means that communications lines are open and not stuck in dynamics of relating that either sabotage progress or curtail learning.

Consequently, there is something implicit here in the *Operative Partnership Methodology*: the democratization of all individuals in the group as equal contributors to the task. As far as facilitation is concerned, all participants are equal and are treated equally. The coach does not favor the opinions of one person over another or help to support the group vs. an individual. The coach's role is to use the tools of the methodology to help transition from one phase to another across the partnership journey. The focus is on the social-dynamic roles that emerge when individuals begin to establish group norms by working together in developing the partnership.

Unassigned Social-Dynamic Roles

Although the individuals of the group have their assigned roles as participants, when they begin to work together they begin to play out unassigned roles which occur unconsciously and are either assumed or not by the participants. These unassigned roles were discovered by Pichon-Rivière through his years of study with groups. They are the architectural construction by which individuals either coalesce into an operative group, or not. The roles emerge from the network of interactions within the group and are actually natural occurrences as the group itself begins to function from its fears and anxieties, trying to resolve the dynamics of inter- and intra-relating. As its anxieties and fears are resolved, the team begins to function better and has greater capacity to face change and challenge. From the third person point of view of the coach, they are simply patterns of communication and relationship that the group expresses as it begins to work together. They are expressed from moment to moment as the group accommodates itself and faces the challenges inherent in cooperating and co-creating together. These unassigned social-dynamic roles are the following:

The Spokesperson

This is the role of the person in the group that voices the implicit challenges of the group in an explicit way and brings awareness to the obstacles the group is facing and having difficulty resolving. This person elucidates what is occurring in the group, the fantasies the group could be experiencing, the anxieties and needs of the group as a whole.

The Scapegoat

This role occurs when the group does not accept what is said by the spokesperson and converts that individual into the scapegoat, rather than addressing the issue at hand. At the moment that it happens, the person will be attributed the negative and unprocessed concepts that the group is rejecting. The activity of scapegoating an individual is an emotional relieve valve on the part of the group that expresses the emerging mechanisms of segregation against that member.

The Leader

In counterbalance to the scapegoat, the leader is the person on whom the members of the group deposit only positive aspects. At times this occurs due to the person's title or position of power in the group, but not always.

Change Leader

This role emerges when the group accepts what the spokesperson says converting them into a member that expresses what the group feels and, from this role, contributes and promotes group work.

The Sabotager
This is the role assumed by a member who makes change difficult by sabotaging the work. Here the person attempts to assume leadership to resist change.

In order for the group to be successful in tackling the challenges of alliance making, or any other collaborative business endeavor, the unassigned roles need to be mobile and flexible. When an individual consistently assumes the *leader role* or any other of the unassigned roles, they structure and solidify group interactions and restrict group flexibility. These roles need to rotate amongst the group as they communicate, interact and relate together. As noted in the previous chapter, a group is never fully formed and as such is not a static entity. Rather it is a phenomenon of constant change and movement that involves a process of structuring, change and restructuring. Consequently, what supports this process is the group's ability to work through its own contradictions and to resolve those contradictions through a dialectic process of holding tensions of conflict and disagreement that help the group arrive at states of flow (e.g. *the Project Phase*, p. 60) and collective collaboration. The group's capacities to address deeper and deeper levels of contradictions through continued conscious and authentic relating allows states of collective flow to emerge more often.

Conscious and authentic engagement is needed because relational tensions tend to function below the surface as a result of unaddressed potential contradictions. This was conceptualized by Pichon-Rivière as the *implicit*, which through the use of the methodology is brought to the surface and made *explicit*. The tensions are not about the competition between opposing strategies but rather, at a deeper level, made of the internal relational contradictions that are consistently faced by members subjectively relating to one another. These contradictions can involve the dialectic and oppositional forces of individual needs vs. group needs, the old vs. the new, change vs. keeping things as they are, and many others experienced by the group. They are always partially elaborated because they are emergent and are part of the dynamics of living systems. As such, the process of partnering is never complete and always in a state of partial disequilibrium and change.

However, should roles become fixed, the group can enter a state of dysfunction. This is evidenced by the leader always being the same person, the one who sabotages always becoming someone that everyone considers to be the nay-sayer. In these circumstances ineffective patterns of relating become solidified and the group loses its ability to self-correct and self-generate ideas that lead the work forward. Pichon-Rivière mentions that in order to avoid structured dysfunction, groups should bring their heterogeneity into the open. Individuals may have similar ethnic and cultural backgrounds but different life experiences, parents, education, and come from varied social-economic realities etc. While heterogeneity supports operative group functioning, homogeneity sabotages productive work. The role of the coach is to help the participants express their heterogeneity and unlock the dynamics of homogeneity that often stifle group progress and operability.

Additionally, if dysfunctions are not property addressed, the alliance may be signed but fall apart later when the cultural dynamics of the initial group is expanded in **T5** (***Sustain & Deepen***, *Chapter 12, pp. 259-266)* to grow the alliance. If not addressed appropriately, dysfunctional and solidified patterns of relating become unprocessed dynamics that leak into the greater system of relationships between the firms and can cause eventual failure. Ultimately, it is the conscious process of supporting productive functioning that helps teams to establish a successful alliance based on a strong partnership and the abilities to respond to the continued challenges of human systems. To do so, the *Partnership Coach* uses the Inverted Cone tool to understand the group's progression toward operationally, the group's ability to put into practice the relational dynamics of a successful alliance.

Inverted Cone to Evaluate Group Progression

To facilitate partnership development, it is important to know what is going on from meeting to meeting and determine if there is progression in terms of the group's operability, i.e., the directionality of group relatedness. The *Inverted Cone* is a tool that helps the coach understand such group progression in a way that can be discerned over time. In order for the alliance to be successful, the group operability must conjoin with the alliances structure. Consequently, the *5-Territories of Alliance Development* are like a map for creating the alliance structure and the *Inverted Partnership Cone* is a map to determine group relatedness and operability (i.e. *Partnership*). The *Inverted Partnership Cone* is made up of *Explicit* and *Implicit* vectors (Figure 6).

The *Explicit* involves all that can be discerned and understood in the context of the alliance group and experienced directly by the coach and others, what is manifest by the group. The *Implicit* involves that which is implied, unexplored and lies beneath the surface, that which is affecting the team's operative functioning, i.e., what is latent in the group (Figure 5).

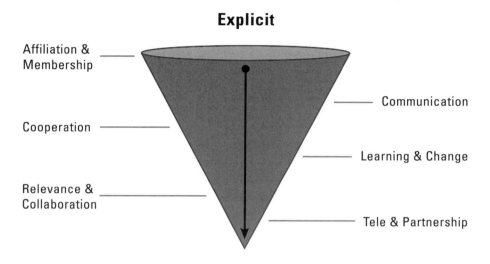

Figure 4 – The Explicit – Inverted Partnership Cone

The *Inverted Partnership Cone* is a visual tool used by the coach to understand group progression over time toward operability and partnership. The progression is qualified from meeting to meeting by the coach and observer (Figure 4).

Affiliation & Membership is the first step groups must take to begin their journey toward operability and partnership. Here, the members of the group become associated with one another by a shared interest in building an alliance. As the affiliation grows, the participants feel a sense of *Membership* as one would expect from a group that begins to commit toward a particular desired outcome or goal. Through their shared *Affiliation & Membership* the groups begin to communicate actively. It is through the rails of the group's *Communication* that they cooperate together. Through their *Cooperation*, the group begins to slowly address the new and develop the capacities to learn together and traverse change. Through their *Learning* they begin to discern what is important and relevant to the alliance, discarding ideas that do not work and accommodating each other's needs and wants. Through their shared state of *Relevance* they slowly incorporate *Tele* (pronounced /telé/), the members' positive or negative desire and emotionality to continue to work well together. According to J.L. Moreno, the *Tele* may be the potential that comes from when individuals truly come together (Fox, 2008, p. 27) and form a partnership. It may never become active unless individuals are brought into proximity, each with a degree of sensitivity for the same *Tele*, from total indifference to a maximum of positive response (Fox, 2008, p. 27). *Tele* refers to a kind of disposition that one has toward another and which resonates with past experiences and/or reactions. Positive *Tele* means people would say they enjoy working with other members of the team and would choose to do so. Should there be a negative *Tele*, people not wanting to work together because of some triggered response to others would result in a very different kind of *Operative Partnership Group*. This is not to say that they would not be able to productively function, but that the relating of the group would be markedly different. Furthermore, negative *Tele* could become an obstacle for the group and the alliance that needs to be worked through. Of course, a positive *Tele* results in a greater capacity for learning and a better overall climate. The group acquires a special structure, a unique operative disposition for the task (Pichon-Rivière, 1985, pp.231-232).

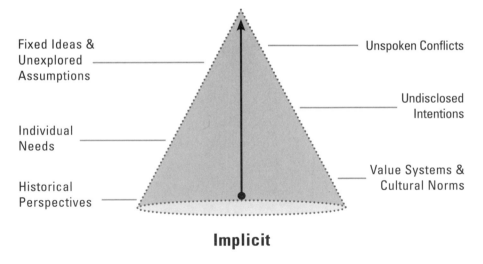

Implicit

Figure 5 – The Implicit – Inverted Partnership Cone

The implicit vectors relate to the unseen and undiscovered elements of the group that operate underneath the explicit and yet are ever-present (Figure 5). When undisclosed, they restrict the altitudinal development of the group (p. 36) from spiraling productively down to deeper levels of relatedness (Figure 5). These implicit forces include the *Unspoken Conflicts* of strategy and ideas that results from *Fixed Ideas and Unexplored Assumptions* about how to develop the alliance. *Fixed Ideas and Unexplored Assumptions* are not disclosed because they inevitably mask potentially *Undisclosed Intentions* and *Individual Needs*. Deeper down the Implicit Cone lie *Value Systems and Cultural Norms* that come from the group's *Historical Perspectives* and also play a role in how the *Tele* is ultimately expressed.

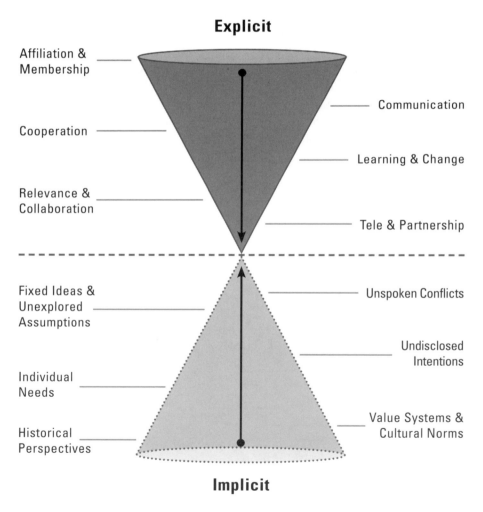

Figure 6 – Inverted Partnership Cone

Consequently, through active and reflective facilitation, the group makes explicit what is implicit (Figure 6). In so doing, it reveals to the group the hidden elements that allow the group to coalesce through transparency and trust into a cooperative and then collaborative partnership. Still, tension does not go away simply because of the united vectors. As relationships deepen, the group's capabilities and capacities to deal with challenges and opportunities become greatly enhanced.

Explicit

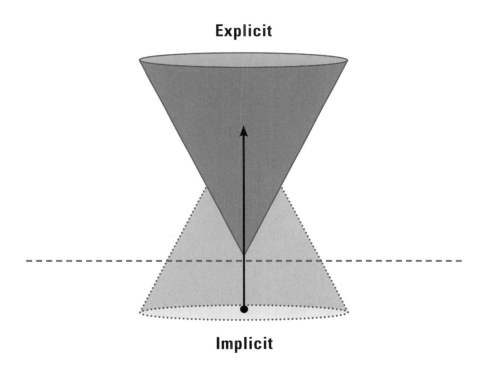

Implicit

Figure 7 –Inverted Partnership Cone Implicit Becoming Explicit

The *Partnership Coach* making the explicit implicit helps to solidify a partnership that has the capability to establish a self-correcting and self-generating strategic alliance (Figure 7). As the group makes the implicit more explicit, it is able to resolve obstacles operating under the surface that curtail group operability.

The Creation of a Group-CROS

It is through active facilitation that the particular *Group-CROS* of the two companies is made over the course of the journey. In **Territory One (T1), Align & Prepare**, (Chapter 8, pp 119-166), the organization develops the capabilities and conceptual understanding of how alliances are built and what they want to achieve as a result of their implementation. These ideas and interests are then shared with the invited party as the opportunity to partner in **T2**. Here the group begins referring together toward a shared understanding of context and vision that helps to build clear and shared meanings for the challenges and opportunities ahead. This conceptual understanding is further developed in **T3** where the group begins to share intentions and goals at a deeper level, as well as to share information referring to core competencies and other business elements that stabilize group understanding. In **T3**, the referential is articulated by the group as it further shares documentation, tests ideas and concepts, and begins to learn together.

The operative elements of the group begin to take hold toward the middle-end of **T3 Learning & Change Phase 2** (Chapter 10, pp. 200-237), as they begin working in unison, discerning what is relevant or not to the alliance. In the process of partnership development, this involves the capacities of the team to focus on tasks and operate effectively to address the challenges inherent in establishing a coherent structure for the alliance and discarding ideas and opportunities to be elaborated after the launch of **T4**. Here, operative refers to the unique dialectic process of working through the conceptual and referential in the real world of developing, structuring, collaborating and accommodating toward a common *Group-CROS*. A *Group-CROS* is made up of a particular alliance structure that comes from a particular team within a particular business context. From here, what needs to be established is the trust and confidence to Negotiate & Launch the alliance in **T4**.

Once the *Group-CROS* is set in place, in this case an alliances group, it is put into practice as a working social-relational structure that has the capacities to evolve over time and expand. Like a social tapestry woven by the interaction of the group, it sets the potential for establishing an alliance that succeeds over time and can achieve further development and evolution well after the alliance is launched into **T5**.

Chapter 5
Discerning the Implicit

Supporting the establishment of the common *Group-CROS* over the journey involves making the implicit explicit and traversing down the inverted cone. As the coach works to make elements of the relating more and more explicit, it gives the teams the abilities to work better together through improved communication, learning and collaboration. Doing this involves the conscious reflective work of the coach and observer to witness group interactions and discern their implicitness in order to employ the right facilitative support at the right moment. The coach surfaces what is implicit in the interactions so that the group can self-reflect, metabolize the facilitation and move into more productive work (Figure 8). The figure below references typical implicit elements that the facilitation helps to surface so the group can be productive. The goal is to help the group become more transparent and forthright in their interactions together, letting go of defense routines in order to better relate and engage together. Relating and engaging authentically are the essential qualities that support group collaboration toward shared work.

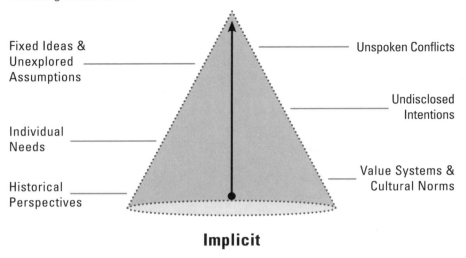

Fixed Ideas & Unexplored Assumptions

Unspoken Conflicts

Undisclosed Intentions

Individual Needs

Value Systems & Cultural Norms

Historical Perspectives

Implicit

Figure 8 – Making the Implicit Explicit

Consequently, discerning interactions requires that the *Partnerships Coach* be able to observe what happens when the group comes together. The coach has to interpret interactions while simultaneously being aware of how the group's interactions impact them. The latter refers in large part to the development of the coach to "get out of her/his own way" and develop self-reflective capacities to ensure clarity of observation, interpretation and facilitative continuity (pp. 112-128). For the purpose of interpreting interactions, the coach must work from a particular frame of understanding that helps guide facilitative interventions.

The focus of this chapter is to review several perspectives on human dynamics and group interactions. These perspectives taken by the facilitator shape the various facilitative interventions that are chosen. They provide a foundation from which to discern interactions that happen between and through people, yet reside down the inverted cone in the latent and implicit realm, unknown to the group (Figure 8).

Human Beings as Open Circles

Human beings make interpretations of the world based on their own internal ways of seeing and functioning. These interpretations are shaped by and through the interactions and bonds people establish with other human beings. In certain respects, people are all open systems with the capacities to connect and resonate with others, as well as reflect, learn and grow (Lewis, 2000, p. 85).

While people can be seen as open systems who resonate with and connect with others, they can also be considered closed systems. As closed systems, individuals interpret and inter-relate with others through their filtering capacities which stem from internal reasoning and ways of being. This occurs essentially through their own internal world which acts as a self-organizing system that contains certain limitations and constitution that arises from within each person (Maturana & Verden-Zoller, 1996 p. 1; Horne & Seagal, 1997, p. 37).

Consequently, the coach working with the alliances group considers all individuals as open circles in that each relates with the outside environment in an open way and internally filters and relates with others through their unique internal structuring like a closed circle. In this sense the coach considers that human beings are the same across all cultures. On the other hand, the coach considers each individual as unique as per their capacities and abilities to interpret things around them. Understanding this allows the facilitation to ask questions directly to the group or to individuals in the group in order to spur growth and change.

The differences lie in our internal functioning. Some human beings function more from their emoting, others function more from their cognition, while others even function more from their physical bodies (Horne & Seagal, 1997, p. 22). Although they may principally function from one of these different centers of intelligence and ways of being, they all emote, think and do respectively. The person whose center of being is emoting is more attuned to feelings, subjectivity, relationship, communication and creative imagination. Those that are more cognitive reside more in their thinking, objectivity, vision, and conceptualizing. The person who is centered more in the physical resides in the doing, making, actualizing and practicality (Horne & Seagal, Ibid, p.27). Being centered in one of these ways of operating does not mean that there is no capacity for the other two. Everyone expresses emotions through the heart, concepts through the mind and does things through their bodies. This is true of all people regardless of culture, nationality or historical origin. In any activities they engaged they do so with their actions, through their emotions and by their intentions. All are interconnected and interwoven in each expression produced, where affect circulates in the form of emotions between people.

Interestingly enough, in biological terms emotions are corporal dispositions that determine actions which are expressed through language and communication (Maturana & Verden-Zoller, 1996 p. 6). Communication in all its forms is fundamentally emotional to the individual and the social sphere of relating. As such, interactions by and between people are always emotional interactions that are conveyed through language where limbic resonance is taking place. This means that self-affecting inter and intra relating emerge from group emotional cohesion and dynamism. As such, body disposition and movements speak louder than words. If there is any doubt as to the clarity of communication, the body is the place to look. It operates under the radar of human consciousness in the human nervous system.

In this sense, every utterance, body expression is a form of communication grounded in human co-creation of consensual activity. Groups produce coordinating actions through conversation and relational actions with each other. For instance, people talk with each other; follow, oppose, propose and reflect on the conversations being held in the moment. Through these actions in conversation, affect is generated, and ways of relating constructed that further a shared and co-constructed reality. Good productive relationships are essentially the rails on which productivity runs (Figure 9) and relationships are established through a network of group interactions involving communication that results in productive or unproductive activity.

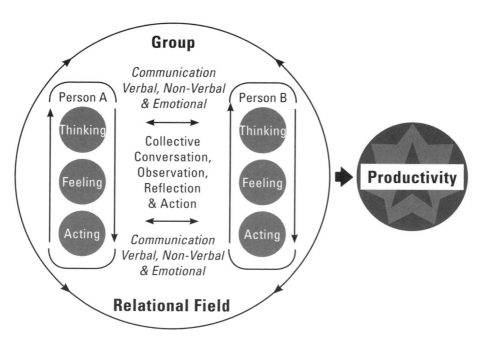

Figure 9 – Group Interaction toward Productivity

However, at times, individuals may unconsciously communicate in mixed messages. They may express something quite simple in language but through prosody and through their bodies convey more meaningfully what is being felt, but not clearly communicated. Sometimes intentions do not match actions of communication because of fears and concerns, coupled with fixed ideas and assumptions which may not be shared openly. Consequently, it is the work of the coach to help the group share implicit assumptions and feelings in order to release anxieties that curtail productivity. Making the implicit explicit and able to be talked about openly, the coach helps the group express conflicts and hidden desires that oftentimes go overlooked in partnership development. Releasing hidden assumptions, emotional concerns and openly expressing interests helps the group avoid possible alliance derailers. Facilitating these productive yet difficult conversations to emerge, the coach helps the group find solutions that meet collective needs and desires.

In order to do this, the coach establishes a relationship of legitimacy, understanding and respect with the individuals and the group. It is the task of the facilitator to communicate with each person and with the group in such a way that demonstrates respect and understanding of human imperfections. He neither considers people to be inherently good or bad, but rather chooses to relate with everyone as equal contributors to the work. The coach provides an opportunity for what all human beings desire—to be respected, to voice their ideas and concerns and to be understood. The coach understands that communication exchanges contain the possibility for conflicts and possibilities for agreement, both necessary for optimal functioning of the group.

Finally, the coach holds a particular and fundamental belief regarding human beings and groups as a whole. All human beings, either in a group or alone, carry within them the capacity for change and the inherent abilities to accommodate to the challenges imposed on them from their environment and life experiences. Still, this open attitude does not prevent the coach from recognizing when the group is in a state of being unwilling to face its implicit challenges. This understanding comes from the coach's awareness of when body dispositions do not concord with what is being said, and when tone is conveyed by the group in ways that are not coherent and perhaps relate to unspoken conflicts or other implicit dynamics at play. When teams move through important conversations and do not spend the needed time to understand the basis for decision making and clarify foundational concepts as a group, it is clear that they are sidestepping the more difficult process of revealing undisclosed fixed ideas and assumptions. So, while the stance toward the group is of being open, the coaching work is directed to what is actually happening in the moment, thus helping the alliance group to see more clearly so that they can operationalize effectively.

Value Systems and Cultural Norms

As groups traverse deeper down the *inverted cone* new implicit challenges rooted in different value systems expressed by the group emerge. These value systems can either coalesce or mesh to produce collaboration when the right combinations come together or collide with and potentially disintegrate the partnership because differing values can be perceived as unsurmountable challenges to the group. Unlike cultural challenges that can be quite complicated and varied in today's global business environment, value systems provide an important contextual structure to work with. In fact, you can find varying value systems operating within a single culture and county, and even within a particular company. Understanding value systems allows the coach to discern opportunities and roadblocks and even plan for them beforehand.

The term *Value Systems* comes originally from the work of developmental psychologist Clare W. Graves who codified in his 20 plus years of research over a thousand people for extended periods of time (1974). He worked to understand human development and reconcile the varied differences in people's world-views and capabilities to function in life. Graves was interested in understanding how people differ in their thinking, in their understanding of the world around them and the foundations on which they take decisions. He essentially worked to reconcile why there was such a difference in people and to find a pattern that made sense of it all. He discovered a spiral-map that clarifies how people make sense of the world around them.

According to Graves, *Value Systems* involve the total psychology of a person or group. In essence these comprise the full scale of their feelings, motivations, ethics and values, biochemistry, degree of neurological activations, learning systems belief systems, preferences for and conceptions of management, education, economic and political theory and practice (Graves, 1974, p. 2). Don Edward Beck and Christopher C. Cowan introduced the concepts of memes into Graves work and named the entire system of ^{V}MEMEs (*Value System Memes*) in their book *Spiral Dynamics: Mastering Values, Leadership and Change*. A meme is an idea, a belief that can be considered the behavioral equivalent of a gene, expressed through culture and residing in people and groups. Memes appear in how people and groups confront, think about and metabolize existence and take action from experience. They come from the work of Richard Dawkins, an English evolutionary biologist who conceptualized them as self-replicating units of culture and behavior. Beck and Cowan called the idea *VMEMEs* "a world-view, a valuing system, a level of psychological existence, a belief structure, an organizing principle, a way of thinking or a mode of adjustment" (Beck & Cowan, 1996, p. 4), which people and groups express.

Consequently, the capacities to meet life's challenges actually begin as a process of adjustment to life. For groups and individuals there exists a need to solve life problems or conditions and, through creating particular values and ways of managing these problems, individuals and societies produce a whole range of solutions which result in management structures, policies, rules, etc. These solutions involve the development of values that subjectively orient priorities and which are expressed and embedded in structural systems. Over time, individuals, groups and societies establish the correct set of values and strategies to be successful in meeting challenges. That productive stable structure only lasts so long. Eventually, people find that previous values no longer work for life's current challenges. Therefore they must reframe their relationship to the original challenges and reformulate their ways of seeing and being to readjust to new life demands. The result is an ever-extending quest for wholeness and integration as people and groups find unique methods to meet life difficulties through changes in their abilities to perceive and act. The work of facilitation is to assist groups accommodating the differing *VMEMEs* that people express, so they can establish the right structure for the alliance.

How *VMEMEs* Work

VMEMEs are ways of seeing and engaging which reside in the people and groups that are expressing them. That is, they act as systems in people. Individuals and groups can express differing *VMEMEs* depending on life circumstances, situational contexts and other pressures. For the purpose of facilitation, the conception is that individuals and groups are both standing in a *VMEMEs* and may have the capacity for change to tackle challenges collectively. This change is conditioned on the team's capacities to hold in the relational field the differences expressed by each *VMEMEs*. This means respecting the unique contribution of each person as they express themselves and working to accommodate and consolidate group thinking. In this way, the group structures an operational partnership both subjectively through its relating and objectively by the alliance agreements and structures it establishes.

^{V}MEMEs work through a dialectic tension of growth that sways from states of independence and self-expression to interdependence and connection. In the state of self-expression, people focus their energies on looking and acting from a self-oriented stance. This can be, but is not always, an egotistical stance. Rather it can be seen as a general interest in personal accomplishment and personal power, where the focus is on individual perceptions of work and contribution, irrespective of others. Conversely, the interdependent stance involves a coming toward others and a toning down of the individualistic focus. This is not necessarily a closing of individuality, but comes more from a need to be part of the group and a desire to connect and contribute in a state of togetherness. In the Spiral Dynamics model, where there are eight succeeding value system levels, ^{V}MEMEs oscillate between from stages of individuality to stages of group collective focus. This does not mean that at each stage there is a lack of capacity to connect, nor an inability to be an individual. It is simply that there is a general orientation toward one or the other; in all stages there is the potential toward connection and individuality. However, it is important to recognize that often one will have priority.

This presents a challenge; meshing of ^{V}MEMEs is conditional on two major factors. The first is a context in which people can actually grow, where the demands placed on them are not so overwhelming that they cannot cope. Where there is fertile ground for growth, there are conditions for development and the creation of new ways of approaching and dealing with life's realities. In the case of partnership facilitation, setting the conditions in the relational field for teams to collaborate together is the act of developing the fertile ground for growth. The second is a person or group's state of openness or closedness. If a person or a group is open to the pressures of reality and is willing to reframe, reflect and learn, the capacity to grow is possible. In as far as partnership facilitation is concerned, closedness challenges a group to traverse the partnership journey and deepen down into the inverted cone, while openness allows opportunities to flourish and learning to occur. Regardless of the orientation of individuality or collectivism, states of openness are where the group can metabolize the effectively differing ^{V}MEMEs expressed and build the subjective relational *Group-CROS* that results in an operational alliance.

Overview of the Spiral Dynamics

Spiral Dynamics is a system that describes eight ^{V}*MEMEs* stages expressed by people and groups, what they value, how they make decisions and general characteristics of what they do. According to the theory, each of the eight ^{V}MEMEs evolves into the other over time, although not in a linear sequence but through emergence. One ^{V}MEMEs grows from the learning and the adaptations of the previous one. This means that teams could be at one level in the spiral and show behaviors of the others that have come before. Depending on their openness they may also exhibit some of the next-stage characteristics. It is relevant to know their existence, to understand their dynamics and how they are expressed. The following are adaptations of the middle five ^{V}*MEMEs* stages in the Spiral Dynamics system (Beck & Cowan, op. cit.). The first and last are omitted due to their very low occurrence rates in groups.

> **The Red ^{V}MEMEs** is interested in immediate gratification and domination through the self (Table 2). It can be considered heroic in its attempt to wield power and unhealthy it can fall to despotism. The ability to reflect and consider options is limited to doing what is required in the moment in order to satisfy immediate concerns that help to express and solidify selfhood. This vMEME simply does what it wants without concern or remorse. This ^{V}MEMEs is depicted in the HBO series *The Sopranos*. All is focused on the use and demonstration of power over others. This ^{V}MEMEs can show itself in others and teams during times of real stress and considerable frustrations when a show of force is perceived as being needed. The healthy expression of the Red ^{V}MEMEs can demonstrate will, garner power and use dominance to unite cultures and tribes supporting upward development. Yet, in its unhealthy expression, the Red ^{V}MEMEs can be predatory and violent (Dawlabani, 2013, p. 52).

> **Basic Theme:** *Might makes Right, Be what you are and do what you want, regardless of the impact on others* (Roemischer, 2002, p. 7).

Orientation (Individual vs. Group)	Focused primarily on expression of individual selfhood.
Degree of Orientation (Individual vs. Group)	High with little to no regard of group.
Strengths	Ability to really fight for their needs as individuals and protect their clan, they can be resourceful and powerful. (Dawlabani, *Ibid*, p. 51)
Blind Spots	Misses much of everything that exists beyond the needs of the self. Can be selfish, predatory and violent. (Dawlabani, *Ibid*, p. 51)
Decision Making Criteria	Decisions are taken on the spur of the moment centered on immediate needs and concerns based primarily on power structure.
Emotion in the field	Power seeking aggression and domination prevail away from group toward individual needs.

Table 2 – Red ᵛMEME Synopsis

At some point, the Red *ᵛMEMEs* begin to realize that the path of the ego does not provide fulfillment and that there must be some coordinating structure to existence and a right way of organizing things. Life and the composition of society do not make sense and there must be some central truth or other knowledge that directs us all to be fulfilled and to provide us purpose. This inquiry leads to the next evolution of the spiral.

The Blue ᵛMEME is interested that things are done the right way, the way things have worked in the past, based on the purpose and systems in place at the company. The right steps are taken and decisions are made by people who have the authority to make them. The group decides hierarchically based on policies and procedures established by management (Table 3).

Basic Theme: *The truth is plain as day, life has meaning, direction, and purpose with predetermined outcomes* (Roemischer, op. cit., p. 7).

Orientation (Individual vs. Group)	Focused excessively on group norms.
Degree of Orientation (Individual vs. Group)	Highly oriented toward group, where group compliance is primary.
Strengths	Is well grounded in the needs of the society and does look for the elements that align well with organizational purpose. There is an emphasis on compliance, equity and uniform treatment (Dawlabani, op. cit., p. 52) under the law or rules established by the hierarchy.
Blind Spots	Can be dogmatic in their approach and rigid in meeting new challenges. There are no shades of gray, everything is right or wrong, black and white (Dawlabani, op. cit., pp. 54-55).
Decision Making Criteria	Decisions taken by those in authoritative position and organizational hierarchy based in part on what has worked in the past. (Shoulds, oughts, musts.) Fearful of group retribution or being shamed by the group or guilty in its eyes.
Emotion in the field	Respectful, toned down and restrained, rule-following.

Table 3 – Blue MEME Synopsis

Over time, the Blue ^VMEME begins to feel burdened by the rules and the methods that *"lead to fulfillment"*. The suit just does not fit any more, the rules established do not seem to accommodate any more, or even make much sense. It is not a fair system based on individual contribution. There must be a better more flexible way of ensuring equality and equity in society. These are the questions of the Blue evolving into the Orange.

The Orange ^VMEME is interested in achieving and winning. The world is full of opportunities. They considers that companies, if they plan and architect their organizations in the most efficient way, will succeed. The focus is on individual contribution and less on group agreement, although decision making is both top-down and bottom-up. This means that leaders in authority positions are involved in decision making as well as managers and other subject matter experts in positions of less authority. Good business is based on shareholder value and payback rates, short-term orientation and a meritocratic model of success (Table 4).

Basic Premise: *Short-term tactical, act in your own self-interest by playing the game to win* (Roemischer, op. cit., p. 7).

Orientation (Individual vs. Group)	Focused primarily on the individual.
Degree of Orientation (Individual vs. Group)	Moderate, individual contribution is favored over group interaction; if group makes right decision, they agree, if not they decide to do things themselves.
Strengths	Very opinionated and decisive, willing to engage in rigorous discussions to arrive at the best possible solutions.
Blind Spots	May not attune well to the feelings of others, either the Blue's needs for direction and respect of hierarchy or the Green's needs for group agreement.

Decision Making Criteria	Decisions are taken based on the best strategic input and "rational" decision making of the group, however may bend strategies that better align with individual ambitions.
Emotion in the field	Open strategic conversation, with challenging discourse and discussion.

Table 4 – Orange ᵛMEME Synopsis

Along the journey, the **Orange ᵛMEME** begins to ask: is this all there is to existence? I have it all now, wealth, prosperity and, yet, there is something missing. What is life really, truly about? How can I be fulfilled as a person as well as make a contribution to society? Is not how I feel and how others feel also important to life? At what expense is all this material and personal success? These are the questions that emerge into the **Green ᵛMEME** (Dawlabani, op. cit., p. 60).

The Green ᵛMEME is focused on the ideals that life is for experiencing each moment. From an organizational point of view it is about coming together to make a real difference for ourselves as a team as well as for society. These people are on a quest to make the world a better place and consider that they have the skills and capabilities as a group to make things happen through the interdependence of human connection (Table 5). Decisions are taken by consensus where everyone has an equal say. While financial imperatives are important for the **Orange** ᵛMEME and remain important in the **Green** ᵛMEME, value imperatives outweigh financial rewards.

Basic Premise: *Seek peace within the inner self and explore, with others, the caring dimensions of community* (Roemischer, op. cit., p. 7).

Orientation (Individual vs. Group)	Focused primarily on the group.
Degree of Orientation (Individual vs. Group)	Moderate imbalance with focus on groups.
Strengths	Values oriented with an understanding of the potential to look for one good solution grounded in relationship and group dialogue satisfies everyone.
Blind Spots	May not listen well to the Orange ᵛMEME's single-minded approach nor be open to excessive individualistic functioning. May also spend too much time listening to everyone's point of view – excessively Green in decision making. Potentially indecisive.
Decision Making Criteria	Decisions are taken with everyone providing equal contributions. Decisions are Green.
Emotion in the field	Can be angry toward those that do not understand them and a bit elitist in their attitude toward others that do not see the importance of subjective issues and collective-decision making. Can be blind to the positive contributions of Blue and Red.

Table 5 – GreenᵛMEME Synopsis

Once again there exists a review of what worked in the past and is not working in the present. The **Green** ᵛMEME does not seem to be working adequately. Decisions take forever and for some reason things continue as they are. Certainly some things change, but not to a great extent. There must be a new way to balance the individualistic leanings of the **Orange** with the group needs for involvement and social responsibilities and connectedness of the **Green** life perspective.

These questions are the shift into the next tier thinking systems demonstrated by the **Yellow** ^{V}**MEME**.

The Yellow ^{V}**MEME** is the most productive to date of the memes stages in Spiral Dynamics. It is most adaptive to the pressures of reality and to the other memes and can help support groups to identify new and innovative solutions (Table 6). The capacity to shift from the individualistic to the collective allows points of leverage in the interactions and the system as a whole. Making a difference can only be done in the here and now; all individuals have a contribution to make in some sense but not equally, and not at the expense of themselves. Balancing financial imperatives are as important as values which only inform strategic action but do not nail it down.

Basic Premise: *Systemic Interdependence, live fully and responsibly as what you are and learn to become* (Roemischer, op. cit., p. 6).

Orientation (Individual vs. Group)	Individual importance, but individual is not always more important than group.
Degree of Orientation (Individual vs. Group)	Low with greater level of integration between individual and group orientation.
Strengths	Can intertwine past and future opportunities and see the connections for present action. Malleable and open to change and to what is happening in the moment. Good leadership is about handling complexity and knowing what to actually do.

Blind Spots	May lose patience with others that do not fully see their point of view or simply allow themselves to only flow with group needs and emergent situations.
Decision Making Criteria	Resulting from productive dialogue and the strategic discourse that emerges from productive interactions.
Emotion in the field	Open, inquisitive, facilitative and directional.

Table 6 – Yellow ᵛMEME Synopsis

Beyond the **Yellow ᵛMEME** there is the **Teal ᵛMEME** which represents such a low percentage of society that it is not really useful to review in the context of partnership development today. Needless to say that that most of the world's organizations are situated between the **Blue** and the **Green** with many of the world's transitioning economies and companies moving from **Blue** to **Orange** and **Orange** to **Green**.

Using Spiral Dynamics to Discern Group Interactions

Spiral Dynamics is a powerful tool for understanding interactions and building the right facilitation approach. Nevertheless, the use of Spiral Dynamics as a lens for understanding must be practiced cautiously. If the coach uses the system to label individuals and the group, and thinks of them as stuck within ᵛMEMEs, the facilitation can become rigid, judgmental in its application and not helpful to the group's operability. Authentically engaging in the role of the *Partnership Coach* takes the capacities to respect the individual contributions of all participants regardless of the ᵛMEME they express and discern the needs expressed underneath their communication. It is of importance to discern how the ᵛMEME's actually interact to support the group to generate a partnership that works. This perspective allows the facilitation to first depersonalize their emergence and then focus on what the group expresses. In so doing, the coach can gauge potential interactions that may occur and be prepared to help the group face them. Because there will be challenges in how ^{V}MEME communicate, cooperate and learn together, the coach may identify participants in emergent yellow to lead specific group tasks that support an integrative approach.

Spiral Dynamics is also useful to discern the challenges faced at the organizational level when one organization with a ^{V}MEME center of gravity will be challenged by partnering with another ^{V}MEME. In many respects, the individuals will express the ^{V}MEMEs of each their organizations: how their organizations function, how decisions are taken and what is valuable to their companies. In this sense, the *Partnership Coach* can help in **T1** to identify the best possible business partners, and in **T2** when making the invitation align with the invited company's ^{V}MEME. While in **T3**, **T4** and **T5**, the aim is to build the accompanying governance and reward structures to mesh differences and operationalize the alliance.

For this reason, the Operative Partnerships Group builds Alliance Operating Principles, Alliance Charters and other documents and tools that express shared mental models to help establish an operating culture that is expanded into both firms. Subsequently, if the ^{V}MEMEs cannot find a way to mesh and establish a common *Group-CROS*, with operating norms and cultural cohesion, the partnership will not survive for long and will be plagued with problems of mistrust and other discontinuities if ever launched. With this in mind, the *Partnership Coach* uses Spiral Dynamics as a framework to conceptualize what opportunities and challenges may occur down the Inverted Cone where the deeper dynamics of value systems are located and new dialectic tensions emerge. When they do, the group will eventually have to produce solutions and group structures that will accommodate ^{V}MEME differences both contextually in the operating of the alliance as well as subjectively in the relational field.

Discerning Patterns of Group Relating

As the group comes together to work on the partnership, participants' interactions can be either entropic to group goals, supplementary to the possible emergence of something new or complementary to its work. Each of these patterns of relating either supports the team's progression through task moments or can become a hindrance. Understanding these relational patterns helps the coach prepare and implement tactics that help the group further in its task.

Entropic relating results when a group is not able to accept, accommodate and use contributions and interactions productively. It can also emerge when the group is unable to work within set limits to produce and sustain productive and effective engagement. As such, entropic relating causes movement into situations of mistrust, incapacity for advancement and general group breakdown. Cybernetics and General Systems Theory have identified several entropic patterns or systems archetypes such as *Shifting the Burden, Tragedy of the Commons and Fixes that Fail* among others (Herasymowych & Senko, 2007, p. 6). *Shifting the Burden* involves teams not addressing the fundamental issues but rather devising symptomatic solutions to a problem (Braun, 2002, p. 4). Entropic relating occurs when the interactions of the group produce negatively reinforcing patterns that result in groups not attaining their goals. In the *Dynamics of False Consensus*, the group fears the leader and rather than expressing ideas openly, members engage in covert conversations and undermining activities while nodding and pretending to agree. The results are continued undermining activities and goal misalignment (Slobodnik & Wile, 1999, p. 4). These dynamics can be seen in group meetings when the group engages in activities that involve not speaking from individual points of view but in hyperbole, or justifying their decisions by referring to corporate policies, etc. In these instances, there is a lack of accommodation to the group task and incapacity to fully engage in the work. Oftentimes, there may be a contradiction between feelings of being safe in relating while not being able to express real concerns in the group. Providing supportive facilitation can help the group to enter into greater levels of trust. Establishing boundaries and norms for meetings promotes better relating, e.g., having the group agree not to share things outside the meeting can be a great way to build greater trust in their interactions. Another way is empathically communicating an understanding of difficulties that speakers may be encountering in meetings.

Supplementary Relating

Alternatively, supplementary relating involves ways in which the group's heterogeneity helps to remedy deficiencies. For example, individual-oriented people working with group-oriented people have the opportunity to produce results which could be markedly different from complementary individuals working together. In contrast to entropic relational systems, positive archetypes produce supplementary results. In the stereotypical entropic system, *Shifting the Burden*, the group knows the fundamental solution but is unwilling to do what is needed. In contrast, *Bite the Bullet*, representing supplementary relating dynamics, results in the group being willing to invest time and money to tackle business challenges at the root regardless of how difficult it is (Herasymowych & Senko, 2007, p. 7).

Complementary Relating

Complementary relating is less about addressing deficiencies and supporting productivity but more about completing and stabilizing group interactions. At times, complementary relating can be supportive toward the end of meeting sessions, but not as helpful in meeting challenges head on. Complementary relating can produce a stabilizing force that results in the group not fully looking for and finding ideas and opportunities for real innovation and creation. At the end of meetings, situations of complementary relating help the teams stabilize themselves in terms of group productivity. If complementary relating is occurring in the middle of the task stage it could prove to be quite ineffectual. Complementary relating would involve the same ^{V}MEMEs working together toward a common goal and addressing challenges from their shared perspectives. In situations where ^{V}MEMEs are the same, the group's capacity to produce new and innovative solutions could be arrested. Group studies have consistently found that when homogeneity of members is promoted in teams it tends to arrest innovation and problem-solving. When heterogeneity is encouraged, it supports collaboration and effective change processes, particularly in times when innovation and co-creation are needed.

Promoting Productive Relating

Spiral Dynamics gives the coach a framework for understanding the inherent complementarity and supplementarity of groups and helps anticipate any possible challenges ahead. According to Clare Graves, ^{V}MEMEs that are odd-numbered (meaning individually oriented) are more focused on growth and changing the environment, while those that are even-numbered (meaning collectively oriented) are interested in consolidating and adjusting to the environment (2005, p. 189). As such, complementarity and supplementarity can be somewhat anticipated. For example, the Green ^{V}MEME would produce a state of general relational complementarity. Since the Green is a consolidating ^{V}MEME, the behaviors and attitudes would be of group participation, insular in nature as well as quite dogmatic. The same kind of complementarity would occur with ^{V}MEMEs expressing the Red, Blue, and Orange systems. Here, the Red engaging with the Red would ensue continued battles of "might makes right". The Blue ^{V}MEMEs would involve hierarchical and bureaucratic systems creating values for the masses, yet two Blue teams may also conflict greatly. The Orange systems would place all the financial burdens of the business on consumers, working to produce the highest returns and shareholder value. The Yellow Meme is different in many respects. It does have the capacity to produce better results and can work more effectively, although may produce solutions unrealistic to the specific needs of the alliance. In short, complementarity can produce rather different results in partnering while supplementarity supports change and innovation. The work of the coach is to help groups enter moments where they can engage together in supplementary relating so that they can create innovative opportunities to build the best possible alliance.

There are activities that can help the teams delve deeper and bring forth greater levels of supplementarity. The coach may present different objective data to help the teams look for better solutions to problems. Also, he may ask the group to consider what others have come up with or help the group decide who else can be invited to help them bring new perspectives into their work. An additional tactic available would be to break the teams into groups and engage in structuring debates to help the teams arrive at new solutions using point-counter point deliberations or intellectual watchdog debates. Both debate structures are used to help the teams enliven their relating and help them to engage in supplementary relating.

Of course, all individuals in the same group having the same ^{V}MEME is highly unlikely. The greater likelihood is that several ^{V}MEMEs will be present in a group and will express themselves as implicit dynamics that need to be productively surfaced. These deeper elements of the inverted cone require both a field of relationship as well as an articulation of the needs which arise out of each ^{V}MEME when expressed. For instance, the Red vMEME has the need to feel powerful and independent from the group. The Blue ^{V}MEME requires the approval of the group and direction from the leader, while the Orange ^{V}MEME is looking for open discussion and deliberation. Finally, the Green ^{V}MEME wants open dialogue where everyone contributes, and the Yellow ^{V}MEME would prefer that there is a balance of interactions where all opinions are voiced, those of the individuals themselves and the group collectively, and where the correct functional decision is made.

There can be a high degree of complexity when you have more than two ᵛMEMEs expressing themselves in a meeting. The usefulness of Spiral Dynamics is to illuminate what occurs between the ᵛMEMEs and to help orient the facilitation using the *Operative Partnership Methodology*. The capacity of the group to overcome challenges inherent in ᵛMEME meshing will reside in its ability to have the conversations needed to go down the inverted cone. The group will also need to address the deeper elements of relating and begin to collaborate to build an operative alliance. Developing the partnership and the alliance structure will eventually require that the ᵛMEMEs mesh in a complementary and/or supplementary fashion. That means they will support each other to complete each other's needs or provide additional competencies for the firms.

Historical Perspectives & Life Experiences

At the deepest levels of the inverted cone reside the historical perspectives of culture, and the life experiences of the people who form the group. As mentioned previously, all individuals are born into relationships and are shaped by the relationships they established at a young age and throughout their lives. When people interact with others, they unconsciously reference these structures which activate patterns of effect. These patterns can become obstacles or opportunities. In this respect, the *Tele* concept where groups express affinity or repulsion toward each other (pp. 67-68) refers to a reencounter in the present with these past references. *Tele* can also be referred to as *empathic resonance*. This is the set of reciprocated interpersonal attractions and aversions that arises when people truly begin to work together (Blatner, 2009, p. 1). *Tele* is a purely subjective phenomenon that can also be seen when groups operate together. In groups, some people "hit it off" right away, others "rub each other the wrong way." Yet, these phenomena are purely subjective experiences that participants have based on personal individual histories, values systems and other inter-relational dynamics. It is a reaction that people experience and which can be facilitated when groups are working together. And further still, while the negative *Tele* can be experienced through the group it may also move as emotional networks within the group's interactions.

Enabling Collaboration

As the implicit becomes more conscious in the group, the capacity for a greater degree of authentic relating grows and the capability to walk down the inverted cone increases. Here, the group moves down the explicit path through communication and into cooperation, towards states of learning and change that bring about true collaboration.

Chapter 6
Facilitating the Emergence of Operative Partnership Groups

The *Operative Partnership Methodology* allows the coach to orient interventions and understand progression from a relational perspective and, in the case of organizational alliance, across the *5-Territories of Alliance Development*. Yet, it is the actual gamut of interventions that produces change and encourages the group to be operative. This is not, however, a mechanistic process where the technician introduces a particular facilitative approach to produce a specific result which then helps the group traverse progress in some calculated fashion. Rather, the coach's function is to understand the group's emotional conflicts and intervene as an epistemologist, attempting to induce the group to launch a more critical analysis of its own theory of operating (Tubert-Oklander & Hernández de Tubert, 2004, p. 101).

The approaches and interventions described in this and the following chapter enable the group to sustain deeper and deeper levels of operability down the inverted cone. A summary version of proven successful methods and approaches to help groups affiliate and build a shared sense of membership, communicate and build a sustainable level of cooperation, setting a foundation for learning and change, will be presented. Essentially, the coach supports the group by helping the members elaborate what is occurring in the field, identifying obstacles and supporting latent elements emerging through the facilitative and coaching process (Figures 10 & 11).

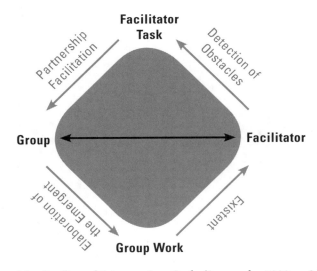

Figure 10 – Facilitated Intervention Cycle (Leonardo, 1992, p. 2.)

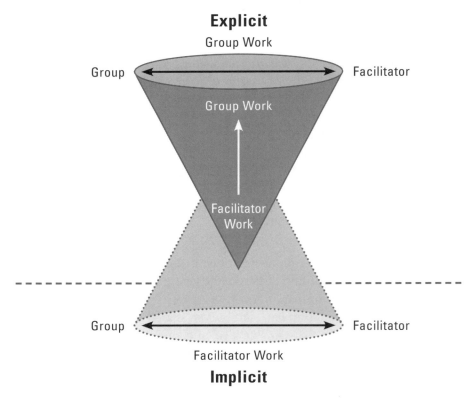

Figure 11 – Facilitated Intervention through the Inverted Partnership Cone

The following section presents the broader use of different meeting structures to the more specific facilitative interventions. Woven together, the meeting structures create the frame and the facilitative interventions create the possibility for successful group productivity.

Using Different Meeting Structures

Meeting structures have an impact on how groups work and set the potential for the outcomes that are generated. Therefore, it is important to choose the most appropriate meeting structure given the set of subjective and objective goals. Subjective goals are those that allow teams to connect and relate given where they are in the alliance development process, making explicit the implicit and building the relational field to engage authentically. Objective goals refer to making decisions, completing tasks and moving forward on structuring the work activities of each territory throughout the journey.

This denotes a continuum in which different meeting structures are planned. In the closed meeting structure, every minute is accounted for and all activities clearly laid out. Presentations are made and discussions are scheduled within pre-defined time slots where specific activities are to take place. In the open structure, meeting topics are generated by the group, considering the group self-regulates its interactions and works to accomplish its goals. Both, however, are applicable and useful depending on the goals, needs and where the team is in the *5-Territories of Alliance Development* process.

For instance, closed meetings are used, more often than not, when there are decisions that have remained unresolved for some time or the tasks are technical and tactical. They are used when the team's subjective emotional resilience is already high and there is a level of authentic engagement that allows the group to be operative. In effect, closed meetings are held after the more open meetings have already occurred and the teams have already established their emotional operative norms. They are not implemented at the beginning of partnering conversations, but can be quite effective during the latter part of **T3** when groups are consolidating their plans and need to get through predetermined pieces of work. This may also occur during **T4** in the final contract negotiations and when launching activities are taking place.

During the initial invitation meetings of **T2**, meetings can be more structured but not closed; in the beginning of **T3**, these become more open and more structured and closed as needed over time. Open meetings founded on dialogue work better to allow the group to get to know itself, build the emotional resilience to tackle obstacles and the opportunity to allow for discourse, discussion and co-creation. Meetings where dialogue is encouraged are more open and allow more freedom of thought and action and, as such, produce the opportunity for more operability. These kinds of meetings can be more emotionally charged, but also allow for the implicit to surface. On the other hand, closed meetings can be less emotionally charged yet, by their very nature of being so organized, can strangle group operability in the early stages of alliance development.

For almost as long as humans have been alive, dialogue has been the foundation of groups facing challenges and working together to create possible futures. In the practice of setting the *Partnership Field of Relationship* there are several dialogic structures to choose from, some more structured than others. The type of dialogue methods chosen for partnerships development needs to take into consideration the goals of the session. The following five meeting structures are good options to choose from. The coach can combine them to create unique meetings to support partnership development.

Open Space Technology The participants are responsible for the development of the agenda, the execution of the topics and the work of the day. *Open Space Technology* was developed by Harrison Owen, a well-known organizational development consultant. He asked whether it was "possible to combine the level of synergy and excitement present in a good coffee break with the substantive activity and results characteristic of a good meeting?" (Harrison, 1997, p. 4). According to Harrison, *Open Space Technology* will not work in settings where there is an autocratic political structure and no room for individual participation and cooperation. If the topics for the meeting are very technical and follow a blueprint of activities, *Open Space Technology* will also not be appropriate. For example, the implementation of a new technical banking platform would not be the right subject for such a meeting structure. It is also inappropriate when the outcome is preset or the sponsors are not willing to change as a result of what happens in the meeting.

However, it would work in the elaboration of potential products and services that an alliance could bring to market together or other such innovative activities during the initial phases after commitment. Here, diverse teams representing several stakeholders can come together to develop and design the potential opportunities of an alliance leveraging each other's core competencies and opportunities in **T3**, Phase 1 (Create). In this respect, the alliances teams do not know all the answers but do recognize that an opportunity exists. It can also be used to address an impasse in the partnership where various opinions and points of view can be used to help resolve questions whose answers are truly unknown to the group (Harrison, 1997). Open Space Technology works by *The Four Principles* and *The One Law*. The four principles are:

1. *Whoever comes are the right people* – the focus is not on the positions or influence of the people who show up, or their number, but the quality of conversations that they have.
2. *Whatever happens is the only thing that could have* happened – this acts as a reminder that for real learning to happen, the group needs to let go of any prescribed ideas and agendas to really create the unexpected.
3. *When it starts is the right time* – this principle introduces the concept that breakthroughs are not time-bound but emergent, they do not adhere to demands of time and space that people place on them (e.g. the meeting starts at 9:00 am and ends at 5:00pm.)
4. *When it's over, it's over* – the time we allotted was more than needed and we can adjourn only when the work is done, not when it was scheduled to end.

The One Law is simple but powerful: if, during the gathering, any person feels they are not contributing or learning from the experience, they must use their two feet and go to a more productive place, perhaps to another of the smaller work groups (Harrison, 1997, pp. 95-99).

World Café

This is a derivative of *Open Space Technology* in that it revolves around Owen Harrison's initial question. The process works similarly in that participants focus on what matters and create the meeting through what is important to them through the conversations that they have. The World Café method is founded on conversation as a core process, involving reflection and exploration, accessing collective insights, discoveries, action planning and implementation with feedback and assessment (Brown, 2005). Like a wheel, the process can be a continued work of creation and discovery of the participants conversing and acting together. The structure of the meeting is set around this circular focus and can be implemented at various stages in the alliance development process.

The World Café begins with the group asking pertinent questions, those that truly matter to them. Those questions are consolidated by the coach to form topic areas that the sub-groups work through together in the Café. The Café is created when the group is divided into smaller table-gatherings set up in the same conference room. Each table takes on one individual topic area. Conversations are then held at each table in Café rounds for a period of 30 to 45 minutes, but normally are no longer than one hour. Participants rotate from table to table, having Café conversations and chronicling their comments and ideas. Each table is hosted by one participant who remains at the table and maintains the continuity of the conversations. Through the conversations, innovative ideas get consolidated into thematic approaches which are further refined into action steps established for further implementation and development. A World Café session can run for between four hours to one day and is generally incorporated into other processes in **T3** to help consolidate and build action planning steps to be further refined.

The brilliance of the World Café is that it catalyzes separate individuals and teams to come together to tackle important issues through the questions they ask and their productive conversations. The process is open enough in that it allows for a group to work together, and begin establishing their operative norms by learning and sharing together, while closed enough to maintain a certain amount of structure to help the group organize activities and follow-up tasks.

Deep Democracy

This is a facilitation methodology based on the idea that there is wisdom and ideas in the minority voice that for some reason or another is not being explored by the group. The approach is, in line with the *World Café* and *Open Space Technology*, meant to open an atmosphere where diverse viewpoints can be shared. Yet, Deep Democracy as a conscious intervention is different in that it is meant to bring out the minority or unpopular viewpoints that remain stuck in the implicit. It is meant to bring out those underlying emotional dynamics that are continuously blocking the alliances group from moving forward (Bojer, et al., 2006, p. 36).

The basics of the approach are to focus on the minority "no", rather than allow for a typical democratic show of votes where the focus is on the majority "yes". The coach asks that the group take time to understand the thinking behind the "no" and consider the ideas and concepts it is expressing. He may also amplify communication of the "no" to ensure it is heard. *Deep Democracy* is meant to allow for the dissenting opinions to be heard so the group can work through them productively. The idea is to encourage the "no" to surface, and to work with the group to amplify its intensity and find the thinking and the wisdom that could be missed if left unchecked. For teams that are stuck, *Deep Democracy* is an important way to help get back on track and ignite supplementary relating. This meeting structure can also be used at different points in the journey to ensure that dissenting views are taken into consideration and no stone is left unturned. Deep Democracy works through the following four steps:

1. Use majority democracy only as a starting point but not an ending point.
2. Search for and open the dissenting "no" that is expressed when people vote for or against an idea or course of action.
3. Spread and share the "no". Allow the group to openly consider and inquire what the "no" is pointing out.
4. Including the wisdom of the "no". Work with the minority to understand what will help them to agree and come together with the majority.

Transformative Scenario Planning

This is a process used when there is a high degree of complexity and where several decisions need to be taken, often simultaneously. The decisions are based on an in-depth review of potential scenarios. This meeting structure is used when the group is in a predicament where it can affect what will happen but could also be affected by many possible outcomes. As such, *Transformative Scenario Planning* offers groups a new way to work together to change the future (Kahane, 2012, p. XV). The meeting structure is based on the work of Pierre Wack at Shell Oil in the 1970s and Adam Kahane's involvement in facilitating the Mont Fleur Scenarios during the early moments of the end of South Africa's apartheid and his subsequent work. The Transformative Scenario Planning process works through the following five steps:

1. Convene a team from across the system.
2. Observe what is happening.
3. Construct stories about what could happen.
4. Discover what could and must happen.
5. Act to transform the system.
(Kahane, 2012, p. 98)

The *Transformative Scenarios Planning* process can be employed for networked systemic alliances that involve a larger set of partners and groups that are facing change and uncertainty. The key focus is working to address the complexity affecting all partners.

Future Search

This concept, designed by organizational development consultants Marvin Weisbord and Sandra Janoff (2010), both resembles *Transformative Scenario Planning* in that it is meant to work with all the actors in a system as well as produce change and collaborative action. The focus is to analyze the past, present and future to get groups to take responsibility for what has been created, what is, and what could be. Unlike the *Transformative Scenario Planning Process*, which can take several months, *Future Search* is created through a very specific three-day structure typically involving 60-70 participants (Bojer, et al., 2006, p. 40). Arrangement of the agenda follows these steps:

1. Review the past
2. Explore the present
3. Create ideal future scenarios
4. Identify common ground
5. Make action plans

Future Search also requires that certain key conditions be met:

1. People from across the "whole system" must be in the room.
2. The "Big Picture" as context for local action is shared and evaluated.
3. Common ground must be built by exploring current realities and common futures, not problems and conflicts.
4. Self-managed exploration and action plans are developed to reduce passivity, hierarchy and dependency on coaches.
5. Everyone must attend the whole meeting.

6. The meeting must be held under healthy conditions, where there is good natural light and enough space to convene and arrange space.
7. The work should last three days to allow things to settle over two nights.
8. Taking responsibility publicly for follow-up actions and commitments grounds the potential results (Bojer, et al., 2006, pp. 42-43).

The elements of these five meeting structures are a basis for enabling successful partnerships. They are not only tactically useful in building partnerships but strategically relevant in that they encourage the kind of relational subjectivity which *Operative Partnership Groups* need to be successful in alliance building.

The first core element they share is that partnerships and alliances are seen as an evolving conversation of independent members of a group who have become interdependent through their shared inquiry, interests and relating. By having conversations that matter and employing the methodology, the group coalesces into a partnership. Productive conversations are encouraged through these meeting structures which share certain commonalities:

1. A spirit of inquiry, reflection and exchange helps groups to arrive at productive solutions and creative ideas for the alliance.
2. Inquiry is created through asking relevant questions.
3. The group is responsible for its structure and its resulting dynamics, both through the commitment that members bring and the kind of questions asked.
4. The concept of participatory collaborative leadership is employed, leadership shifts around the room based on what conversations are being held and the expertise and perspective of the group.
5. Strategic direction and subsequent actions are jointly developed and agreed to.
6. The circle is used several times as an operative structure that fosters equality and shared learning, where power is distributed and collective insights are mined.
7. Facilitation occurs in all dialogic structures and supports group operability through varied methods creating a frame and field of play.

In as far as partnership development is concerned, it is the role of the *Partnership Coach* to set the field of play by designing and structuring the sessions. Oftentimes meetings are structured as a two-to-three-day work-shop, other times as working sessions that can last a full day or a few days, and finally as a meeting that lasts from one to three hours. Their application, duration and structure are chosen based on where the group is along the alliance development process and the objective and subjective intentions of the reunions. For example, during the initial meetings in **T2**, the meetings are shorter in duration and involve a more closed structure. As the teams progress into **T3**, a structured and well-organized *Partnership Innovation Session* is held which uses a dialogic structure over the course of several days involving a larger group of 15 to 25 or more people to begin structuring the alliance. These innovation sessions use elements of each structure reviewed above. As the teams move through **T3**, techniques from *Open Technology* and others are employed till the alliance is developed and the final negotiations take place. In regards to moments where the alliance has launched and is not meeting expectations, and/or there are significant challenges ahead, elements of *Deep Democracy* and *Transformative Scenario Planning* or *Future Search* may be employed. Again, this is the work of active and conscious facilitation, understanding where the group is along the five territories and ensuring that once meetings are held, follow-on activities support the group to maintain traction and continuity toward the group's objectives.

Working with and Clarifying Purpose

Supporting the group to clarify purpose occurs to varying degrees throughout the journey. For instance, at the end of **T2** (pp. 181-190) the purpose is simply to commit to invest resources toward the designing of an alliance. That purpose is combined with the contextual information shared on why an alliance should be formed. However, as the group progresses from one work activity to another, as in **T3** (pp. 191-227) and beyond, the group articulates the purpose of those particular meetings, e.g., creating the collaboration and governance structure, developing roles and responsibilities, testing, piloting, etc. Intentions are communicated openly. In this respect the coach uses purpose as a way to guide the group to focus on the work-tasks and as a reference point to ensure productive progress across the 5-Territories.

Additionally, as the teams work through **T3** (pp. 191-227), they begin to divulge their unique interests in deeper and clearer ways. As this occurs, the overriding purpose for partnering is created. This overriding purpose sets the larger contextual framework for the partnership and is used by the coach to focus and re-focus the group's attention to the tasks where the group may be stuck or in unproductive disagreements. As the purpose becomes more and more refined, it is used to build the Alliance Charter and other tools for launching the partnership.

Contracting, Setting Rules of Engagement & Establishing Operating Principles

Contracting is the process by which the group begins a meeting and agrees to the tasks at hand, including how they intend to do the work. Building consistent rules of engagement during working sessions supports the group in operating effectively by clarifying how it wants to be together. Rules can be used at different times of the alliance development process. For instance, during the partnership innovation sessions held in **T3** (pp. 191-227) rules such as *No Spectators* are used to ensure that everyone participates fully in the meeting. At other times, there may be the need to use rules that help to frame the kind of interaction that supports the group to progress in its task. For example, *Share Your Thinking* can be used for groups that may be advocating certain positions but not allowing for productive dialogue to emerge. Subsequently, rules are sometimes imposed by the coach depending on the purpose, tasks or place along the journey, and also are co-created with the group's input.

Alliance Operating Principles tend to emerge from operating and engagement principles that are repeatedly used over time. They are also larger in scope and depth than contracting and rules of engagement. They are created in the Consolidate Phase of **T3** as a dynamic interplay of purpose, metaphor and substance that helps the alliance consolidate around a unique social contract. *Alliance Operating Principles* elaborate the shared and individual characteristics of each company which become reference points for negotiation, as well as operating the alliance. Over time, these principles help the group consolidate its unique alliance culture and norms that help deepen and expand the alliance's potential in **T5** (pp. 248-254).

Helping to Clarify Language

Helping to clarifying language is a process by which the coach actively assists the group to agree on the meaning of terms used. Undoubtedly, throughout the process there will be terminology used by one company that refers to the way that firm measures and conceptualizes the business. The other company may use different terms that have similar but unequal meanings. The coach helps the group identify terms that bridge differences in business culture and also supports the teams in establishing shared meanings. This intervention involves identifying moments when there is unclear use of language that leads to either misunderstanding between the groups or instances where language is being used to hide the implicit. Nuances in language and unclear communication serve to disperse emotion, support individuals who wish to hide interests and to indirectly maneuver around sensitive topics. These situations, if not addressed, can build up over time and become real elements of derailment in the future.

As such, helping teams to clarify language supports them in creating shared mental models and a clear understanding of intentions and ideas. To do this, the coach supports the active creation of shared nomenclature, e.g., writing the meaning of key words or phrases on flip-charts. In so doing, the group begins to build a meaningful shared vocabulary that will support deeper inquiry and, as a result, learning together. In this sense, the group through its emotional relatedness discards old ideas and discerns what is important.

Optimizing Learning Capacity through Emotions

Learning for the group is change and change is learning. In order for learning to happen individuals must be open to it. They must be willing to drop, let go and re-organize old knowledge (ideas, concepts, and ways of doing or approaching things). Fundamentally, learning is a process of change, emotionally charged, both positively and negatively depending on the group orientation. Oftentimes, a group is fixed on ideas and concepts which it considers to be right and true. As the group begins to question previously acquired knowledge through its interactions, it unavoidably runs into emotional dynamics of attack, defensiveness and/or feelings of possible loss. At deeper levels, individuals and groups hold to ideas and concepts of what is considered to be true. Concepts and ideas are the basis of the way we observe and understand the world around us. Thus, when new concepts or ideas emerge, the group must adapt to that learning process.

However, optimizing group capacity for learning demands that emotions flow. As gateways to learning, emotions need to circulate in the group and be openly communicated. Allowing them to be expressed enables productive inter-subjective work to occur. Through language and emoting, real and authentic conversations take place. Anger, frustration, happiness, joy: all emotions are always the right emotions to have. No emotion is fundamentally "negative" or "positive". It is in the leaking or acting out of those emotions, in mixed messaging, verbal attacks, hyper-happiness and other unproductive ways that the group reduces its power to mobilize real learning and adaptive change. Ambition, competitiveness, anger, envy, aggression and fear reduce group intelligence and restrict the domain of openness in consensual conversation (Maturana & Verden-Zoller, 1996, p. 6). However, no group can change and learn if "negative" emotions are just bottled up or put under the table, and monitored or policed by rigid policies of engagement introduced by the facilitation. Groups cannot mobilize if the "positive" emotions are held back either. All emotions are needed for real and true learning to emerge, through consensual conversations focused on co-creation and problem solving (Maturana & Verden-Zoller, 1996, pp. 1-8). Consequently, the group establishes a field of relationship that has a certain emotional depth and amplitude created by emoting together. The result for the group is an opportunity for learning and becoming together as they work though different domains of reality in their interactions with others, explicitly or implicitly, according to the flow of their emoting (Maturana, 1988, p. 22).

Through the implementation of group practice methods such as *Principles of Engagement*, all emotions can be expressed in productive ways so that the group can come into learning and change together. At times, *Principles of Engagement* can be used by the group to quell emotionality and reduce productivity. Using them requires conscious facilitation to ensure the most supportive principles are in place and not ones that restrict emotions from being voiced. The aim is to create neither a space of judgment, nor one of parental dynamics, where the coach berates the unruly children. Avoiding these allows the group to hold the emotions and experience their usefulness in making decisions and entering a state of relevance and team collaboration. Additionally, the coach can help to work with the emotional interplay in the room. This can mean shifting the emotionality in the room by incorporating humor, lightness and play when needed, or working with the team to hold the tension in moments when the group is avoiding and not fully processing. Appropriate interventions by the coach support the group to ultimately deepen the emotional resonance in the field to produce team learning.

Additionally, in times when the group is entering learning and change but is having difficulty (which may be most acute in **T3** Phase 2, Change & Learning, pp. 210-221), the coach can help organize work so that the learning can become more and more depersonalized, while still remaining effective. Storyboarding and mapping of alternatives are productive ways to help the teams look at ideas and alternatives from a different perspective. Constructing games for the group to experience allows learning in different ways through the fun and inquisitive conversations achieved. Finally, simply respecting and allowing emotionality to be present in the field is foundational. Through emoting in conversations, the group learns and moves through change. Thus it becomes able to discern what to do, how to work more productively and how to innovate as a coherent unit.

Chapter 7
Enabling Group Flow and Reflective Learning through Facilitative Leadership

Group flow is an experience of group co-creativity, learning and collaboration. It occurs when the conditions are set for the group to productively work together, encouraged, at each meeting and from meeting to meeting, by the *Partnership Coach* and by the *Observer*. Group flow is in many respects the ultimate state of group collaboration characterized as an energized collective focus on tasks when entering the *project phase*. This possibility requires ongoing reflective strategies.

The task of the *Partnership Coach* and the *Observer* is to help build the capacity for group flow through specific strategies, which, consistently applied, create the potential for collaboration to occur in group work-sessions. They also help the group establish productive relationships which, over time, become an important part of its operating norms and culture.

Additionally, the work of the group is to establish a productive rhythm by keeping the lines of communication open, both in working sessions and in between them, to create a continuous flow of learning and purpose. Pichon-Rivière, who wrote his theory in Spanish, referred to this process as *"retro-alimentación"*, which can be translated as *"feedback."* In Pichon-Rivière's conceptualization this refers to feedback that enriches and sustains the process. As such, the key aim is to create a continuous cycle of repeated enriched feedback within the group to foster communication, cooperation that leads to experiential learning. To accomplish this, the *Partnership Coach* and *Observer*, through various strategies and the use of the *Alliance-CROS*, support the group to become productive.

Enabling Group Reflective Learning

Group Reflective Learning is a process for facilitating groups to become operative. It is a strategy implemented throughout the alliance development process that supports groups to face the dialectic tensions experienced as the *Operative Partnership Methodology* is employed. The group must traverse the conflict between the concrete experience and abstract concepts of the alliance and between group observation and actions. Another tension occurs as the group works to adapt and accommodate while assimilating experiences into existing conceptual structures (Kolb, 1984, p. 29). The *Partnership Coach* supports the group to work through these tensions by helping it reflect on its progress, as well as discover in clearer terms how it is addressing the challenges of its collaboration.

Additionally, *Group Reflective Learning* is enabled when the *Partnership Coach* helps move the conversational space from monologues to conversation, and thus into collaborative dialogue, in an appropriate and timely fashion. Through action, reflecting and inquiring, the dialectic nature of learning and adaptation turns into a praxis defined by Paulo Freire as "reflection and action upon the world in order to transform it" (Kolb, 1984, p. 29). In this respect, the group optimizes its potential for success in the alliance. In a continuous cycle, the process is one of consistently connecting to the contextual challenges faced by the group in meeting collective goals. The *Partnership Coach* and the *Observer* support the emergence of collaborative leadership, which opens the potential for group flow.

All group members, as well as the *Partnership Coach* and *Observer*, reflect as they engage in their work. The *Partnership Coach* and the *Observer* review and reflect on their task to support the group, while the group itself is given information and guidelines to support its own reflective learning. Such learning and the potential for growth at the individual–group–organizational levels are key for successful group partnership and company alliances.

Group Action Reflection & Inquiry

Group Action Reflection & Inquiry refers to the learning strategies used by the *Partnership Coach* and the *Observer* to support the group to become centered on its task. From the *Operative Partnership Methodology, Action Reflection & Inquiry* assists groups to reflect on their work together and inquire into assumptions, mental models and other latent elements that affect group operability. The goal is to create an opportunity for increased collective learning and group development which opens the potential for group flow.

Action Reflection comes from the work of Kurt Lewin (Kolb, 1984, p. 21), and *Action Inquiry* from Chris Argyris and Donald Schön (1989), John Heron and Peter Reason (1999) and Bill Torbert (2004). *Group Action Reflection & Inquiry* as used here involves the full range of strategies used in the moment and, after situations have passed, to help groups operationalize. Lewin proposes a four-stage integrated process for learning in which he considers the "here-and-now" followed by the collection of data and observations which is analyzed and fed back to the group. Argyris and Schön pioneered the idea of double-loop learning where groups enter an exploration of the foundational thinking and values that leads to their behavioral patterns. Congruent to this, Heron and Reason suggest that individuals who engage in research should also become the subjects of that research. In this way, they reflect on how they affect their own research as participants and simultaneously enhance the possibility of their own learning. Double-loop learning interventions create an opportunity for groups to reframe their assumptions so that they may produce different results. Expanding on Argyris and Schön, Torbert developed *Action Inquiry*, which is "a way of simultaneously conducting action and inquiry as a disciplined leadership practice that increases the wider effectiveness" of individual and group actions (Torbert, 2004, p. 1). The method introduces triple-loop learning where people ask themselves "how do we decide what is right?" (Alia Institute, 2013, p. 10) and "what actions to take?"; i.e., questions that help seek out the origin of behavioral patterns.

Through the *Group Action Reflection & Inquiry* strategies, the *Partnership Coach* and the *Observer* help groups identify the mental models that promote change before new behaviors can be put in place. This process helps the group progress deeper into *the implicit (Pichon-Rivière)* which the coach maps using the *Inverted Cone* (Chapter 4, pp. 69-74).

Circular Processes of Group Action Reflection & Inquiry

The Partnership Coach and the Observer facilitate the group around four simultaneous learning processes where action reflection and inquiry strategies are consistently implemented and refined (Figure 12). Each of the circles refers to the action reflections that occur at each level: individuals and group, facilitator and observer.

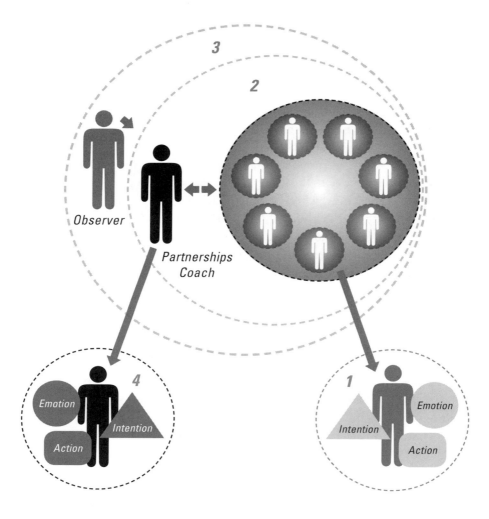

Figure 12 – Circular Processes of Group Action Reflection and Inquiry

One process involves a first-person reflection at the individual level. The task is for individuals in the group to become aware of their own intentions, emotions and actions through self-reflection and inquiry. Participants can be assigned a journaling activity practice to reflect upon the activities of the day, and how they contributed or not to the group task. This can be used as a strategy when there is a high degree of tension in the group, or the group is stuck during a meeting.

The second learning process involves the group itself. Following Lewin's four-phase *Experiential Learning Model*, this includes checking-in and planning activities, working through communication, having concrete experiences as a group, as well as reflecting on the outcomes of working sessions. In line with co-operative inquiry, the *Partnership Coach* helps the group analyze its perceiving, acting and remembering, at times reframing and launching concepts, while also supporting the group through the anxieties stirred by inquiry (Heron & Reason, 1999, p. 2).

The coaching process can help the group shed light on blind spots. To do this, the coach poses questions to the group, makes observations or provides enriched feedback that leads the group to reflect and inquire into what is happening. Through reflection-in-action the group takes inputs, makes changes to its approach, its ways of conceptualizing issues and working together. As work proceeds, the *Partnership Coach* interjects and facilitates to further stimulate reflection and inquiry, thus, enhancing operability. The goal is for the group to change the way it is communicating and working together.

The third learning process is promoted through the *enriched feedback* of the Observer, who operates as a silent participant incorporating both the *Partnership Coach's* facilitation of the group as well as the group's reaction to the interventions. The Observer chronicles the meetings and at the end of each working session reads the chronicle out loud for the group to reflect on.

The chronicle briefly describes the group process: the challenges, the capacity to change, learning, as well as the disposition of the group to be task-centered. The goal for the group is to articulate, reflect and organize for the next session. On an individual member level, participants reflect on their own contributions to the outcomes and operability of the group.

The fourth action reflection circle pertains to the *Partnership Coach* and *Observer*, if there is one, to function in reference to the *Group-CROS* and the challenges experienced in the task. During partnership meetings, the *Partnership Coach* enters a moment by moment Action Inquiry process of thinking, feeling and acting to support the group's operative functioning. From the third-person perspective, the *Partnership Coach* experiences the group: what is being communicated, where the group is in its trajectory down the inverted cone, the task-phases, the goals and activities of the meeting. At the same time, the *Partnership Coach* is attuned to the impacts that those interactions are having on them, on an emotional-relational-conceptual level. As an instrument of change, he uses all his/her capabilities in service of the efforts of the group, avoiding relational spaces that curtail group functioning.

After each working session, the *Partnership Coach* conducts a conscious and structured reflection process incorporating the *Operative Partnership Methodology* and working through his/her own personal inquiry. To do this, they reflects on what happened in the meeting including any important thoughts and feelings that came up for them during the facilitation. Then he chronicles the most significant issues to enter into a deeper inquiry into what happened. The *Partnership Coach* reflects on what they were trying to do for the group?", "how they responded?" and "what facilitative or coaching strategy was implemented?". As the coach reflects deeper into their own operability, they also inquire into why they felt the way they did and what informed them to take on the decisions they took, as well as what they could have done to improve the situation. Both action inquiry and action reflection open a level of personal understanding and into the Alliance-CROS so that he may grow in capacity to enable group operability.

As part of his/her task, the *Partnership Coach* analyzes group operability by chronicling each meeting and mapping the group's progression through the *Inverted Cone*. The coach reviews the emergent roles and determines the group's progression through the task, pre-task and projects phases *(Chapter 4, pp. 61-64)*. In doing so, the *Partnership Coach* asks themself questions that support this process, such as whether the group is truly progressing or simply delaying the more difficult conversations. Is the group resolving differences or glossing over them? What else could be occurring within the group? What is a potential obstacle to success? The information is then used to prepare for follow-up meetings in order to ensure continuity and determine the best structure for future facilitations. In a continuous spiraling circle, the group becomes more productive and, over time, establishes its own operability as a result of these strategies.

Meeting chronicles, prepared by the *Partnership Coach* or the *Observer*, if there is one, serve a double purpose. The first is to recount group occurrences from previous meetings to help the group reflect on progress and coordinate activities. For the *Partnership Coach*, they are a key tool for analyzing, as well as recounting the activities and work done, framework and observations of the group that include communication, points of contention, disagreements, positions and emotions. The *Partnership Coach* is guided by the *vectors* of the inverted cone to construct the chronicle.

Consider the following example of a chronicle of a group meeting. In this case, CompanyX, a major international bank, and CompanyY, a major retailer, are pursuing an alliance across six international markets. They have already signed a *Mutual Commitment Agreement* (pp. 189-190) and are in the beginning stages of the **T3**, where they must map the roles and responsibilities of each firm. The assigned activity is meant to take no longer than two to three hours.

Chronicle

Companies: Partnership between Company X (three participants and Company Y (four participants)
Date: Thursday - 08/15/2013 - 9:30 to 12:00 (Mexico City)
Where in the 5-Territories: Territory Three
Task at Hand: Mapping Roles & Responsibilities

The meeting began on time at 9:30am. The group is now comfortable with the check-in process and is voicing the alliances teams' progress, issues and concerns that remain important. The group reviewed the chronicle of the previous day's events. In general, the group agreed on the activities of the day. Additional concerns were added to the day's agenda. The group then reviewed the tasks of the day and goals to accomplish.

In order to work through the roles and responsibilities of the alliance, the *Partnerships Coach* opened the conversation asking the group to determine how it would like to work through the details. The group suggested mapping the core competencies of each organization to clarify in more general terms the capabilities of each company and, from that work together, draw out the roles and responsibilities in operating the alliance. The group did not feel completely comfortable with formulating the roles and responsibilities and made several attempts to redirect into other conversations. The group spent a good deal of time discussing the best approach to producing the roles and responsibilities of each party. In previous meetings, the same issues did not seem as difficult to work through as they did today.

After some deliberation, the group finally decided that reviewing core competencies would be good, but added that there were some roles where both companies could provide value and input. As they began to map their activities, the obvious differences in roles were easily determined. However, middle areas such as marketing and customer support quickly became heated topics where both sides wanted a role.

The group then decided to table those conversations and produced a list of activities meant to be discussed at a later date. The meeting wrapped up with a check-out. The group made plans for the next meeting but no exact date was agreed upon.

Analysis of Meeting using Operative Group Methodology

Companies: Partnership between Company X and Company Y
Date: Thursday - 08/15/2013 - 9:30 to 12:00 (Mexico City)
Where in the 5-Territories: Territory Three
Task at Hand: Mapping Roles & Responsibilities
Participantes: David (x) – Carlos (x) – Elizabeth (x) – Andrei (y) – Maria (y) – Dona (y) – Sandíp (y)

The meeting began on time at 9:30am. The group is now comfortable with the check-in process and is voicing the alliances teams' progress, issues and concerns that remain important. The group reviewed the chronicle of the previous day's events. In general, the group agreed on the activities of the day. Additional concerns were added to the day's agenda. The group then reviewed the tasks of the day and goals to accomplish.

Inverted Cone Review – *The Explicit:*

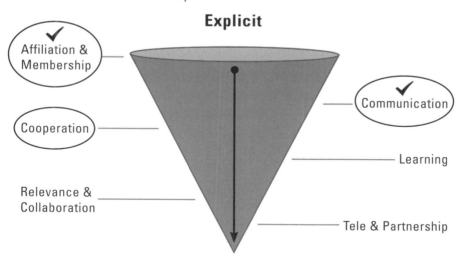

Figure 13 – The Explicit – Coach Analysis of Inverted Partnership Cone

The facilitator uses the tool to reflect on the meeting and check how each of the Inverted Cone's vectors were expressed in the meeting (Figure 13).

- Affiliation & Membership: Although they represent different companies, the group presented good affiliation and membership in their check-in. Participants started to make jokes and refer to each other in new ways. David joked with Elizabeth about the "touchy, feely" check-in process; nevertheless he was forthright in voicing expectations and thoughts openly. This sentiment seemed to lighten the mood a bit, but revealed that an underlying tension could be present.

- Communication: The communication seemed to pattern out in a back and forth way, with the more senior company people doing most of the speaking. Interactions were becoming rigid, only three participants were directly involved.

- Cooperation: Cooperation was limited, even though the group was able to find new ways to review roles and responsibilities mapping by adding a new role-category. But as soon as they began working, they appeared uncomfortable and, rather than face the challenges, resorted to putting the issue on hold.

- This is the first time the group postponed a conversation for another time and did not accomplish its goals.

Participantes: David (x) – Carlos (x) – Elizabeth (x) – Andrei (y) – Maria (y) – Dona (y) – Sandíp (y)

Inverted Cone Review – *The Implicit:*

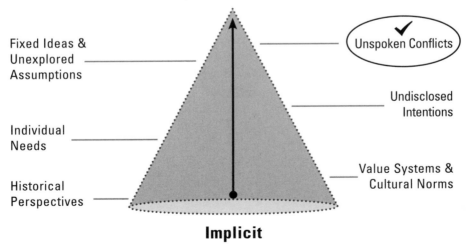

Figure 14 – The Implicit - Inverted Partnership Cone

As before, the facilitator marks the elements of the implicit that either emerged in the meeting or should be the focus of upcoming work-sessions (Figure 14).

• Implicitly, the group used humor to relieve some kind of pressure. The jokes were about individuals in the room, but were nevertheless stereotypical, relating to individual's functional roles and not about anyone's humorous personal characteristics. The humor served to cover the underlining tension in getting to know each other.

• It was almost like they were not interested in getting to know each other beyond the superficial.

• When the group started working with the roles and responsibilities of the alliance, it seemed as though it was afraid of what it wanted, perhaps knowing that different roles implied differing levels of investment and return.

• Perhaps there are some unspoken conflicts and even fixed ideas and assumptions to be explored in the next session.

Participantes: David (x) – Carlos (x) – Elsie (x) – Andrei (y) – Maria (y) – Dona (y) – Sandíp (y)

Unassigned roles mapping:

Scene 1

• Carlos proposes action, team scapegoats Carlos.

• Carlos becomes quiet and accepts role.

• David proposes action, team supports David and confers him as leader.

• David accepts leader role.

• Group stalls on the work and begins to disorganize.

Scene 2

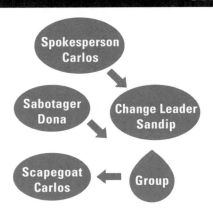

- Sandip expresses that the team is not being productive
- Group agrees and accepts Sandip as Change Leader.
- Dona, expresses that she does not understand what they are doing and sabotages the work of the group.
- Carlos, tries to provide input and is dismissed by the group.
- The group stalls a second time, remaining in pre-task.

Scene 3

- Group looks to David to save them.
- David proposes mapping the activities into a list.
- Group begins to start working.
- Dona, mentions that time is running out.
- David suggests having the meeting rescheduled when there is more time.
- Carlos remains quiet but is visually agitated.
- Group agrees and quickly adjourns.

Figure 15 – Unassigned Roles Mapping Example

As the facilitator reflects on the meeting, he maps the interactions to determine how the emergent roles were expressed in the group (Figure 15).

Task Phase Review:

Figure 16 – Pre-Task, Task & Project Phases

Reviewing the interactions, the Facilitator maps when and how the group entered the various task phases to discern progression (Figure 16).

• The pre-task phase occurred in the beginning of the meeting when the group began deliberating about the validity of reviewing core competencies and scapegoated Carlos.

• When the group entered the task phase, it turned out to be a red herring. The group was 90% of the time in pre-task.

• After some deliberation and discussion the group stayed mostly in pre-task; finally, at 40 minutes before closing, entered the task phase. Teams remained in task phase for only 10% of the total time.

• The group showed difficulty discussing the more substantive issues, placed many into a parking-lot list to be reviewed at another time.

• The group returned to pre-task phase at 15 minutes prior to the end of the meeting and adjourned at 12:00.

Coach Analysis of Group
The group is facing difficulties in building the fundamentals. Roles and responsibilities are not typically a difficult undertaking with two firms in such different industries. Yet there remains incapacity to work through the suggestions of the entire group. Carlos was scapegoated, and no-one on the team asked Carlos to explain his thinking.

Carlos accepted the scapegoating role and did not advocate further. David accepted the role of leader, in this case sabotaging the task. As a result the team is expecting him to resolve all the group's issues.

Planning for Next Session

Next session the assignation and assumption of fixed group role is the key to helping the group to focus on its task. The implicit tension between Carlos, as the scapegoat, and David, as the leader of the "no-task", needs to be worked by the group. The *Partnership Coach* will support views and ask the group to reflect longer and express ideas in order for the group to become task-centered. Planning a review of the interests and goals of each team could help to unlock the fears underneath about sharing too much, which seems to be hindering cooperation.

Maintaining Facilitative Continuity

After each working session, the *Partnership Coach* helps to maintain engagement, connection and communication space within the group. To sustain productivity between working meetings, particularly when there is more than three to four weeks between them, they keep a history of their decisions, actions, shared purposes, chronicles and narratives, principles agreed to and used, intentions shared and "a-ha" moments from one meeting to the next. For instance, after the *Partnership Innovation Session*, in **T3**, Phase 1, a synopsis of the outcomes, photos of materials and transcripts of meetings are provided to both teams and woven into the follow-up working sessions as reminders and topics to explore in the future. This approach leads to continued productive engagement between the teams, as well as a continuous weaving of the group narrative, and development of key ideas and relational patterns. It also provides teams with materials and documents that can be used to share information with important internal stakeholders of each firm.

Additionally, group reflections and interventions (e.g. use of chronicles and analysis etc.) proceed along the alliance process. They become more engrained in the practice of alliance-making from **T2** to **T5**. For example, in **T2** interventions occur mainly on the surface as accounts of tasks accomplished. In **T3**, the strategies (e.g. check-ins, check-outs and chronology reviews) are intentionally used to establish the group's operability. In **T5**, when the *Sustain & Deepen* elements of the alliance are set in place, it is the task of the group to continue perpetuating these practices into the future operating norms of the alliance.

Facilitative Leadership

Partnership coaching and facilitation is at its core a practice of facilitative leadership. In this respect, the *Partnership Coach* acts as an instrument that enables the emergence of *Collaborative Leadership* which paves the way for self-correcting and self-generating strategic alliances. When facilitating and coaching, the *Partnership Coach* must learn to contain the unconscious desires of the group, thereby helping them to operationalize their relating, as well as communication, to allow a productive field of relationship to emerge amid an atmosphere of trust. As a result, the *Partnership Coach*, aware of the challenges inherent in coaching groups, develops the capabilities and capacities to employ the *Operative Partnership Methodology*.

The central challenge of the *Partnership Coach* is to give an account of the *Alliance-CROS* (Chapter 4, pp. 54-55), i.e., from where they functions, the whole system of knowledge and the attitude they use when working in relation to the world and to themselves (Tubert-Oklander & Hernández de Tubert, 2004, pp. 47-52). Once they have a clearer understanding of their own operative functioning and a sense of how to *"get out of their own way,"* they can begin employing the methods and techniques of *Operative Partnerships Groups*. According to Pichon-Rivière there is a dialectic relationship between the facilitator as subject, interpreting the world around them, operating in that world and creating in it as well (Pichon-Rivière, 1985). This implies that good facilitation requires the *Partnership Coach* to become both skilled in the methodology and tools proposed, as well as a conscious active participant in their application. As such, the *Partnership Coach* understands their own interpretation of reality, how they understand life around them, and how they assign meaning to their perception and interactions affect group collaboration.

Additionally, the *Partnership Coach* needs to become aware of the psychological and relationship pitfalls and traps that occur with groups in order to be effective in facilitating them. Wilfred Bion identified certain group patterns which obstruct group capability to focus on the task at hand when a third party is present (1961). Based on his work, groups tend to fall into three dynamic ways of acting and relating toward facilitation and coaching: *basic assumption group, dependency group and fight or flight group*. In the *basic assumption group*, the participants work to remain and survive as a group by making the coach into the leader and focal point of their interactions. In the second group, *the dependency group*, the group acts as if the leader is there to provide security and protection to the group. In the third dynamic, the *fight or flight*, the group acts with the purpose to preserve itself irrespective of the task. Here the group persists by aggressive action, such as scapegoating, withdrawal or passivity. In any of these three cases, the coach/facilitator can turn into the subject that hinders group progress on the task. As such, he/she has to stay aware and conscious to these hidden obstacles, which can affect his capacity to coach the group if he/she accepts the assigned role. In this sense, his/her needs to cultivate a quality of active detachment, staying attuned to the potential relationship pitfalls the group tries to put him/her into, while, at the same time, actively helping the group operationalize.

Consequently, thoughtful facilitative intervention requires understanding that there are limits to group's capabilities to traverse the implicit. These limitations refer to the dynamics stemming from the group's capacities to integrate learning and maintain the relational space where authenticity can occur. Sensitivities emerge through the process that can arrest transitioning into new areas of relational understanding, alignment and progression along the *5-Territories of Alliance Development*. Possibility in the partnership resides in the group's capacities to integrate varied sensitivities and dialectic tensions and to reconcile them by accommodating to each other's needs and ways of problem solving. This means that there is always a place where groups will be able to work together and where there will be a lack of readiness. It is the *Partnership Coach's* work to locate the place where the team can build an alliance and a partnership. They work to understand and identify those limits so that the right balance between tensions can be struck both operationally and subjectively. To do this, they essentially become an enabler of *Collaborative Leadership* as it relates to the productive functioning of the group from a subjective point of view.

Accordingly, the *Partnership Coach* works proactively to produce the most authentic interactions possible between them and the group. In this respect, they learn to discern their own reactions to group patterns expressed through communication, emotions and corporal dispositions (Figure 17). As such, the action reflection loop involves the facilitator's own internal reflection in coordination with the action reflection and inquiry that they engage in with the group. From that awareness and understanding he produces a way of engaging that is meant to produce the outcomes of an *Operative Partnerships Group*.

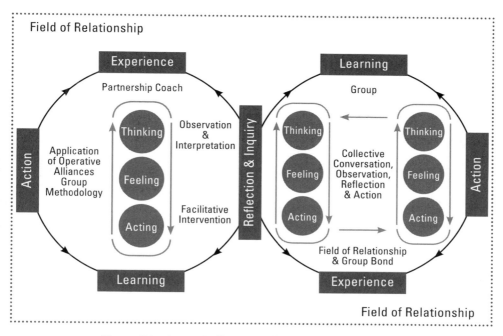

Figure 17 – Action Reflection and Inquiry Coaching Loop

Thus, for authentic engagement, the capacity of the *Partnership Coach* to engage with the group in the most real, aware and honest way possible is critical. It is a matter of remaining consciously engaged with the group thinking and feeling, while at the same time noticing what is occurring in themself while facilitating; always working in support of group learning and collaboration. Therefore, authentic engagement requires that the *Partnership Coach* contain, deepen and engage with the group to help bring forth the kind of relating that supports collaboration along the *5-Territories of Alliance Development.* Working accordingly, they productively support *Collaborative Leadership* to emerge by applying the methodology.

In this way they model for the group a way of being and communicating that opens a possibility for increased relatedness. For the group, authentic engagement becomes a continued practice of facing reality and engaging together in such a way that emotions can be expressed, differences can be worked through and disagreements can be overcome in a realistic and honest way.

Section Three
5-Territories of Alliance Development

The **5-Territories of Alliance Development** is a meta-process for alliances development that can be applied to any business collaboration that involves a multi-year agreement where two or more firms work interdependently on goals that they determine will meet their individual and collective strategic intentions. Through its five territories, a partnership team invites another firm or several firms to join them in developing the alliance. They work together, with the support of the *Partnerships Coach*, across a defined set of activities that help the teams to frame and consolidate their collaboration. In each of the territories, the teams work on a specific set of activities to establish a self-sustaining and self-generating alliance (Figure 18).

5-Territories of Alliance Development™

Figure 18 – The 5-Territories of Alliance Development

Territory One, Align & Prepare, involves ensuring that executives are clear on the goals for building alliances based on organizational strategic fit and how to carry them out. This includes ensuring the strategic alliance business has executive support and is fully oriented with short-term and longer-term strategic goals of the organization. Preparation involves developing the capabilities for alliances either by establishing the alliances business unit team or by building the competency across the organization. This is done by ensuring executives are properly trained and have the tools and models to engage in the identification of the best possible partners and the preparedness to approach them.

Territory Two, Invite & Commit, involves the process of approaching the possible alliance partner and working with that partner to commit to pursue a possible alliance. In **T2**, the team who went through the preparation makes an invitation to the company identified in the first territory. Over the course of the **T2**, teams commit to work to create their potential business collaboration, acknowledging that initial ideas may change in the process. In this territory tools are used and methods are put into practice to make the invitations and documents to help solidify commitment.

Territory Three, Create & Consolidate, refers to the group work of solidifying the strategic vision for the partnership. This involves working productively to develop the alliance by elaborating on respective roles and responsibilities based on strengths and core competencies. This means conducting research, running pilots, developing governance and alliance cooperation structure and formalizing terms. In this territory, the group undergoes a process of change and learning, which, if not addressed and developed appropriately, can lead to a failed opportunity for true collaboration.

Territory Four, Negotiate & Launch, involves the final contract negotiations and formal launching of the alliance.

Territory Five, Sustain & Deepen, involves ensuring that the ongoing alliance structures are in place and relationships are fostered through measurement, communication and collaboration.

Chapter 8
Territory One:
Align & Prepare

The foundational step for implementing an alliance building process is where companies must gain sight of how alliances will be employed in their businesses, and align internally on how and where alliances may be employed before they prepare themselves on how to do so. Often, companies are caught off guard and are approached by firms wanting to develop strategic alliances, not knowing how those opportunities support the organization's strategic objectives or their alliances strategy. In many instances, firms spend time on opportunities that are completely reactionary rather than productive, vision driven and organized around groups working together. Taking the time to prepare, establish an alliances strategy, and perhaps an internal alliances function and alliances team helps organizations to distinguish between the kinds of alliances that will help them grow and discard potential business partnerships that do not make sense. Aligning internally on the opportunities afforded through strategic partnering can help to focus resources on possible partnerships that make sense but also advance organizational capabilities. Building alliances as a core competency within an organization can itself turn into an important element in establishing collaborative advantage in the market-place. That means being able to leverage shared risk and resources through collaborative business arrangements.

Today, alliances occur across various parts of a company's value-creating activities and can be struck in a variety of ways. From research alliances to major supplier alliances, through to co-marketing, sales, business development, distribution and co-production, they can span across almost every activity of a company's value creation undertakings. In many respects, companies can have partnerships in all their key activities outsourcing most, if not everything, to other specialized players. Many companies work more like integrators of several strategic suppliers, combining their efforts to produce products, while others collaborate across industries, and even types of organizations (e.g. non-profit, NGOs, private and public companies and public entities). Such combinations exist in all kinds of forms, from financial service companies making alliances with airlines, to beverage firms collaborating with furniture manufacturers, public-private partnerships, and many others across a geographic region or within a particular country.

To be effective in their development of alliances, companies need to discern for themselves what business relationships should remain as simply supplier/vendor accords, and which are more suited to become strategic collaborations. Some business relationships are organized as alliances and others, perhaps, developed as a joint-venture equity arrangement. Each relationship type requires different levels of management and oversight, including the kind of contracts used, the level of decision-making, governance, and financial agreements. In general, the more strategic a relationship is to a firm's business, the greater amount of investment that is made in resources to ensure alignment and success.

In this preparation phase, executives need to engage in setting the alliance's strategy, working together to align it with organizational goals and then to establish the corporate preparedness for successful alliance building. All organizations have a process for establishing a view of where the industry is headed, what trends are affecting them and where they in strategic terms would like to go. The *Align & Prepare* phase involves a process of working with internal groups to agree on the shared desire of where to go and from a strategic alliances perspective, to prepare on how to arrive at organizational goals. In this respect, internal groups agree on the strategic goals of the firm and discern where strategic alliances fit. Like any group trying to accomplish a task, there must be desire for something and then a focus on effort to prepare by obtaining knowledge, skill, capability and tools. In synthesis, the work of **T1** is to set sights on a goal and get prepared for the journey ahead.

Phase 1
Setting the Alliances Strategy

The alliance strategy should flow directly from the organizational corporate strategy. Typical decisions in strategy focus on either buying a particular capability through a merger or acquisition, building the capability by investing internally or partnering through strategic alliances. In some cases, where the company sees alliances as core to their business, the alliances strategy and organizational strategy will essentially be one and the same plan. However, this is uncommon in today's organizations. Instead, for a majority of today's companies, an organizational strategy should employ collaborative alliances as a key strategic element for executing goals.

The organizational strategy is a road-map for building business by accessing new markets, new technologies or other capabilities that the company foresees will further its objectives, without having to make the full investment. The alliance strategy is a piece of the corporate development puzzle which will help a company accomplish the organizational goals it sets. The *organizational strategy* is the *"what,"* and the *alliances strategy* forms a piece of the *"how"* the organization will get there. The *"how"* involves determining which parts of the organizational strategy can be accomplished either 100% in-house or which pieces may be developed through partnerships. However, choosing between what can be done in-house vs. with alliances partners is an over simplification in an age where businesses can operate quite successfully within a business network or an ecosystem of interdependent and interrelated actors.

Deciding where to Employ Alliances

Determining areas where alliances should be implemented in a company's organizational strategy requires clear understanding of what *strategic alliances* are as distinguished from other types of business relationships. First and foremost, *strategic alliances* are collaborative relationships between firms to fulfill strategic goals of partners by pooling organizational capabilities. What distinguishes them from transactional business is that *strategic alliances* tend to be longer lasting than simple business transactions which complete when value is exchanged. Transactions have a very clear beginning and a distinct end. In contrast, *strategic alliances* are business relationships that span from three to ten years in duration or even longer. They are developed over longer periods of time in order to take full advantage of the market opportunities possible between the collaborating firms. Alliances, unlike typical business transactions, relate to several activities that can be quite varied. For example, an alliance may be formed to collaborate on logistics with the same firm you already do co-marketing and advertising activities with, even though each company sells different yet complimentary products. Additionally, the exchange of value in alliances is not clearly defined by traditional business roles of buyer and supplier. Rather, the role is more adequately defined by collaborator or alliance partner, a business relationship consummated by equals. The different roles correspond to the varied activities that are shared between the partners. As such, the shared work product requires a good deal of joint work between the entities, from infrastructure to managing decision making and execution. These attributes of *strategic alliances* help leaders distinguish which business relationships to develop as alliances and which to remain as simple transactions. Upon aligning, a company can then work through which elements of the value chain can be developed through strategic relationships and which are better managed through simple transactional deal-making.

There are essentially two basic alliance business structures used to combine resources that generate shared opportunities and shared value. The structures can be either equity-based arrangements or not. Equity-based arrangements involve the merger or acquisition of a company or the forming of a completely new-company, *"newco."* In the case of forced acquisitions where a company is taken over, a *strategic alliances strategy* and process in this case would not apply. Certainly, the *Operative Partnership Methodology* would, but the *5-Territories of Alliance Development* would not. Acquisitions do not normally go into Invite & Commitment (**T2**) and Create & Consolidate (**T2**), but rather, enter into strict negotiations after a period of financial and strategic business discovery or a straight forward stock purchase and take-over. The new company established by the alliance applies when it is not a takeover but rather collaborative venture. Here, there exists owner-ship of some kind, either shared ownership or unequal ownership between the partners.

In non-equity partnerships, cooperation happens in commercial business de-velopment activities, which may include co-marketing activities, co-branded services or sales channel relationships. A non-equity strategic alliance strat-egy can also be applied to cooperative research agreements found in the bi-otech industry, long-term strategic collaboration relationships found in key supplier alliances seen in the automatic industry and consortiums or net-works where several companies cooperate as part of a larger alliances net-work or platform. Lastly, there exists informal cooperation between firms that work without binding agreements. This book is primarily focused on strategic partnerships that are contractual, yet much of the process and the schema for developing partnerships is applicable to non-contractual alliances as well as joint-venture alliances, public-private partnerships and collabora-tions with NGOs and not-for-profit organizations.

The key distinctions between alliances and other business relationships and the three possible structures help leadership determine what alliances are and how they may be employed. However, these distinctions help but do not in themselves provide the formula for developing the alliances strategy. The de-cision to build an alliance capability and seek out partners or even treat stra-tegic suppliers as partners is not based on a methodical, cost-benefit analysis. Leaders are deceiving themselves if they believe an alliances strategy can be developed purely on rational cost-benefit analysis and not on the subjective elements, ideas, shared norms and corporate culture from which strategic decisions are formed. The decision to embark on alliances and partnership is based primarily on the culture of the company and its approach to business. Corporate culture involves how the company thinks about itself, and builds the structures and strategies which it executes in the marketplace.

Oftentimes, outside market pressures push companies to form partnerships and alliances. However, market pressures do not in themselves cause entire organizations to formulate and employ alliances. Executives developing alliances must take into account the company's capability to employ alliances as it confronts market challenges. Forcing an alliance onto an organization can have dire consequences if the organization is not culturally prepared and skilled to succeed. Studies from the Association of Strategic Alliances Professionals (ASAP) dating as far back as 2000 have consistently pointed to a real gap between the potential of these alliances and their actual success rate. According to ASAP, 50% to 60% of alliances fail, and 50% of those that survive do not meet expectations. They stated that culture is a major reason for such low success rates, since these rates only increase marginally after establishing an alliances functional area within companies (Duysters, De Man, Luvinson, & Krijnen, 2012, p. 9). They consider organizational culture between firms as the key reason for failure.

Ultimately, choosing where to employ alliances is a question of executive leadership and wisdom. Thoughtful alliances executives determine where strategic partnerships will fit into the organizational strategy, within the corporate culture; the fit has to be close enough to be successful, while still stretching the organization to open itself to the market pressures of doing business in entirely different ways. There are many executives today that see alliances as core strategies for meeting today's exciting and worthwhile challenges. Chief executive officers and their teams are establishing new business approaches, new tools and alliance functional areas that reach out and profit from the interconnected and interdependent nature of business today. The question for corporate leaders is to choose *"where"* to first employ such a strategy. Deciding, then, becomes no longer a question of *"what"* but a question of *"how."*

How to Establish a Successful Alliance Strategy

To develop a successful alliances strategy, it is important to consider where the organization is in its evolution toward greater and more inclusive stages of business collaboration. These evolving stages represent the organization's capacity to have a more expanded viewpoint of itself as an actor in an industry and within a large network of market players. In the first stage of development, *Firm-Centric Stage*, there is willingness to partner only in the immediate future and within a limited part of the current business.

In the second stage, *Post-Modern Corporation*, a company is more able to shift its perspective to meet future market demands and partner more broadly along its supply and value chains. In the third stage, *Emergent-Enterprise Stage*, the firm sees itself as being in the business of creating shared value within an interconnected and interdependent world. Here, the company lets go even further of the need to control the business and minimize risks, and operates as an integral actor in a larger network of activities. All three stages provide insights into the company's cultural capacity, value system and general ability to develop alliances and partnerships effectively.

The goal is to employ an *alliances strategy* that the organization is able to effectively develop and metabolize in its processes and organizational plan. Determining which parts of the supply and value chains can be developed through an alliances strategy, and which will be accepted by executive leadership and the organization, is not only important, but wise. Building alliances that force an organization to enact change is likely to be why 50% of alliances fail (Duysters, De Man, Luvinson, Krijnen, 2012, p. 9), as well as lack of organizational cultural capacity for alliances and lack of internal leadership buy-in. It is, therefore, very important to gauge where the organization can build alliances that have the chance to be successful. If there is no internal executive support for developing an alliances strategy, or even closing a particular partnership, and there is no real internal alignment established in this phase, then it is hard to think that a potential partnership once signed will actually bear fruit. The fundamental question for executives is how is the alliances strategy established?

The short answer is by knowing where the organization is in its development and determining in which areas alliances may be employed. The more willing a firm is to forgo control and therefore take risk and collaborate (i.e. liberalize), the greater potential there is for extensive use of alliances across the supply and the value chain to meet organizational goals. However, if a company's cultural orientation is not toward collaboration but instead toward controlling all aspects of its business, the areas where alliances can be employed will invariably be lessened. Take for example a bank operating in retail financial services. The bank may not be willing to build a partnership to pool its compliance and audit functions through an alliance with another competing bank because culturally it would never have those activities occur outside its doors, however lucrative and valuable that could be.

To build the alliance strategy, the alliances team and the CEO must know where the organization is willing or unwilling to partner. The analysis here is not purely from a rational and clear business opportunity perspective, but also from a cultural and political point of view. There are most certainly areas where partnerships could be developed but where the organization would simply not be culturally or developmentally ready. What leaders need to account for is the scope of perceptions about control and risk that underlies the range where partnerships and alliances could be implemented (Figure 19). As the graph shows, the company would be more willing to partner in the lower left quadrant than the upper right because it perceives that both the desire for control and risk perception would be low.

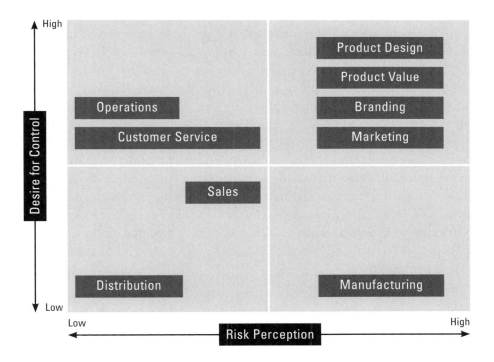

Figure 19 – Control/Risk Matrix

The *Firm-Centric Company* would experience the desire for control and for risk in more areas of its supply and value chain than the *Emergent-Enterprise* operating as a networked organization. For example, a toy manufacturer who is *Firm-Centric* would want to control real-estate by owning all the distribution facilities, although the risk in partnering or even simply outsourcing that function is low. Following the matrix, the area where there is high desire for control and high-risk perception would be considered a company's core competency. It is the role of executives to determine where the perception of risk lies in order to develop an alliances strategy that the company is able to sustain (Figure 19).

However, the *Post-Modern* Company is more oriented toward strategic growth goals and opportunities. While alliances may be seen as a complement for shifting costs and risk in the first stage, in the second stage the more strategic companies use alliances as a means to extend reach, to provide the market and customers new services, products, and functionalities. The reason to partner comes from a desire to create, grow and find the right partners to make real the potential opportunities in the horizon. It is a reaching out, an extending and building value, rather than a pure orientation toward operating efficiencies. Here, companies focus on building competitive and comparative advantages through alliances and partnerships. In comparison to the Emergent Enterprise of the next stage, the *Post-Modern* company remains attached to the concept behind core competencies and unilateral alliance building, rather than focused on networked alliances where many actors participate in a more open system. *Post-Modern* companies continue to consider product design and product value in the upper areas of the control/risk matrix (Figure 20).

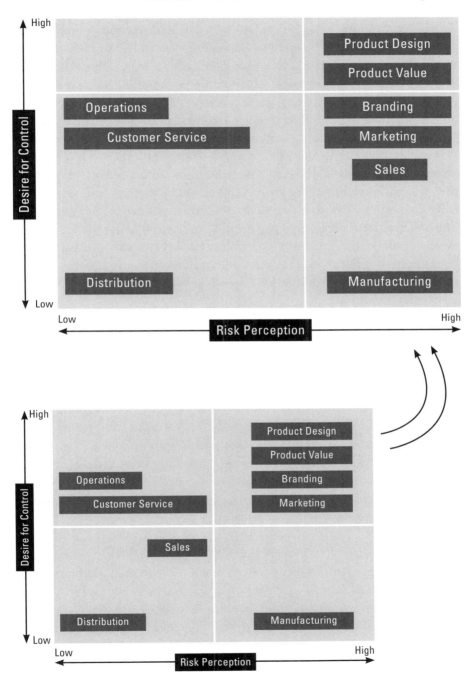

Figure 20 – Control/Risk Matrix Change

As the *Firm-Centric Company* enters the *Post-Modern* stage it amplifies its capacity to accept risk by opening perceptions and lowering need for control; thus, opening more places where alliances can bring value (Figure 20). The firm becomes more flexible, adaptive, open and oriented toward collaborative business opportunities. An organization that places partnerships and alliances at the forefront of its strategy becomes apt to change and to address the needs of today's business environment more quickly than competitors. "Asking what combinations of resources —yours and others'—might better serve customer's needs" (Lewis, 1990, p.30) in the future is invariably part of this process toward building an effective alliances strategy and opening the collaboration space of the lower-left and lower-right quadrants (Figure 20). The organizational capacity to partner with other companies increases when there is greater tolerance for risk and less need for control. This genuinely opens opportunities to develop alliances and find new and innovative solutions that provide value to stakeholders across business networks, ecosystems and society as a whole.

In the last stage, the *Emergent-Enterprise* develops strategic thinking where alliances business strategy and the organizational strategy become one and the same plan. Here, the direction is to partner and collaborate within and through an interconnected and increasingly interdependent world in social systems and within business networks. The company here is more flexible and agile. As an organization, it increases its capability to make strategic decisions based on the interconnections of its supply and value chains. As a result, it arrives at an entirely new way of approaching business; that of shared value creation in networks and social ecosystems. The basis for shared value rests on *"the business of relationship"*, a new understanding of businesses as an actor within a greater whole in commerce and society.

Kramer and Porter (2011) assert that all business operates in relationship. Companies and organizations operate in relationship to their customers, suppliers and partners, as well as to the employees and communities where they work, and the culture and societies in which they are embedded. These actors function in relation to each other systemically, one maintaining the other while supporting the whole in an intricate and organized way. Their assertion is that "companies, themselves, remain trapped in an outdated approach to value creation... continue to view value creation narrowly, optimizing short-term financial performance" (Kramer & Porter, op. cit., p. 4). The narrow short-term financial view is dictated by an overall conception of control and risk, and other inter-subjective value systems that coordinate to bring about activities in the global competitive marketplace (e.g. *Firm-Centric* and *Post-Modern* companies). Companies, then "optimize short-term financial performance in a bubble while missing the most important customer needs and ignoring the broader influences that determine the longer-term success" (Kramer & Porter, op. cit., p. 4).

The emergent stage involves ecosystem and network orchestration. Network orchestration is "a multiplier that increases the reach and effectiveness of the organization" (Fung, Fung, & Yoram, 2009, p. 17). This final stage does not preclude the activities that continue to exist within an organization. The company includes those activities from previous stages and, yet, goes beyond them to involve new skills, approaches and methods that can be applied to opportunities based on social and business network needs. In fact, "network orchestration extends standard business processes to a broader network but requires skills that are distinctive to network orchestration" (Kleindorfer, & Yoram, 2009, p. 313) in alliances and partnerships.

Alliances Strategy at the Edge of Corporate Growth

Leaders need to determine at what stage of development their companies are in to establish an alliance strategy that can be implemented successfully over time. They can see that over the course of their company's growth, changes in risk and control perceptions will open up a range of possible business allianc-es. From this perspective, leadership can determine what alliances to engage in first and which ones to pursue in the future as the company develops. This way of determining the alliances strategy will help to increase the chances of success and making the chosen alliance support the company's natural progression from one stage to the other (Graph 1).

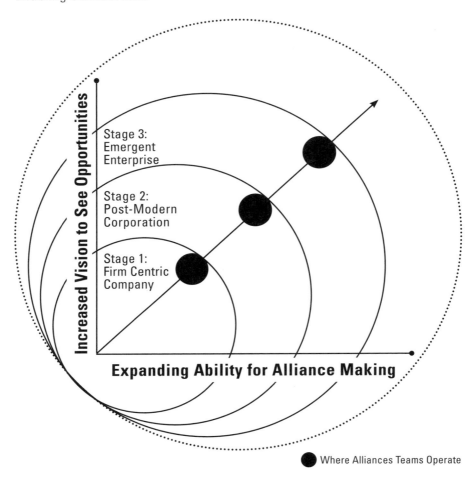

Graph 1 – Corporate Stages of Development

For the alliance executive each stage represents a place of readiness for the company to employ an alliances strategy based on an expanding ability for collaboration. These stages where *Circles of Influence* and *Circles of Concern* coincide for an organization demonstrate an increased reaching out from an atomized self-focus toward focused partnership and out to networks of alliances and partnership within society as a whole. As the organizations move from *Firm-Centric* to *Post-Modern* to *Emergent*, the arcs of space at each stage increase toward corporate development that extends beyond and includes the previous stage. This demonstrates an increase in leadership and cultural capacity, coupled with growth in new skills and capabilities (Graph 1).

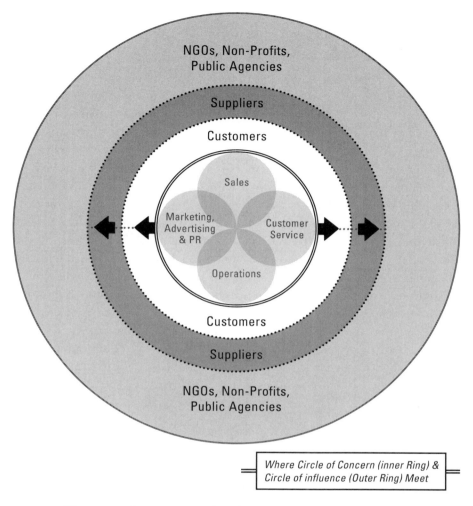

Figure 21 – Increasing Circles of Concern & Circles of Influence

The capacity to build alliances and partnerships must be developed by the alliances team as the organization develops the capacity to metabolize them. Alliances from this stand point can be seen as the purest way to grow corporate capacity at the edge of each line (Figure 21). The key challenge for executives is to devise a strategy that will be successful based on their current stage of development while preparing for future alliance capabilities. The right alliances strategy must correlate the plan to the development stage of organization operability and its respective level of readiness. Based on readiness, leaders can build partnerships and alliances across supply and value chains and beyond into business networks and into the social sphere establishing newer and newer forms of value creation (Figure 21).

In *Stage One, Firm-Centric,* the state of the modern 20th century corporation, the process to build an alliances and partnership strategy requires review of the supply chain and discernment of where the company is willing to share control and the perception of risk is least. It is in effect the most conservative place within a company to begin an alliances strategy. At this stage, the most effective area to develop alliances is in profit-making partnerships, or partnerships where the organization is willing to forgo control, i.e., where the perception of risk is relatively medium to low. For the *Firm-Centric* company, developing alliances that support the organization to achieve efficiencies through better partnerships and consolidating market share is best. These kinds of alliances demonstrate calculated risk-taking. Over time, stretching the organization to shift its view of control and risk will open its willingness to grow to the next stage, where alliance strategy can become more important to the entire business.

In Stage Two, the organization begins its journey toward a more progressive, almost post-modernist 21st century approach. The strategy in these circumstances can begin to build alliances that cover a broader spectrum of the supply and value chain activities, and areas where business collaboration can take place are increased. At this stage, an organization will be more willing to accept and implement an alliances strategy that develops new and unique structures of business relationships to resolve gaps between strategy and performance. At this point, the organization is more able to metabolize greater levels of collaboration through its value chain and partially beyond, resulting from lower control and risk distribution across a variety of business activities. Here, the organization has a heightened understanding of its interconnection and interdependence, although is limited in scope and capacity for execution. The alliances unit can execute across several parts of the supply and value chains, from product development, to research as well as more upstream activities such as sales, marketing and advertising.

The third stage, *Emergent-Enterprise,* involves building an alliances strategy that looks to establish new businesses based on shared value concepts and enabling clusters and networks of interdependent actors to cooperate and support the vibrancy of the systems in which the organization operates. At this level, the alliance and partnership strategy is the core corporate focus.

The company sees that "the world has become more networked, the competencies that are important are not so much the ones a company owns as the ones it can connect to" (Kleindorfer & Yoram, 2009, p. 9) and the networks it can establish. The central focus is the business of relationship, where the company undertakes work at greater levels of complexity and opportunity and establishes public-private partnerships. This could mean developing and participating in networks and other hybrid projects to help society prosper, as well as the company and network to grow economically. Here, the level of concern is systemic, deeper within an organization's own internal functioning as it develops partnerships among its own departments and employees, as well as into the outer context, beyond suppliers and customers, with communities, business networks and other social systems. Stage Three involves moving the "focus from the firm to the network, a shift in management from control to empowerment, and a shift in value creation from specialization to integration" (Kleindorfer& Yoram, 2009, p. 310).

The *Emergent-Enterprise* possesses a wider orientation toward society and business networks, from the province or county to a region, to the globe, and deeper into human challenges. Alliances that are built around an ever-expanding orientation are used when an organization is prepared "to create economic value in a way that also creates value for society by addressing its needs and challenges" (Kramer & Porter, op. cit., p. 4). At the most fundamental level, if communities are healthy, then companies that depend on them are also healthy. If the community where customers, employees and suppliers is not strong, then it stands to reason that neither will the company be. They are intricately intertwined and interdependent. As companies, there are opportunities to provide services to underserved communities, not only for profit reasons, but also to meet unfulfilled areas of demand. These businesses that revolve around social opportunities can include financial services for the disadvantaged distributed through cell phones, or micro-insurance products for short-term use. Where the needs of society converge with good businesses, emergent collaborative partnerships are developed that promote social good and profit based on business models that take into account all actors in a social system. As the concept for shared value through shared partnership expands, new opportunities that touch all elements of the value chain can also emerge, while simultaneously a new conception of the value chain can be redefined. In establishing business networks, the alliance orchestrator is "focused on designing the best possible processes across a global network for delivering the right product to the right place at the right time and the right process" (Kleindorfer & Yoram, 2009, p. 314). They are also focused on doing all this for the right reason.

The Collaborative Enterprise

The capacity of a company at the individual and team level to collaborate and partner internally affects its capability to partner well with other firms and, even more, to participate effectively in open networks. When a company's own internal functioning goes contrary to collaboration, its capability for developing collaborative businesses is clearly diminished. In these instances, marketing is always fighting with finance, sales and marketing constantly compete for relevance, operations is always hoping to get noticed and human resources never has a voice. For some reason, many companies have taken their competitive nature and applied it to their internal functioning as well. The *"winner takes all mentality"* is brought inside in the hope that the company will be better for it. Perhaps a company's outward way of doing business is just a reflection of the inward way it functions.

The path to becoming an *Emergent-Enterprise* requires that internally teams employ the tenets of partnering within their own organizations. This means choosing to participate in practices that build internal collaboration capability. From authentic engagement to dialogue to establishing shared commitment, the collaboration challenge is as much about internal partnering as it is in external alliance building. Here the *Collaborative Enterprise* can implement a wide variety of strategies. These include a fair distribution of value for work that supports the ongoing healthy and sustainable functioning of the immediate resources a firm uses. This may mean paying strategic suppliers more than market rates to ensure that they remain resilient. Maintaining closer ties that increase communication, stabilize market cyclicality, measure outcomes, and develop a management structure congruent with their interdependence. Support in strategic decision-making may also help suppliers to be better at what they do.

The strategy can also include developing internal human capital policies that redefine the partnership between employees and owners or shareholders, and even the company and its customers. This may include providing varied profit incentive plans to workers, training and career rotations, and support, while improving the overall longer-term commitment of employees to their companies. With customers, this may not only include a robust loyalty program, but shared ownership of the business as well as annual profit sharing. In effect, this new partnering orientation can be used within and through the corporate supply and value chains, from human capital to suppliers and vendors. This is not to say that the *Collaborative Enterprise* exists only at the *Emergent-Enterprise* stage. It means that at the Emergent Stage there exists a greater and more expanded perimeter where *Circles of Influence* and *Circles of Concern* coincide. A Collaborative Enterprise can certainly exist in the *Firm-Centric Stage*, just to a lesser degree. Perhaps there are no partnerships with NGOs or public entities, but there are some well-established relationships with employees.

The Alliances Strategy

The process for creating the alliances strategy is not as straightforward as one would like. Given the percentage of alliance failures over the years, this methodology proposes that the setting of strategy is based on a company's capability and willingness to enter alliances in the first place. This process involves working through the organization's readiness to forgo control and share risk as it considers alliances along its supply and value chains. In this way, executive leaders can test where alliances make the most sense. This does not forgo the need for actual hard number analysis and strategic research which are also important for making such decisions. For the purposes of the framework, the key element is that preparation requires that a company be developmentally prepared and culturally committed to alliances.

Essentially this involves having internal conversations and testing the cultural atmosphere for alliances in the organization and, also, determining the kind of shift that is needed to further evolve thinking and capacity to react to market changes. "Strategizing is the search for combination of choices about such [alliance business] decisions that, together, generate strong performance," (Kleindorfer & Yoram, 2009, p. 186), is strategic to the organization's longevity and development. Strategizing between the possible alliances alternatives with what can be executed, both from a resource perspective and a cultural point of view, is where real organizational commitment to alliances lies. Commitment is then demonstrated by investments made in resources, time and effort. With true commitment, the firm can focus on organizing the alliances business unit or ensuring the capability is developed across the company.

Phase 2
Shifting from a Selling to a Partnering Approach

It is important to draw distinctions between selling and partnering because, so often, a sales process is used when partnership approach is called for. Additionally, once there is an understanding of the differences, the company building an alliances business unit can hire the right team members, design the appropriate tools, and follow the alliance development process that ensures a much higher likelihood of success.

Let us elaborate the differences between selling and partnering by first clarifying a common misconception about sales. In today's hyper-competitive "sell everything" business environment, there is a faulty concept that selling is involved in everything you do. You have to sell to get ideas heard, projects invested in and always in a dynamic where others must "buy" your concepts, ideas and even your personality. That is not selling. That is convincing, influencing, communicating and relating, among other activities, in order that others should agree with a point of view or recommended action. In selling, what one is actually doing is specifically exchanging a good or service for payment. The acts of convincing, influencing etc. for which the term "selling" is misused occur in both sales and in partnering regardless of whether clients, stakeholders or partners are involved. In partnering, as well as in sales, these acts of communication are always being used. In partnering, however, you may not necessarily be exchanging a good or service for payment. You may in fact be collaborating toward common goals and common objectives. What is important is to distinguish between knowing when to use a sales approach and when to use a partnering approach. Each approach is used in different circumstances, contexts and sets different goals and objectives.

Let us clarify the difference a bit further. Wikipedia defines selling as: "Selling is offering to exchange an item of value for a different item. The original item of value being offered may be either tangible or intangible. The second item, usually money, is most often seen by the seller as being of equal or greater value than that being offered for sale" (http://wikipedia.org/wiki/selling, Sept. 25, 2013).

According to the *Oxford English Dictionary*, to sell is: "To give up or hand over (something) to another person for money (or something that is reckoned as money); esp. to dispose of (merchandise, possessions, etc.) to a buyer for a price; to vend" (http://www.oecd.com/, Sept. 25, 2013). Selling therefore involves a company which has an item and/or service which another company would like to purchase with money. The goal is to conduct a transaction where one company or person is the buyer and the other the seller.

On the other hand, partnering involves the act of coordinating together toward a common purpose and/or mutually supportive interests. According to Wikipedia: "a partnership is an arrangement in which parties agree to cooperate to advance their mutual interests. Since humans are social beings, partnerships between individuals, businesses, interest-based organizations, schools, governments, and varied combinations thereof, have always been and remain commonplace" (http://wikipedia.org/wiki/partnership, Sept. 25, 2013).

The *Oxford English Dictionary* defines partnership "as the fact or condition of being a partner; association or participation; companionship" (http://www.oecd.com/, Sept. 25, 2013). Therefore, a partnership is an arrangement in which parties agree to cooperate to advance their mutual interests but not necessarily in exchange of a good or service. The goal is to establish an ongoing business relationship founded on interdependence and operative human relations.

To elaborate further, sale tools and selling and partnership tools and partnering are used in very distinct situations and within different market conditions and contexts. As such, one must keep in mind several important considerations in order to determine which approach is best suited: one that involves a transaction or one that involves an ongoing business relationship.

Strategic considerations are "a major reason for choosing a partnering approach rather than a selling approach. "In Strategic Alliances firms cooperate out of mutual need and share risks to reach a common objective. Without a mutual need companies may have the same objectives, but each can get there on its own" (Lewis, 1990, p. 1). That is the core strategic consideration in choosing a partnerships approach. Jordan D. Lewis in *Partnerships for Profit – Structuring and Managing Strategic Alliances* (Ibid) points to several areas where partnering is used. These include working with companies that help to increase an ability to create new products and services, finding possible partners that provide access to new international markets and finding other potential allies that bring new technical know-how or share know-how to build entirely new businesses. There may be potential alliances that provide value-added services jointly to customers, partners that help to shift core expenses and reduce costs to get ahead of competitors and even cooperate with competitors in specific instances. Steve Steinhilber in his book *Strategic Alliances – Three Ways to Make Them Work* (2008, p. 2) speaks about the broad and deep initiatives that Cisco uses to identify and characterize strategic alliance relationships. "Broad and deep initiatives to me means 'several,' and deep signals 'significant' initiatives within the alliance that cut across the value chain of both companies". The final strategic consideration involves understanding if there is significant value in terms of real ongoing and sustainable revenues or savings in the project. All these taken individually and collectively help the executive determine if there is high or low strategic value in the potential business.

Why implement a partnering approach here and a not selling one? One good reason is simply because in these strategic instances it is not clear who is doing the selling and who is doing the buying. There exists a high level of interdependence that obscures the traditional business roles of buyers and sellers. It is also unclear who pays whom. Additionally, it is possible that in instances mentioned above, neither party pays the other; rather revenues come from shared customers. This helps to elaborate on another distinction between using a sales vs. a partnering approach, when the roles are of equal collaborators and not of buyers and sellers.

When the business transaction is limited in time and space, i.e. where it contains a clear beginning and a clear ending, it is best to use a selling approach. Partnerships require greater continuity and ongoing management of the business relationship in the form of cooperation/governance structures, shared metrics and dashboards. In sales, when the transaction is completed, there is no need for ongoing maintenance. This may include the purchase of a building or even the acquisition of a business. In these instances, when the sale goes through and the money is exchanged, the professionals involved will never see the other party again. On the contrary, when the business is ongoing, when there needs to be coordination and collaboration, a partnering approach is best used. The key reason is that the structures for collaboration and ongoing management require co-development and joint implementation. This points to a second distinction between partnering and selling; when the business requires a deeper level of collaboration and coordination between the parties, it is best to use a partnering approach rather than a selling one. The human relations that underpin success in this type of business practice are of real importance, while in sales they are not as pertinent. Partnering is about building operative human relationships that lead to ongoing success and selling is about completing a business transaction.

A final consideration for choosing the right approach is establishing if the opportunity involves an equal *Balance of Power* and *Shared Risk* and *Shared Reward* between the parties. *Equal Balance of Power* relates to the potential for partnership between the parties. Both partners understand that both have other possible alliances. This balances out market power and increases the potential for interdependence. In the case of *Shared Risk and Shared Reward*, determining if these are equally shared by each partner will help to identify what approach to take. In the scenario where there is unequal balance of power and an unequal risk and reward, some firms opt toward a selling approach, although a partnering approach may have been more suited. Ultimately using a sales approach in partnerships could be a major reason why many alliances fail to meet expectations.

Taken as a whole, if the business opportunity is not limited in time and space and, as such, there is significant interdependence of activities between the firms, power and risk are high and somewhat shared, using a partnering approach is best. Neither approach is better than the other; rather different circumstances and contexts require different approaches.

But what really makes them different?
How is a sales process different than a partnering process?

A sales approach is made up of the following activities:

1 Prospecting; involves the process of finding buyers for your product or service.
2 Qualifying and Analyzing Needs; determining if the buyers you have prospected actually want and need your service and ensuring that what you are selling actually will work for the client.
3 Providing Proposals; documenting a proposal to the client that contains the needs you identified along with the pricing you offer.
4 Negotiating pricing and specifics.
5 Closing the deal, and committing to implementing solution or completing transaction by delivering product.

Whereas a partnering approach involves the following process:

1 Aligning and Preparing; involves the process of aligning alliance strategy to organizational plans and obtaining organizational commitment. This is prepared for by identifying the strategic needs of the company and identifying the potential partners that would benefit from a shared and mutual strategic need. This step involves linking corporate needs and aspirations with the potential needs of an identified firm.
2 Inviting and Committing; inviting the identified partner or partners to engage in a potential partnership conversation and committing together to pursue the proposed partnership.
3 Creating and Consolidating; the process of bringing together various actors across each organization to develop the alliance's structure, establishing the roles and responsibilities based on core competencies, as well as developing the ongoing governance framework and basic financial projections.
4 Negotiating and Launching; closing any loose ends and finalizing the actual contract. The major reason why contract negotiations occur toward the end of the process in partnership development is due to the importance of the common *Group-CROS* that needs to be established before negotiations take place, in contrast to a more transactional relationship characteristic of a sales process (pp. 52-74). The need here is for launching, bringing the alliance to market, implementing what was created and ensuring the ongoing management and development of the business relationship.

5 Sustaining and Deepening; this ensures that the alliance is meeting expectations and may be expanded into other potential business collaborations between the parties.

Some key differences between the two processes:
- The sales process is more clearly defined around a core product or service being offered, while in the partnership process the opportunities are more broadly defined.
- The sales process involves formal (legally binding) proposals while the partnering process involves conversations and the exchange of jointly elaborated (not legally binding) documentation.
- The sales process involves someone purchasing something and someone buying something; in partnerships there may not be any buyer or seller.
- The sales process involves agreeing before you close the sale by transferring the good or implementing the solution, while in partnering you make agreements throughout the process.
- In sales you negotiate in the beginning and in partnerships you negotiate at the end after both parties have built the basic alliance structure.
- In sales the agreements struck are almost never exclusive, while in partnerships many times they can be.
- In sales the focus is closing the deal and in partnerships it is building the right relationships and establishing the right structure.
- The sales process is simpler than the partnership process which is more complex.
- In partnering there is opportunity to include a variety of business opportunities that are discovered along the way which may be missed when a sales approach is used.

What to do differently?

In sales, there is a standard process of going back and forth. In the more structured selling situations the initial steps are essentially scripted, orchestrated to every minute detail. The intention is to win the hearts and minds of the possible clients. The power differential is palpable: "the client is always right". What did the presenters do? They talked about how great their company is, the size of their business, discussed their geographic footprint, elaborated on about how great they are and how excited and grateful they are about the opportunity to present. The more sophisticated of these presenters do not refer to themselves "salespeople". They instead refer to themselves as "solution specialists" or "trusted advisors." Regardless of the nomenclature used, the activities of partnering do not involve these kinds of hopeful presentations. What alliances executives do is completely different. Their focus is not about convincing the prospective partner about how great they are and how much they will gain by partnering. Alliance developers do share the company's background and capabilities. Executives will also present ideas, data and influence the other person or team on how they see the trends in the industry and opportunity for collaboration, but what they will not engage in selling. There are no proposals provided, just ideas shared and conversations had. Of course it goes without saying that *request for proposal* processes where buyers ask several vendors for their best proposal is completely antithetical to partnering and is akin to a reverse sales approach.

Effective partnering is about opening a conversation with your identified potential partners about the possibility of an alliance that can be created together. In sales, people concentrate on the needs of the client alone with the intention to close a deal. In sales everything is closed-ended. Close the deal, execute and then charge the client for the product or service. Meanwhile, in effective partnering the focus is searching for complementarity between the inviting company's strategic needs correlated to the realities and needs of the invited partner. The activity of partnering begins more open-ended. It is more about recognizing and acknowledging that the inviting firm does not know everything in the front end, certainly they may have a vision, but they do not have all the answers. Those answers are in part provided by the invited partner and discovered along the process through joint collaboration which results from the conversation held. In partnering, the partnership developer expresses the sentiment that both companies are open to figuring it out. It is about solving (through collaboration) problems that exist in the marketplace and/or creating something new, something that springs forth from your mutual, soon to be discovered, interests, rather than about consummating a transaction. It is about deepening the relationship as you develop business opportunities together.

Partnerships are used in entirely different situations and contexts. The people involved in them will require different and unique skills, and the tools, processes, methods involved will also be different.

Navigating the Gray Space

There are gray spaces between the two approaches which involve opportunities to choose either a sales perspective or a partnering perspective. Each approach results in very different outcomes. Both approaches have their strengths and weaknesses and the use of each reflects in large part the kind of company you are and the kind of company you want to be.

Take for example co-branded credit cards in the financial services industry. In these projects, a bank sells a credit card through an affinity/loyalty program relationship offered by another firm. This second company also places its brand on the credit card. The American Airlines (AA) Citibank Credit Cards are a perfect example of this kind of business relationship. Here, obviously American Airlines does not want to become a bank and Citibank cannot become an airline, yet there is opportunity here for the companies to work together.

Citibank recognizes the size of the financial portfolio that can be developed with AA, since they are the largest airline in the US. The strategic consideration is obvious; they are huge and doing a deal with them can certainly bring in a lot of revenue to the bank. However, the project is not necessarily broad and deep since here each firm would essentially execute separate activities for the co-brand to operate. The bank issues the cards and the airline awards miles for flights. Apart from co-marketing, there is not much scope for real and true collaboration. It is also obvious that there are many good banks that AA could partner with in the US and only a few airlines that Citibank could partner with. So the opportunity to partner is lop-sided, AA having more choices and Citibank having less. This results in AA having more power in the relationship. In this scenario AA could be perceived as the buyer with Citibank being the seller of the credit-card services. However, the project is not really limited in time and space. Citibank and AA have been working together for over 25 years and, as such, one could consider this a partnership.

The bank bears most of the risk as it has to issue the cards, run the credit checks, etc. One could argue that AA has some risk if its customers are never eligible for the cards and the bank cherry-picks only the best customers, but that can be worked through. Conversely, Citibank is not responsible for AA operating on time, etc.; and it can be argued that certain basic conditions could be put in place, e.g., that AA keep a majority of its routes. This business collaboration does not align perfectly with either a sales or partner approach as identified previously. Yet, it is strategic to the bank because of the significant size of the potential cards sold to AA travelers, as well as strategic to the airline due to the importance of their loyalty program and the revenues that result from the card. However, the project is not broad and deep enough. It is unclear if Citibank and AA collaborate beyond the credit-card into lending and other services that they could develop together. If the business relationship was deeper, with more products and services offered through the alliance, then a partnership would be more suited. There is risk, but not equally shared; there is an imbalance of power in the relationship, yet it is a multi-year project not limited in time and space. Either a sales or partnering approach could be applied.

Looking at it from the AA's point of view, choosing the right bank may not all be about the dollars and cents, although airlines have struggled financially over the years. For AA, the project is strategic because it is a core differentiator and important to retaining customers and keeping them loyal.

Here a sales approach and process would seem appropriate. After all, AA essentially has all the power in the relationship; they can easily become the buyer. Using a sales approach, the bank would engage with AA executives to perhaps qualify their interests, analyze their needs, and most certainly, make a presentation. The presentation would be strong, providing ample pricing per mile for the co-brand card and possibly entertaining a share of the other banking fees the cards generate. In this situation the bank is essentially crossing its fingers that it will provide AA with the best offer. However, engaging in a partnering approach could be a better option. There are weaknesses and strengths in each approach and related costs and benefits (Table 7).

Strengths of Partnership Approach	Weaknesses of Partnership Approach
• More open-ended, with the potential for more opportunities to be discovered. • Relationship-centered approach that establishes more flexible role-taking between the teams and more capacity for collaboration. • Relational approach disarms the potential for the abuse of power.	• Much longer time frame because more time is spent upfront aligning mutual needs and wants (**T2**) and developing the business (**T3**). • Involves an unclear set of stakeholders.
Strengths of Sales Approach	**Weaknesses of Sales Approach**
• Clear cut process and clear roles and responsibilities. • Involves a clear set of stakeholders that work on the opportunity from each company. • Shorter expected time frame.	• Socially and operationally fixed roles of buyers and sellers which results in restricted conversations and team interactions. • Process could miss opportunities. • Over-emphasis on distribution of power and financial negotiations. • Could result in one party taking advantage of the other. • Could result in establishing unhealthy and resentful business relationships that derail business when launched. • May involve greater investments of time and energy.

Table 7 – Partnership Approach and Sales Approach Comparison

Choosing between a partnering or a sales approach is not a simple feat, it requires balancing the weaknesses and strengths, and costs and benefits which characterize the more objective side of taking the decision, with the more subjective elements of choosing the best course of action (Table 7).

> When in the gray space, consider some additional fundamental questions:
>
> - Which business relationships are potentially the most fundamental for the growth of the business?
> - How will the company develop, foster and establish the self-generating and self-correcting business relationships that are fundamental to my company today and in the future?
> - Which approach and therefore which outcomes do I want that will allow my business to grow sustainably over the years?
> - In strategic areas, what kind of business relationships does my company not want to be involved in? What do those relationships look like?

There will be times when a strategic alliance opportunity shows itself and the balance of power shifts from one firm to another. One company may act like the "over-dog," demonstrating a culture of dominance, treating everyone like a supplier, trying to squeeze every ounce of power and money at every meeting. It is at these critical moments where executives have to choose what kind of business relationship they are willing to have and at what cost. The core tenet here is beyond the act of choosing. It is traversing the gray space which is fundamentally an act of leadership, business values and taking into account the kind of company that executives want to create and be a part of.

Phase 3
Creating the Alliances Business Unit

This chapter presupposes that executives recognize the importance of collaboration and are committed to establishing an alliances and a partnerships capability. Leadership is prepared to invest in alliances, not with eyes closed but open to the possibilities that a well-established partnering business unit can bring. A dedicated alliances business unit provides organizations a place where alliances learning may be maintained and optimized. At the same time, such a unit increases external visibility in the marketplace, provides internal coordination capability, and eliminates accountability problems and intervention issues when alliances need improvement (Dyer, Kale & Singh, 2001, p. 4).

As previously mentioned, the same core competency for establishing alliances has to be developed for the alliances team. They must have the capacities, the competencies and the action logics to successfully implement alliances and partnerships. The team must be developmentally prepared to support the organization's growth. Finally, once the business unit is consolidated, it must be given the authority and capability to work effectively across the organization.

Alliances are complicated businesses and individuals really need a strong combination of social and emotional capacity coupled with strong business competencies, and a willingness to grow and change to be successful. As an alliances business unit, the team's capability to tap into its heterogeneous intelligences will help it to become operative and more capable as a team when building partnerships.

The *Partnership Coach* can be an effective support to the alliances team to become operative. The coach helps the team build the capacities to improve performance. Promoting these capacities, through a good facilitation process on the part of the coach, will allow team members to productively disagree and to dialogue together. Applying action-reflection practices, the coach helps the team learn to work well together. Over time, the alliances business unit improves and is able to expand its capabilities for entering a variety of alliances and, perhaps, begin taking a portfolio approach to their alliances making.

Capacities, Key Skills and Action Logics

Creating the alliance business team involves recruiting alliance professionals with certain capacities, skills and action logics, which can be inherent or developed. These capacities are related to the intelligences of individuals who help build the competences in developing, sustaining and deepening partnerships. Certain key skills employed across the alliance development process are important regardless of alliance type. Action logics relate to the different ways in which individuals conceptualize the world around them in order to make decisions in a particular domain.

The capacities below are the inherent intelligences of individuals that can be developed and grow to become more effective in managing the complexities of alliances development.

> **Emotional Intelligence** comprises self-management and relationship skills. Self-management skills include:
> 1 Self-awareness— knowing your strengths, weaknesses, and emotions and their impact on others
> 2 Self-regulation—controlling disruptive impulses and channeling negative emotions for good purpose

3 Motivation—having a passion for achievement for its own sake and for constant improvement.

Relationship skills include:

4 Empathy – understanding others' emotional makeup, and

5 Social skills – building a rapport with others to move them in desired directions (Goldman, 2004, p. 1 & 3).

Relational Intelligence involves the ability to relate effectively and deeply with others by maintaining a level of empathy and understanding that allows for clear communication, capacity for honest disagreement and simple human connection and bonding.

Perspective Taking "comprises the developing capacity of a [person] to become aware of and consequently take or seek the perspective of a real or hypothesized individual or group with the intent to use the information about the object dimension enacted for some instrumental purpose" (Fuhs, 2013, p. 8). Perspective taking allows alliance executives to understand the point of view and perspective of a potential partner and internal stakeholders. This is an invaluable skill to help establish an agreement that is fair and equitable from all points of view.

Systems Thinking is the ability to see the interconnected elements of mental models, human relating and team functioning, the whole "interconnected set of elements that is coherently organized in a way that achieves something" (Meadows, 2008, p. 11).

Cognitive Intelligence comprises the ability to learn something new, to think rationally and recall what you learn as well as apply what you learn toward new problems.

Somatic or Kinesthetic Intelligence involves the capacity to use body awareness to access deeper levels of knowing within oneself and understand the body language of others, their emotional reactions and perspectives.

The following general skill areas are foundational to alliances development:

Partnership Negotiations includes not only knowing the *"Getting to Yes"* tactics and techniques of negotiations but also being able to employ a negotiations strategy that finalizes agreements without detriment to the relationship. As distinct from normal negotiations, partnership negotiations employ a different engagement model described in **T4** (pp. 240-257).

Team Coaching & Team Reflection involves being able to coach individuals within the team to improve their capacities in relation to the tasks at hand, as well as engaging together to continuously reflect and improve on performance.

Strategic Planning involves both developing a coherent alliances strategy and outlining the alliance's future evolution.

Strategic Influencing refers to the ability to influence stakeholders both horizontally and vertically in an organization to garner support for alliances being developed. Also, it involves the capability to use a variety of influencing tactics when working with partners.

Financial Modeling is critical regardless of the kind of alliance that is developed. The costs and benefits and other financial considerations need to be modeled and interpreted as part of negotiating the alliance.

Project Management is mostly used during the latter part of **T3** (pp. 211-224). It involves assigning resources and ensuring that commitments between the operational teams are being met, while, at the same tracking progress to timelines and deliverables.

Legal Contracting refers to the importance of having legal support that understands partnering and recognizes that contracting is only a part of a larger, more integrated alliance. Understanding alliances governance and ongoing decision making structures are also important here.

Action Logics alludes to how individuals interpret their surroundings and take action based on those interpretations, and how they function as members of the alliances team. These include how individual executives take their capacities and competencies and form them into their functioning selves, the way they move in the world, how they make sense of the world, take decisions and interact within themselves and with others. "Different [individuals] exhibit different kinds of action logic-ways in which they interpret their surroundings and react when their power and safety is challenged" (Rooke & Torbert, 2005 p. 3). An important part of establishing the alliance business unit is choosing the right individuals that support the organizational goals based on the company's stage of development. Action logics provides a useful tool for recruiting the right alliance leaders for an organization.

The statistically validated Leadership Development Profile Assessment describes the seven action logics (Rooke & Torbert, Ibid. p. 3) (Table 8) and their fit or discord with the three stages of corporate development. The first three, the *Opportunist, Diplomat,* and *Expert* lack the needed action logics to be successful in building and maintaining alliances businesses because they lack the capability to act more freely within an organization and take advantage of opportunities that come from a broader view. The last four, *the Achiever, the Individualist, the Strategist* and *the Alchemist* are best suited for developing successful alliances and partnerships.

Action Logic	Strengths	Characteristics for an Alliance & Fit	Effects on "Alliance Business"
Opportunist	*Wins any way possible* - Good in emergencies and in sales oriented activities	Lacks the action logic that can move or manage an alliance relationship. Unprepared and not ready for alliance work.	Can be more interested in winning than co-creating with Alliance Partner – results in a win/lose relationship

Diplomat	*Avoids overt conflict* - Brings people together in the office, yet tends to avoid conflict and wants to belong.	Best for a transactional based relationship but not as effective for a partnership relationship where conflict cannot be avoided. Unprepared for alliances work.	Can be a protégé for future development in an Alliances Career; however avoidance of conflict can be a major barrier.
Expert	Rules *by logic and expertise* - Seeks rational efficiency	Good as an individual contributor, yet may require coaching to build better relational capacities. Unprepared for alliances work.	May not have the capacity to foster deeper relationships with alliance, however can execute tasks effectively.
Achiever (Alliance Manager/ Developer)	*Meets Strategic Goals* - Effectively achieves goals through teams; juggles managerial duties and market demands	Well suited to managing an alliance relationship, the roles required, taking effective action and achieving the alliance goals. Supports the *Firm-Centric* Organization to expand alliances capabilities	Participates effectively in the formation and ongoing managing of an Alliance Relationship. Focus on the end game, supports the alliance but only so far.

Individualist (Alliance Manager to Alliances Executive)	*Interweaves competing and personal action logics* - Creates unique structures to resolve gaps between strategy and performance	Effective in establishing new alliance relationships and supporting the alliances business. Enables best the transition from *Firm-Centric* to Post-Modern.	Can open the alliance to new ways of approaching opportunity and can function effectively with conflict and cross functional teams.
Strategist (Alliances Executive to Chief Alliances Officer)	*Generates organizational and personal transformation* - Exercises the power of mutual inquiry, vigilance, and vulnerability for both the short and long term.	Effective at developing the alliances business unit and building the tools and strategies for success. Is excellent for supporting the transition from Post-Modern to Emergent.	Can transform the alliance business and is highly effective change agent who can weave idealistic visions with programmatic, timely initiatives and principled actions.
Alchemist (Alliance/Partnering Mindset for entire eco-system)	*Generates System Wide Transformation beyond boundaries* - Integrates material, spiritual and societal transformation.	Good at organizational, and system-wide change for partnerships and alliances. Builds the *Emergent-Enterprise* and works with society at a larger level.	Has the ability to reinvent themselves and their organizations in historically significant ways.

*Adopted from Harvard Business Review 7 Transformation of Leadership 2005 Article & Bill Tolbert Action Logic

Table 8 – Action Logics

Building the right Alliances Team

The alliances team can be made up of a group of individuals from Achievers to Individualist to Strategists to Alchemists (Table 8). Working as a team they can take on the roles of managers of alliances, directors or executives. The roles and the size and scope of the alliances business is relative to the stage of development of the company and the strategic plan being employed. Table 9 is a representation of the scope of the alliances business through the differing stages.

Company Stage	Achiever	Individualist	Strategist	Alchemist
Firm-Centric Company	Will benefit from a team made up of Achievers and Individualists. The team will help the company move into a Post-Modern state while developing the needed alliances that support a more conservative approach along its supply and value chain. Roles here may include Alliance Managers and the Alliances Executive/Director.			
Post-Modern Corporation	Will have a team made up of Achievers who act as Alliance Managers, Individualists who manage a set of major alliances and Strategists who look to enable greater opportunities by building networks of alliances and supporting the organization to become an *Emergent-Enterprise*.			
Emergent-Enterprise	Will be comprised of Achievers, Individualists, Strategists and Alchemists who see the business as actors in networks and creators of new ecosystem-oriented businesses. The organization will comprise all the activities of the company.			

Table 9 – Action Logics Mapped to Corporate Stage of Development

There are two key alliances roles within the alliances business unit: the teams that do the approaching and development and the alliances manager who manages and develops the alliance once it is launched. There are not specific roles beyond that of management and development, just varied organizational levels where there may be more layers of alliances management. There may be three levels of managers that are responsible for one alliance reporting into a director who manages a group of partnerships within an industry or network who, in turn, reports into an executive role. Additional to the alliance management roles are subject-matter experts who support the alliance, either as members of the team or by reporting to other parts of a company, depending on the kind of alliances being developed. These can range from marketing and advertising, to finance and accounting, operations and even legal.

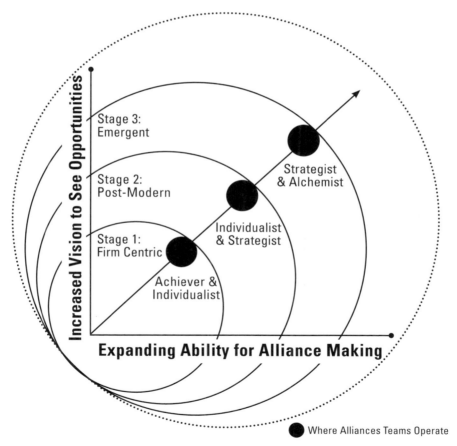

Graph 2 – Corporate Stages of Development

The alliances organization is made up of leaders at various action logics to help the organization grow from one level of development to the next (Graph 2).

Achiever & Individualist – from Firm-Centric to Post-Modern

The *Achiever* is a good fit for the *Firm-Centric Company* which is starting to implement its alliances strategy. *Achievers* are "open to feedback and realize that many of the ambiguities and conflicts of everyday life are due to differences in interpretation and ways of relating. They know that creatively transforming or resolving clashes requires sensitivity to relationships and the ability to influence others in positive ways" (Rooke & Torbert, op. cit. p. 4). Achievers can be alliance managers responsible for one major alliance, or even several, for a company in the *Firm-Centric* Stage. They can be successful in developing the structures needed and leading a team to implement the alliances strategy over one to three years. The *Individualist* is better suited to helping the *Firm-Centric Company* grow into a *Post-Modern* Corporation and expanding the alliances business to include NGOs and other types of organizations in the outer reaches of a company's supply and value chains. However, through coaching and focus on individual development, the *Achiever* can grow to meet the challenge of growing the alliances business unit and can develop and grow with the company.

As a more experienced alliances director, the *Individualist* can be made responsible for defining the vision and main strategic objectives of the alliances business unit. This means setting goals that cut across more areas of the supply and value chains while beginning to consider ways in which the unit can form business networks that involve a set of expanded interdependent actors. Their role is to act as a business architect for alliance programs and initiatives. Individualists "put personalities and ways of relating into perspective and communicate well with people who have other action logics" (Rooke & Torbert, op. cit. p. 5). They can provide a full range of opportunities for partnerships and alliances with companies that are operating at the *Firm-Centric* level, as well as establish networks of alliances. Individualists have the capacity to manage various achiever-managers, while helping to expand the overall strategic direction of the organization.

Individualist & Strategist – from Post-Modern to Emergent Organization

The *Individualist* can be very successful in helping a firm traverse the bridge from being a *Firm-Centric Company* into a *Post-Modern Corporation*. He can tie into the needed networks and structures to effectively manage a series of alliances that cut through the value chain as well as develop shared value with non-profits and others.

Strategists have the ability to transform the alliance business because of "the ability to be highly effective change agents who can weave idealistic visions with programmatic, timely initiatives and principled actions" (Rooke & Torbert, op. cit. p. 6). They can formulate entirely new networks of businesses that involve a group or groups of players supporting the ongoing development of emergent businesses. Working pragmatically, they build through their networks realizing new ways to create value through a shared ecosystem of activities. They are highly effective at expanding reach while shifting the subjective drivers of change within teams and across organizations.

The Strategist to the Alchemist – from Emergent and Beyond

The *Strategist* can help catalyze the *Emergent Enterprise* and establish the sustaining structures for a networked organization operating through an ecosystem of companies and entities collaborating together. The *Strategist* builds the business to turn the company into a partnering organization that sees itself as part and parcel of the interconnected and interdependent fabric of business and society. The *Alchemist* can integrate further in new forms of collaboration that are as yet unseen.

Creating an Operative Alliance Team

The *Partnership Coach* can either be part of the alliances business unit or an outside consultant. As discussed in Section Two (pp. 24-33), there are pros and cons for both. The *Operative Partnership Methodology* coupled with the *5-Territories of Alliance Development* provides the alliances business unit a foundational understanding for developing their approach and capability.

Regardless of how the role of the *Partnership Coach* is organized, the alliances team needs to develop the capabilities to address the challenges of human relating. Facilitation and coaching helps a group of people understand their common objectives and assists them to plan to achieve them without taking a particular position in the discussion. It involves the competency to understand operative teams and to help move conversations to allow unseen problems to be addressed productively while helping the alliance partners to work through the difficult topics. In facilitation, the task is to remain objective while at the same time alive to the opportunity that both companies are committed to creating. It is fundamentally about helping the alliance teams to leverage their core strengths toward a common and joint purpose. At the alliance business unit level, the *Partnership Coach* can help the team develop the capabilities to work effectively together by helping to build the skills to authentically engage in rich conversations, team explorations and group reflections. This helps the team build the internal capabilities to traverse the pre-task, task and project moments incorporating the practices of the *Operative Partnership Methodology* that is employed through the *5-Territories of Alliance Development*. Coaching and facilitating help the alliances team to coalesce, and come together as an operative group that learns through their group practice what it takes to build real partnerships. As they build the internal capacities for internal partnerships, they build group capability for when they engage with potential alliance partners.

Establishing the Organizational Structure

The increasing development of the business's capacity to see opportunities and build alliances beyond itself is defined by the stages, *Firm-Centric*, *Post-Modern* and *Emergent*. The first two are characterized by the state of becoming competent at alliances while the last is a state of being a partnering and alliances enterprise. For the *Firm-Centric Company*, alliances occur only with particular partners of the supply chain. For example, a local supermarket chain may form an alliance with a strategic supplier like Coca-Cola, but not necessarily with a food-bank in their state. The *Post-Modern Corporation* will likely implement more partnerships across more parts of their supply and value chains. However, for the *Post-Modern Corporation* the alliances they develop will extend only so far. In both instances, there are fewer resources dedicated to doing partnerships and alliances than in the *Emergent Enterprise*. As such, the first two stages require a more consolidated alliances structure and team, while the final stage will require capability to be spread across the organization. In the last stage, corporate activities are networked and the ecosystem focused. Therefore a majority of the work is centered on groups collaborating; many people are building alliances and partnerships on a platform or across several platforms.

Two key distinctions need be made here., One is that alliance business units as formalized teams make more sense in the *Firm-Centric Company* and in the *Post-Modern Corporation*. Organizations at the *Emergent Stage* of development function in less formal structures with more informal mechanisms based on distributed authority. Therefore, establishing an alliance business unit in the *Firm-Centric Company* and the *Post-Modern Corporation* involves building the direct relationship to leadership but also distributing alliance knowledge and understanding horizontally across the organization. In this case, the alliances unit focuses on developing capacity, knowledge and expertise, while managing some of the alliances directly. For the *Firm-Centric Company* direct reporting to the CEO or having a Chief Alliances Officer is best. In the *Post-Modern Corporation*, alliances can become an integral part of a larger function and still report into corporate leadership. In both cases, a matrix reporting structure that works horizontally across the organization is needed. For the *Firm-Centric Company* this helps the organization transition to the Post-Modern stage, while for the *Post-Modern Corporation* a matrix reporting structure is generally business as usual.

Metrics and Goal Setting of the Alliance Business

Following the developmental structure, it is critical to establish the goals and the ways of measuring the success of the alliance business. For the *Firm-Centric Company*, goals may be more conservative and generally more profit-based since less of the supply chain and value chain are being risked on alliances. For the *Post-Modern Corporation* metrics that include both tangible and intangible value make sense since certain alliances do not hit the corporation's bottom line but do contribute to its success in other ways. For example, Unilever's alliance with Rainforest Alliance mentioned in the introduction would be measured based in terms of brand value but not necessarily on hard dollars hitting the income statement. For instance, an *Emergent Enterprise* that is networked can be measured in terms of social good and other shared value concepts. The key element is to develop the executive support for alliances and ensuring that the right and appropriate goals are set with the right measurement tools in place to measure success and retain relevance.

Identifying Potential Partners and Preparing the Tools

Identifying potential alliance partners that the alliance team will approach stems directly from the alliance strategy discussed and developed earlier in **T1** (pp. 126-142). The alliance team prior to identifying potential partners has determined the kind of alliances it will be developing as well as how far down the supply chain and up the value chain it expects to develop partnerships. The kinds of alliance may include a contractual strategic collaboration between key suppliers or alliance/partnership consisting of greater interdependent activities and revenue sharing; another possibility is an integrated joint venture/equity alliance where a new company is formed between the parties.

The step of identifying potential partners is fairly straightforward. Best practice is to use a *Partner Selection Tool* that begins with a strategic analysis of why the particular alliance or set of alliances is being pursued. The *"why"* simply states why alliances are being developed and *"for the sake of what"*. The answers to these questions should coincide directly with the organizational strategy and any industry or other contextual challenges that the company is facing. The context involves the industry trends that are affecting the business and very likely potential partners as well. This context can include economic changes affecting the country, demographic shifts and other systemic issues that challenge the firm or open particular opportunities. The second element is drafting the goals that the alliance is trying to achieve. These goals organize the team's thinking about the preliminary methods that will be used to measure the alliance and to help solidify the goals of the partnership. Although these may change or perhaps expand as both partners share information in **T2**, this step provides a good starting point for the team.

The second major step is to develop an assessment grid used to discern the attributes that will help the alliance team decide which partners to invite first. These grids are typically fashioned around two specific areas of inquiry. These are the more objective business-oriented elements that distinguish one potential partner from another and the more subjective element relating to the potential partner culture and way of doing business (Table 7). Both should be equally weighted in order to determine which best-fit partners are available. Two important caveats here: firstly, the information that is sourced from third parties, even though authoritative reports such as 10K reports and other Securities & Exchange Commission (SEC) filings should be double-checked in the questions and answers documents shared in **T2**. Secondly, subjective rating should be counter-balanced when the team actually meets with the invited company's executives. In this way, nothing is left to chance, the team checks information from the source and experiences first-hand the invited partner's potential for partnership.

Regardless of market or industry, the steps for choosing the right partner are similar, yet for extremely technical fields such as bio-tech and aerospace specialist knowledge is important and needs to be added to the rating grid. In this case much deeper due diligence will be needed in **T2 Invite & Commit** and possibly in **T3 Create & Consolidate**.

1. When determining who to partner with, break candidates down into key industry groupings, including NGOs and other kinds of organizations. The market is full of many different kinds of players.
2. Develop a grid of partner attributes that are important for your business and rate each according to industry groupings. The grid should contain objective attributes, such as geographic footprint, revenues and profits, market-share, etc., and subjective attributes such as mission, vision, employee ratings etc.

Industry Group: *Retail*	
Objective Attributes	**Subjective Attributes**
Size of business in terms of revenues, profits, and customers	Cultural fit and market reputation
Geographic footprint	Employee satisfaction ratings
Core products and services	Brand relevance and fit with your brand
Core competency that the partner must possess and you critically need (e.g. design and engineering know-how)	Corporate stage of development (*Firm-Centric*, Post-Modern & Emergent)
Other partnerships in their business that either support or conflict with your business model.	Mission, vision & values
Major investors and other key actors	Auxiliary—non-profit / environmental work etc.

Table 10 – Partner Grid

The goal in creating a partner assessment grid is to identify all the key areas that will support the outcome of the potential alliance business and complement the strategic alliance plan developed. Consider creating a rating scale of one to seven, with seven being the most important attribute and one the least. Assign each point on your list with a rating, then sort the list from highest to lowest. This helps to rank the priorities when looking for an alliance partner. It also allows to distinguish between different potential partners and share findings with others, or consolidate the findings of several involved stakeholders.

Numbers and ratings do not a potential partner make. This is only a guide to help alliance teams prioritize partner selection. However, alliances teams know better who to partner with when they actually meet for the first time in **T2** and work though the steps to reach commitment. Teams need to take into consideration that just because one company has a slightly lower rating than another, that does not mean that it should be ruled out. It can wind up demonstrating a better fit for the alliance once the first meetings are held.

3. Rate the top players in the grouping. With a list of industry groupings in place, identify the five top players per industry grouping. The top players in this case are the ones that fit best to the priorities determined in Step 2 above. Take each potential partner and run them through the matrix of key attributes. Based on how they score in the matrix, identify an appropriate ranking for each potential partner. The higher-scoring partners will be approached first.

4. Research the top partners in greater detail by downloading 10K reports, annual reports, and other recent postings. Determine whether they partner already with others, and if so, with whom. Find out whether they have a vice-president of strategic alliances or CAO (Chief Alliances Officer), etc. Determine how important their partnering strategy is. Figure out how they make money. Understand at a basic level their need to grow and how the potential vision to partner would complement their growth strategy.

5. Learn about the leaders of the company, where they come from, who they are, where they have studied, etc. This background knowledge will be helpful to formulate the approach.

6. Frame-up a whole picture of each identified and target potential partner. This includes adding the contextual story-line elements, ratings and other information from research on the partner's business and leaders. This is essentially a partner profile that can be used to prepare the approach (pp. 173-178).

Success here is predicated on good preparation and sound thinking to arrive at a set of potential partnerships that the business leaders can commit to approaching and, then, the alliances team can invite. Many times a potential partner not listed or thought of reaches out to enter into an alliance. In these cases, it is still important to research the company and complete a partner profile. Teams should enter into conversations with stakeholders to align thinking when approached by an unexplored potential partner. Alignment to strategy and organizational planning, not to mention being in agreement with internal leaders, is always good practice to ensure the partnership journey starts off on the right foot.

Finally, the process of determining the best potential partners is a continued conversation with internal stakeholders who meet on an ongoing basis to measure an alliance's success and continue looking at how alliances can fit into the supply and value chains of the company.

Prepare Tools

As a final step in **T1**, the alliances teams should make sure that they have all the tools prepared for use throughout the territories. These tools include having the financial models ready, documents that will be shared with the partner at each stage, including templates that may be used to establish the *Collaboration and Governance Structure*, roles and responsibilities, and any other basic templates that may be needed. These may also include internal documents used to inform internal stakeholders on progress along the process, etc.

Chapter 9
Territory Two:
Invite & Commit

Territory Two is the beginning of deploying the alliance's strategy for the inviting company. It sets the initial tone of the potential partnership which will evolve into the relationship dynamics leading into **T3**. In **T1** the work is within the company to align and prepare (Chapter 8, pp. 131-181), whereas in **T2**, it is the implementation of that strategy in the real world. In this respect, the team makes use of the *Operative Partnership Methodology*, as well as the information gathered and tools developed in **T1** which initiates the invitation to partner.

Throughout this territory, both teams, from the invited company and the inviting firm, begin a conversation based on the contextual challenges they face and the potential opportunity to partner. This conversation continues through a process as joint inquiry and productive dialogue. They share information, learn about each other and begin to cooperate together in ways that sow the seeds of the partnership and the alliance (Figure 22).

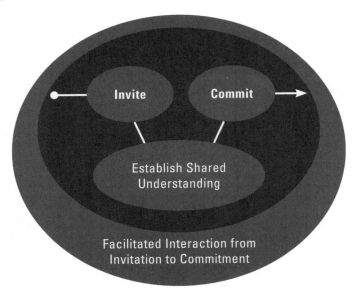

Figure 22 – Territory Two Invite & Commit

From a subjective point of view, both companies' teams start building the relational attitudes that will support an eventual commitment toward a cooperative future. Each person as a participant member of a team engages in the task of determining if an alliance is possible. As the group progresses, the initial elements of the *Partnership Field of Relationship* begin to emerge, shaped by the group's interactions and the work of the *Partnership Coach*. This field lays the groundwork for the group to begin discovering the opportunities to partner. The *Partnership Coach* supports these interactions, while the group works through the specificities of the possible alliance: sharing ideas and concepts while taking the time to consciously address challenges to arrive at shared intentions.

From an objective point of view, the group reviews specific documentation and contextual information about each firm to help frame the opportunity to partner. In this respect, the group constituted by the companies' teams makes its way through toward the end of **T2** until a state of commitment to move forward is reached. The subjective elements of shared meaning and relatedness combined with the objective possibilities of the alliance result in a clear commitment to proceed into **T3**. It thus demonstrates the willingness of the teams to work together as a group and their companies to invest resources, people, time and effort to create the alliance.

Phase 1
Preparing the Approach and Making the Invitation

Preparing the partnering approach is about consolidating the information gathered in **T1** into an organized and thoughtful invitation. Framing the meeting as an invitation supports two key goals. First, from a relational perspective, this reduces the power-plays typical of sales presentations. Here, there are equal parties in a conversation which through shared ideas, points of view and meaning discover if the opportunity really exists and is possible. This approach sets both parties as equal participants in a relationship where joint interest, responsibility and cooperation are foundational to success. One party is inviting the other to participate actively in search of what is possible between the two companies. The invited party needs to take a figurative step forward into relationship. They do this by engaging in the conversation that is interwoven into the invitation. The second goal is laying the groundwork of relational attitudes and norms toward collaboration through communication and mutual inquiry.

The invitation itself is structured into a planned conversation between the future alliance teams. Organizing the approach as a conversation helps in two important ways. First, it provides time for the invited team to interact in a particular way that slowly and deliberately lowers team defenses and begins seeding the spirit-du-corps needed to succeed in developing the alliance over time. Secondly, the teams begin practicing the behaviors of shared inquiry and cooperation.

Conversations and dialogue are critical elements of success in alliances and **T2** is the first time where conversational methods are employed as a tool for joint discovery. Beyond **T2**, there will be disagreements and discussions between the parties, but having the collective muscle to engage in productive and authentic conversations goes a long way to helping the teams resolve conflicts. The invitation formulated as a conversation sets in place the dynamics of giving and taking, advocating and inquiring, and searching together for common solutions and creative ideas.

Drawing Meaning from Information Gathered

The initial step involves organizing all the information gathered in **T1** into its more important elements. Generally, there are four sets of information clusters used:

1. *Contextual Information* made of industry trends and other information that affects both companies;
2. *Approaching Partner Profile Information* made up of data on how the company partners, business fundamentals, etc;
3. *Potential Partners Profile Data* compiled in **T1**;
4. *Opportunity for Collaboration*, which naturally extends from all the data gathered (Figure 23).

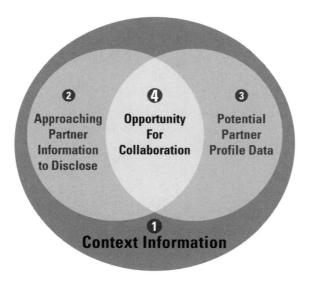

Figure 23 – Information Clusters

It is best practice to start organizing the data regarding the industry context and work through how the challenges and opportunities affect both firms. This sets in place the overriding environmental elements in which both companies are embedded. From these data-sets, shared challenges or possible opportunities can be found for each company. If the firms are from two different industries it is likely that the specific challenges are dissimilar; however, there are always macro trends that affect both firms. There could be new opportunities as a result of changing demographics, new technology, changes in international political environment, regulatory changes etc. where collaboration is warranted.

The key questions that guide the consolidated contextual information are: *what* and *why*? What makes this information valuable and important to each partner? Why is the invitation so concretely compelling? In what way do these affect the businesses of both partners? It is important not to be too broad in discerning what contextual facts support the partnership opportunity for establishing a compelling invitation. If the contextual challenges are too broad the impact of the invitation could be diluted... The idea is to make contextual opportunities and environmental challenges relevant so they are manageable and can be acted upon in pursuit of the possible alliance between the companies.

The second data-set is fairly straightforward since much of **T1** was about setting the reasons for building alliances. This involves organizing thinking regarding intentions for partnering and the opportunities seen ahead for the inviting company. At this stage, the alliances team should again inquire *what* and *why* to help bring the relevant information to the conversation. Why is my company interested in this partnership? What is my company's vision and mission? What intentions does my company have to address the contextual opportunities and challenges in which we are both embedded? With what resources and core capabilities and competencies can my company address the identified opportunities?. This data-set includes information not known to the partner but relevant to share. This sharing allows the partner to learn more about the firm's mission, vision, business fundamentals, partnership strategies, etc.

The final step refers to the contextual challenges and opportunities that could be affecting the potential partner. This includes research from the media, obtaining 10K reports for US companies and researching other annual reports and documents available, etc. The information compiled from the three data-sets needs to become a narrative, presented to the partner as a meaningful invitation.

Creating the Narrative

A narrative is a spoken or written account of interconnected events, ideas and themes delivered to convey a message to an audience. Its purpose is to connect the thematic elements from compiled information in a purposeful and meaningful way. A well-constructed narrative fosters group connection and helps make sense of information. It is a highly recommended tool for producing a compelling invitation, which can also be used throughout the 5-Territories to communicate important topics. "Stories fulfill a profound human need to grasp the patterns of living – not merely as an intellectual exercise, but within a very personal, emotional experience" (McKee, 2006, p. 6). The story is purposefully meant to share the partnership opportunity in an emotional way and connect to the possibility of an alliance.

Actually, the foundation for the narrative began when the alliances strategy was being devised, the inviting team formed and the context of potential alliances partners conceived. The narrative is contextualized by the inter-section of the inviting firm's *Circles of Influence* and *Circles of Concern* (pp. 20-21) with those of the invited firm. It describes the massive change taking place and the need to deal with opposing forces. It calls on the inviting team to dig deeper, work with limited resources, make the difficult decisions, take action despite risks and, ultimately, discover the realities and opportunities of partnering together. The team being approached will be compelled to understand that they are also facing similar if not complementary odds of success and opportunity. The narrative is not an impersonal account of two companies joining forces, but rather an invitation to co-create and meet the opportunities and challenges of the group. The potential partners reflect on the opportunity at hand and the possible challenges faced if they con-sider alliance. Therefore, the narrative is strategic, yet personal, emotional and aspirational.

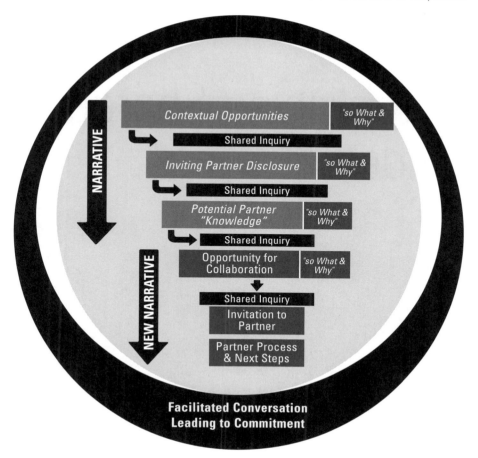

Figure 24 – Making the Invitation

Taken together, the invitation conversation encompasses the shared context and the convergent information and shared opportunities of the two partners (Figure 24). The narrative is created initially by the inviting team and as the invited team decides to engage and contribute, a new narrative is generated by the group. As such, the invitation conversation when delivered openly and authentically establishes the right foundation for the partnership. It helps the group to become operative and, as the new narrative is co-created, it increases the likelihood the partners will reach a state of commitment to working together.

Phase 2
Establishing Shared Understanding

The second phase refers to the process of creating a common set of knowledge for the partners. It involves reviewing and testing assumptions, as well as relevant information leading the way toward commitment. Both companies need to go through a structured and systematic process of sharing important data, taking the time to meet, discover and deliberate on the information's relevance. As part of this, the group formed by the companies' teams, must also walk through a relational process that helps it discern from a purely relational perspective if there is capacity to work together in partnership. The goal of this process is to gauge if there is opportunity to partner, and if each partner has the resources, strategic attributes and other capabilities to develop the alliance.

To accomplish this, the partners work on four specific goals. The first is to gauge if the other partner is reasonable, fair and reciprocal in their dealings. The second is sharing relevant information about each other with the goal of understanding each other's businesses and the intention of seeing what opportunities lie ahead. The third one is to begin establishing the relational group norms for sharing information, clarifying questions and inquiring deeper into the partnership's potential. Finally, the fourth goal falls to the *Partnership Coach* to discern how the partners are beginning to learn and interact together and support them through the territory.

There are tools used in accomplishing the first three goals. The first tool is commonly referred to as the non-disclosure agreement (NDA), which protects confidential information that will be shared between the partners. This is generally provided by the inviting company doing the initial partnering invitation. Generally one party will supply the NDA and the other will make any needed changes. The second tool is referred to as the questions and answers document (QAD).

The NDA provides the receiving company insights into the first goal: the potential partner's reciprocity and fairness. If the document's language is reciprocal in nature and the covenants and structure provide equal protection, the receiving partner gets a clear vision into the legal and business culture of the engaging company. However, if the NDA is one sided and unilateral, it is important to reconsider moving forward. A unilateral NDA is a sign that there are potential problems which stem from business culture and potentially differing intentions. The parties need to navigate these discontinuities and ensure that language balances out reciprocity in the NDA.

The second tool is the QAD. This is a reciprocal questionnaire that each provides to the other to better understand their business models and to further inquire into the potential for partnership. Generally, it is the inviting party that provides the QAD to the invitee. However, many times upon receiving the QAD, the invited party shares a similar document.

The QAD needs to contain specific questions that reflect the information necessary that will help the inviting team test specific assumptions from their initial research. Two key elements need to be kept in mind. The first is being able to identify specific opportunities of the partnership by asking for specific data (e.g. supply chain and value chain details) in order to initially measure or monetize the opportunity. Secondly, there is a need to ensure that there is fit between the two firms' long-term strategic goals. A well-structured QAD breaks the business questions into several core areas (Table 11).

Core Areas	Broad Questions	Specific Questions	Trending Questions
Market Share & Competition	How would you characterize the competition in your market today? What key issues are you facing?	What is your current market share, by product and by country?	What has been the trend line in % growth or decline of your markets share over the past three years and where are you expecting it to go over the next three years?
Customers	Who are your key customers? How many customers do you have in total? How would characterize your best customers?	How do you segment your customer base? What is the spending pattern over the last three years?	What is the trend line in customer segmentation looking into the future over a three-year horizon?
Key Partners/ Suppliers	Do you currently have a partnering or alliances function? How do you see the evolution of partnerships in your business?	Who are your key partners? Who are your key suppliers? Which key resources do you acquire from your partners? Which key activities do your partners perform?	Are your partnerships meeting expectations or failing? How do you typically measure and sustain your current strategic business relationships?

Table 11 – QAD Structure

Summarizing, the key point at this stage is to learn about each other, asking the needed questions, sharing relevant information to test assumptions and begin determining where potential challenges and opportunities lie. Open-ended questions may be added such as: "Is there anything else you'd like to share that is important for us to know?" or "How would you see this alliance fitting into your strategic goals?" This can provide additional information that may not fit formally into the document's structure but may reveal opportunities not seen previously.

The entire process of sharing information, by way of the NDA, the QAD and meeting to discuss findings etc. is a process that helps to enable the basic unit of interconnectedness. Karl Weick, an organizational theorist, describes this basic unit of interconnectedness as the *"double interact"* (1969). A double interact consists of three elements: act, response and adjustment. Through the process of sharing information and conceptualizing, individuals begin to build the interconnectedness needed for the partnership to move forward (Griffin, 2003, p. 264). This basic unit of partnership begins here and is fostered throughout the 5-Territories supported by the *Partnership Coach* using the *Operative Partnership Methodology*. Once all the contextual and strategic information is shared, it is consolidated and reviewed in meetings and working sessions. The teams, constituted as a group under the coordination of the *Partnership Coach*, elaborate on new insights, discuss new opportunities and any potential challenges not seen before.

Phase 3
Consolidating Shared Thinking and Reaching Commitment

Consolidating shared thinking is the final step before commitment. It involves taking all the contextual and strategic information and combining it with data and insights shared between the partners to frame the opportunity. In meetings, the group elaborates on new insights, discusses new opportunities and any potential challenges not seen before and over the course of Phase 3. Thus, it determines that an opportunity to collaborate exists. With the assistance of the *Partnership Coach*, the group consciously works though the more subjective cultural elements of the possible collaboration between their companies. This work supports the group in considering possible future obstacles not envisioned previously (Figure 25). As the figure demonstrates, both companies are embedded in a context and through sharing and learning about each other, they identify an opportunity for collaborating.

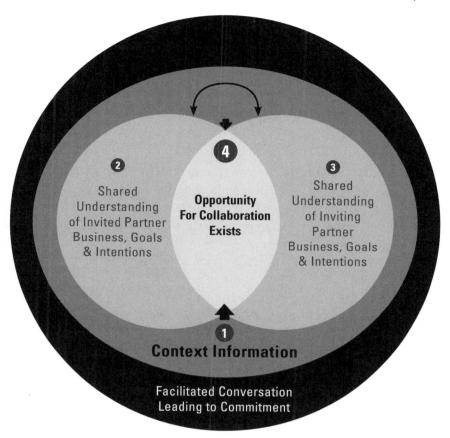

Figure 25 – Consolidating Shared Thinking

Oftentimes, when subjective differences between the partners are overlooked and problems of culture fit are not adequately discussed, alliance contracts may still get signed, but the alliance fails to meet expectations. For this reason, the *Partnership Coach* takes on an important role in helping the group work through obstacles. This does not necessarily remedy the cultural differences between the companies, but rather illuminates them so that the group can consider strategies to avoid misunderstandings down the road.

At this point in the process, what is most important is the group's commitment that it will be heading toward a particular goal. From an operative partnership perspective, the group has to hold *Affiliation and Membership* steady. The coach measures this in every meeting using the vectors of the Inverted Cone (pp. 66-70). The goal is to become affiliated to the group individually and collectively to meet the task of forming an alliance. Throughout the facilitating, the *Partnership Coach* remains objective and open to the potential challenges that could derail the alliance in the future. This facilitative stance is crucial to ensure that things are not missed and problems that need resolution may be uncovered in **T2**. Generally these are problems of vision, clarity of intentions and strategic business considerations that are not fully articulated.

The *Partnership Coach* helps the group walk a careful line to operationalize around the potential of the partnership, without letting them plunge into structured negotiations. The key focus is to help the group build the necessary trust to reveal its concerns, interests and ideas, so that it can establish the basic relational foundation that will contribute to the group's ability to build the alliance structure in **T3** and, through continued trust, negotiate productively in **T4**. Oftentimes in **T2**, groups resort to negotiating because they are experiencing trouble managing the dialectic tensions of *letting go vs. controlling, immediacy vs. working through a process*. These dialectic tensions are managed by the *Partnership Coach* by using a dialogic and inquiry method (pp. 42-52; pp. 96-111) which allows the group to settle into productive conversations.

Additionally, the need for facilitation becomes paramount because consolidating shared thinking is as much a process of pointing out where there is opportunity as of clarifying understanding of where there is disconnect and where potential challenges lie ahead. The work of the *Partnership Coach* is to point out these challenges and allow the group to resolve them in time. As pointed out in Section Two (pp. 23-121), there are defense mechanisms at play which produce a veil between what is actually a problem and what is a relational challenge that the group must overcome. At times, what is perceived by the group as a structural business problem could be a different challenge. For example, oftentimes it is the invited party who must come further into commitment; as such, its commitment carries a greater amount of emotional charge that can be misunderstood as a business problem and can sometimes cause derailment if not managed productively. So that this does not happen, the *Partnership Coach* employs the *Operative Partnership Methodology*, aware of the ebb and flow dynamics of the group as it manages these dialectic tensions. As such the *Partnership Coach* helps enlighten the convergence of mental models and consolidated shared thinking while allowing the possible obstacles underneath to emerge productively so that the group can work through them (Figure 26).

The Path toward Commitment

The path toward commitment continues with facilitated conversations as a core process. At the same time, the group consolidates its thinking by framing the opportunity based on information shared between the partners and engaging in a core-competencies discussion. The group works through a facilitative process to identify the strengths of each firm, what each brings to the business in addition to information shared thus far. This additional step is often used to help stabilize thinking and settle anxieties such as whether the right partner has been chosen. The goal at this point is to help the group consolidate all elements of the possible partnership and alliance.

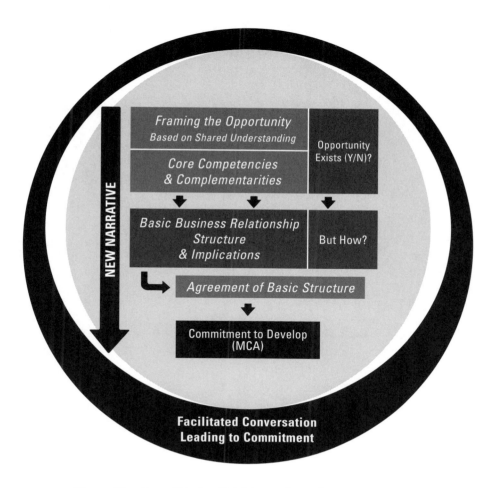

Figure 26 – Consolidating Thinking and Reaching Commitment

By framing the opportunity, both teams organize what they learned and through a facilitated discovery process come to a shared conclusion. The group takes the core learning from shared data and meetings and places them side-by-side where key concepts and general shared observations are canvassed.

Core Areas	Partner A Sharing About What They Learned (Partnership Potential Etc.)	Partner B Sharing About What They Learned (Partnership Potential Etc.)	Facilitated Intersection Of Shared Comments, Observations And Core Competencies Mapping
Market Share & Competition	"so what commentary"	"so what commentary"	Complementarities & Supplementarities Identified
Customers	"so what commentary"	"so what commentary"	Opportunity For Collaboration
Key Partners/ Suppliers	"so what commentary"	"so what commentary"	
Shared Contextual Data	"so what commentary"	"so what commentary"	

Table 12 – Framing the Potential Partnership

The *Partnership Coach* works with the group to draw out the strengths and fundamental expertise and capabilities of each firm. This core-competencies conversation assists the group in articulating how these two companies can combine their strengths to meet complementary objectives or work together to find supplementary opportunities (Table 12). The results of this inquiry are sometimes further refined in **T3** and used when roles and responsibilities are mapped and the collaboration and governance structure is developed (pp. 223-229).

Agreeing to Basic Business Relationship Structure

Once the group frames the business and elaborates on shared competencies, they will invariably begin to question *how*. "How does this work? What kind of business relationship makes sense here and how would a partnership here actually work and operationalize?" In these instances, the *Partnership Coach* follows the Conceptual Model (Figure 27). This is a useful tool that allows teams to understand the implications of different types of alliances they can develop together. The tool helps the group understand how the alliance can be operationalized and the implications of each level. It is an additional way to help the group come to an understanding on the path to establishing commitment.

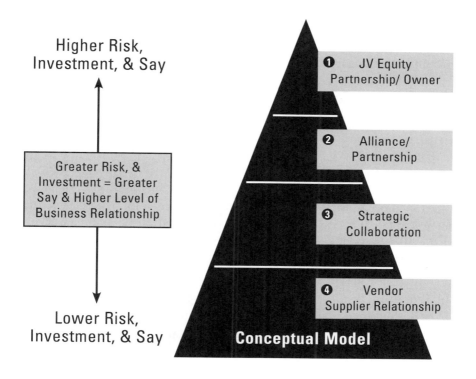

Figure 27 – Conceptual Model of Business Relationship Structure

The conceptual model shows four levels of increasing integration and interdependence of the partners (Figure 27). The lowest of these is the **Vendor/Supplier Relationship**, which does not really apply in the present framework. In a **Vendor/Supplier** relationship, there are no special rights granted to either party and there is no ongoing governance/collaboration structure in place. The financial structure is a simple fee for service model reminiscent of sellers and buyers doing business. In the second more integrated business relationship, the **Strategic Collaboration** scenario, there is some governance, potentially revenue sharing and possibly some form of exclusivity. There is greater risk taking, greater investment, interdependence and decision-taking for each partner. In the third level, the **Alliance/Partnership** relationship, there is an increased level of interdependence. The agreement is long term and involves an integrated governance cooperation structure that is more robust than in the **Strategic Collaboration** relationship. The **Alliance/Partnership** can be an exclusive relationship with clear shared strategic goals and metrics, often based on a profit-share financial agreement. This differs from the **Strategic Collaboration** which is structured through top-line revenue share. The final and most integrated relationship is the establishment of a new company, called a **JV Equity Partnership/Ownership** structure. There is an entirely new company, with significant co-investment and a completely integrated stand-alone structure. Based on ownership of the firm, board seats and c-level positions are created (Figure 27).

The work of the group is to consider these varied relationship types, discuss the general pros and cons of each and agree from a conceptual standpoint which represents the kind of alliances structure and relationship that would work based on all they have learned so far. This is not a negotiation, but a meeting of the minds where the groups come to a strategic understanding of the direction to take as they create and consolidate the alliance in **T3**. What is highly important at this juncture is close agreement between the partners. If they decide on an **Alliance/Partnership** Relationship and **Strategic Collaboration**, the differences can be easily resolved in **T3**. However, if one partner is looking for a **Supplier/Vendor** relationship and the other an **Alliance/Partnership** agreement, the differences are too large and continued conversation will be needed. They cannot be more than one level apart. If they are, it is better either to work on reconciling those differences or not continuing toward commitment.

Reaching Commitment

Reaching commitment is about agreeing to spend time, energy and resources oftentimes on an exclusive and confidential basis for an agreed period of approximately three to six months to develop the alliance's structure. Reaching commitment signifies a major milestone at the end of **T2** for the alliance team who began in **T1** with a list of potential alliances partners. While they are not necessarily halfway into the process, it is an important starting point for the two teams to begin functioning as a group. Commitment is characterized by the focused engagement as a group, as well as corporations deciding to proceed down the alliance development path. Commitment does not mean that the structure is completely developed or that the roles and responsibilities and product/service road-map structured. It shows that the two partners are concertedly interested in moving forward with the energy and dedication to make the alliance a reality. The intention is to work through, and in the near term, establish the specific structures and agreements for ongoing success.

The problem with commitment is that the group must be willing to determine if there exists commitment to proceed. There needs to be a balance between the partners, where each sees and experiences the commitment of the other to work towards building the alliance. In this sense, commitment is not only found in signed contractual agreements, but also in the emotional commitment of the group to create the potential alliance. At times, agreements may be signed in **T2** and still the alliances derail. At other times, no signed agreements are used in **T2** and the deal comes to fruition after investments in time and resources have been made. As such, both teams engaging in the alliance making have to gauge if there is indeed commitment. It is a shared felt experience between both teams, the one who made the initial invitation and the one who accepted it.

However, best practices are that an agreement be in place to signify commitment at the end of **T2**. In alliance parlance, agreements typically used are **Letters of Intent** (LOIs) or **Memos of Understanding** (MOUs). Still, LOIs have no real connotation of commitment and are oftentimes meaningless because there is no promises of time and investment of resources. MOUs, like LOIs, oftentimes carry no real tangible agreement. The **Mutual Commitment Agreement** (MCA) is the best tool for formally putting in place a record of the efforts being made for moving forward.

The basic elements of a Mutual Commitment Agreement are:

Structure: many times the MCA is written as a letter to the CEO or other key alliance executive from the inviting partner. In addition, key stakeholders are copied from each firm. While structured as a letter it is a legally binding agreement diligently executed by both company executives.

Introduction: the introduction speaks to the work that has been done and both parties' commitment to continue down the path of the alliance development process. It may include some elements of the partnership relationship structure the teams will work toward creating and other preliminary concepts that have been shared.

Time Bound Exclusivity: a key piece of the MCA is an agreement to work together on an exclusive and confidential basis for a determined period of time. During this time, neither partner will seek an alliance with another firm in the same industry. The exclusivity clause of course is industry specific and project specific. The alliance team would have to determine if it is necessary.

Partnership Development Process: the MCA continues by describing the partnership development process in its next three territories and the process for continuing down the development path. The timing of such stages may be included, with milestones delineated. Engagement Teams: the teams, their roles and negotiation rights are listed to ensure that both companies invest the right resources in building the alliance.

Shared Expenses and Investments: the parties agree to invest 50% each in having workshops, conducting research and piloting any product or services being contemplated. Each party is of course responsible for its own travel and other related expenses.

Confidentiality: considering NDA was signed at the beginning of the T2 much of the same language simply refers back to that agreement.

Proprietary Information: here the parties agree to share ownership in ideas developed jointly while respecting data and information that is owned by either party. These are industry-specific guidelines that need to be discussed and agreed to in **T1** by the inviting team.

Legalese: this refers to other legal warranties and covenants added by each company's lawyers.

Final Commentary and Signature: as a closer to the MCA there is a signatures section.

Once signed, the alliances teams are ready to begin the work of **T3**.

Chapter 10
Territory Three:
Create & Consolidate

Create & Consolidate are the main concerns of the alliance group in **T3** as it works together to discover innovative possibilities, review alternatives and solidify the alliance structure. Building a workable alliance involves two domains. In the first one, the *Partnership Coach* works with the group to establish the norms of interaction which help to conjoin and coalesce the two teams – the inviting and the invitee – into one *Operative Partnership Group*. The second sets the alliances structure which involves agreeing to the product roadmap of services, establishing the roles and responsibilities, completing the financials and agreeing in a signed *Term Sheet* to the fundamentals of their collaboration. This corresponds to the explicit work of the group in establishing an alliance. While the second domain contains elements that comprise the alliance structure, the first focuses on the relational interactions that give life to the alliance's success. Both of these activities are connected through the operative work of the group and comprise the meta-process all groups traverse when creating an alliance, regardless of industry or geography.

The journey through **T3** contains opportunities for the group to innovate together, as well as possible challenges to make its ideas become a reality. **T3** goes through three phases that can last from two to four months each, or longer depending on the complexities and size of the potential alliance (Figure 28) and the speed at which organizations work together. The first phase of the journey, **Create**, is experienced by the group as a kind of "disorganized innovation" due to the intentionally divergent nature at its beginning – a planned and well-orchestrated *Partnership Innovation Work Session*. As the group progresses through the first phase, ideas are further elaborated, work plans are organized and creative actions taken that pave the way forward.

Phase 2 emerges as the group begins to learn and change. It is a chasm of sorts that occurs between the create and consolidate phases. It requires the group successfully maneuvering differences of vision and goals that begin to appear.

In the third phase, consolidate, the group finalizes roles and responsibilities, defines a collaboration and governance structure, runs financial models and puts in writing all key terms of their collaboration into an *Alliance Term Sheet*. Once signed, this represents the formal completion of **T3**.

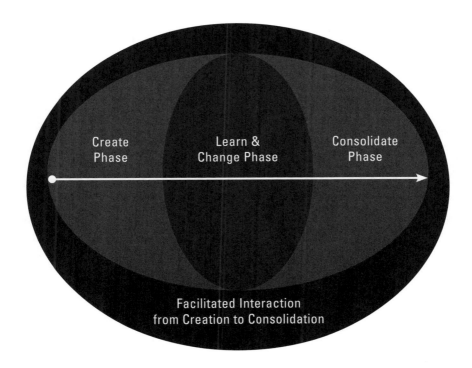

Figure 28 – Overview Map of Territory Three

Phase 1
Create

The first phase, **Create**, starts with a "kick-off" meeting, the *Partnership Innovation Work-Session*, where teams review materials shared in **T2** and work together through a structured work session to map all the possible ways to collaborate together. The innovation session serves three important purposes. First, it brings the working teams into a meeting where they begin to break down the barriers of "my company" and "your company" and starts the process of thinking and acting as a group. The work session enlarges and deepens the field of relationship by involving other participants important for building the alliance. Generally, these include stakeholders and front-line personnel from each company who are important to the project, and who will champion the alliance along the process. Depending on the industry and other specifics, such as operations, technology, finance, marketing, and sales, all key departments and people could be involved in the meeting. The second goal is to focus on identifying all potential opportunities for the collaboration, determining where resources could be placed and organizing follow-on activities. For the coach, the aim is to orient the group toward shared goals, assisting the creation of the initial foundations of a socially cohesive unit. As such, the *Partnership Innovation Work-Session* is meant to produce creative collaboration in the group that begins to establish the relational dynamics and cultural glue needed to create an *Operative Partnership Group*.

Designing the Partnership *Innovation Work-Session* requires the coach to plan a meeting that brings the group together to become productive. The goal is to develop key opportunities and potential areas for strategic collaboration between the two (or more) partnering companies. This enables the group to have shared dialogue that builds common meaning and leads toward coordinated activities and group learning. As participants share their knowledge and insights, stimulating and innovative thinking builds a community that allows the teams to explore possibilities surrounding real issues and questions foundational to the alliance. During this initial work session, the teams conduct in-depth explorations of key challenges and opportunities. People who meet for the first time engage in productive conversations where the group relationship deepens and key alliance goals, direction and deliverables are shared.

Based on the needs of the group, the complexities of the alliance and other factors, the *Partnership Coach* organizes the meeting. Better practice is to design the innovation session with input from participants. Structuring the meeting involves working through a series of questions (Table 13):

Underlining Social Relationships:
When reviewing the chronicle from previous meetings held in **T2**, what key social dynamics and patterns are present?
What is perhaps being left unsaid and unexpressed by the group?
What social roles are being taken on by the members? Are they stuck or fluid?
Has the narrative surfaced? If so, what is the narrative and what shifts in narrative are needed at this point in time, if any?
Are there new metaphors that will help shift the group toward greater collaboration and learning?
Where is the group operating from in Spiral Dynamics Terms (Chapter 5)? What is potentially attempting to emerge from the group? As a result, what challenges will the groups face?

Goals of the Session:
What goals are set by the participants themselves?
What key questions are needed to be answered?
What tools will help the group to arrive at the stated goals? Room design, flip-charts, cognitive tools/models, writing instruments etc.
Session Attendees:
Of those who are attending, who is new to the group?
What "ramp-up" information should be provided to the group, both the new entrants and the original group?
Session Location:
Where can the group meet that provides an atmosphere for working together that is within budget and allows for no interruptions and supports the goals and social contracts being struck?
Session Length and Structure:
How much time is needed to arrive at the goals of the session?
What kind of meeting structure will best fit into this situation?

Table 13 – Structuring the Partnership Innovation Work Session

Workshop design involves reviewing the timeline, processes and practices to arrive at concrete goals for the partnership. This includes designing facilitative interventions and using a variety of meeting structures that support group progress. Innovation sessions can be broken down into one to three full working days or longer depending on the project. These sessions may involve different forms of Open Space Technology such as the World Café (Chapter 6, pp, 97-106). Since no partnership or alliance is the same, no two innovation sessions should be duplicated. The *Partnership Coach* can choose from a variety of strategies to use in the initial work session and may also apply them in other meetings throughout the create phase.

Setting the Mission & Vision for the Alliance

One possible exercise for the session, setting the Mission & Vision, involves articulating the overriding reasons for partnering and clarifying a future view of what the alliance will become. Each organization comes into the possible partnership with a different reason for developing the alliance that reflects each firm's *Circles of Influence* and *Circles of Concern* (pp. 18-20). These circles coincide with one another in a place of complementarity and/or supplementarity between the companies. Working with each team to answer *"for the sake of what?"* they are partnering and this helps convey the deeper reasons why the organizations are pursuing the partnership. Each company's mission is shared with the group to identify a common mission that brings them together and which can be accomplished in a meaningful way. Once put in writing, this mission may become part of the metrics used to measure the alliance. It can be socialized internally in each firm, as well as serve as part of its Public Relations (PR) launch campaign.

The second part, building the alliance vision, helps to ground the mission in more tangible ways. The process involves projecting into the future what the alliance could become, what value it would be producing, etc. This involves contextualizing as much as possible. Once documented by the group, the vision can be used to solidify metrics further, and lead to provisional agreement on contract length, as well as opening additional opportunities for future development that may be added to the alliance road-map.

Finally, the Mission & Vision facilitation helps the group to begin consolidating its narrative. The story they are co-creating can be used to socialize the alliance in each company and in due course helps to maintain the partnership over time. Socializing is the process of introducing the opportunity to different parts of each organization, keeping it top-of-mind and ensuring buy-in and progression along the journey. Like any social contract, the practice deepens the level of commitment of the group, brings meaning to the collaboration and starts to weave the group's operative collective culture. Oftentimes, the group encapsulates the Mission & Vision into a graphic representation accompanied by statements to bring commitments to life. However, these statements are only as good as the companies' abilities to continuously work together toward applying them as they collaborate. Well-meaning written words are made real through the authentic relating and group operability that result in a productive partnership.

Mapping Core Competencies, Assets and Strategic Relationships

This process may have occurred in **T2** and can be reviewed once again as new participants join the group. The exercise involves placing the names of each company side by side and identifying the strengths each brings to the alliance. These may include marketing, finance, processing and operations, specific technology and know-how, as well as the key relationships each brings to the alliance. The strategy of mapping helps to work through a variety of opportunities. It helps to determine how the firms can partner by recognizing each other's areas of strength more clearly as well as grounding their respective roles and responsibilities as they structure the alliance.

The true value that each organization brings to the alliance becomes clear. Sometimes, one team may be covertly questioning the capabilities of the other company and yet may not have all the data available to make such assertions. This may lead to a team remaining silent. In these instances, the process illuminates areas of supplementarity and complementarity and helps to clarify and uncover hidden perceptions and assumptions.

Cultural Review

A third strategy, reviewing each organization's culture, can be a valuable exercise in understanding possible obstacles and devising ways to manage differences. Cultural review refers to the management practices that the companies use to make decisions and move their organizations forward. It can include such dimensions as how decisions are made, the key measures used in each organization to gauge success, and the business drivers that move the organization forward. It includes the formal and informal systems, supervisory and work practices in each company. Cultural review also involves understanding the subjective value systems and cultural norms based on the Spiral Dynamics mapping of each organization (Chapter 5, pp. 80-90).

As a cluster of activities, the *Partnership Coach* can discern possible challenges that the group must make explicit and face together due to the differing value systems expressed by each company and the management practices each employs. For example, a hierarchically organized Blue ^{V}MEME company (Chapter 5, p. 85), where management decisions flow from the top down, have a very different culture than a more Orange ^{V}MEME company. The Orange ^{V}MEME firm (p. 86), could be more horizontally organized with matrix reporting structures and decision-making diversified between functional teams.

Consequently, discovering these differences will aid the group (made up of the teams from the different companies) to find ways to work together in the Create phase and down the path be prepared for challenges. Additionally, when designing the alliance governance and collaboration framework in the Consolidate phase, the group will have to take the different organizational cultures into consideration. The insights from this exercise allow building the right structures to respond to these differences. They will be used in the launching of the alliance and through to the Sustain & Deepen activities of **T5**.

Cultural reviews can be conducted as an open inquiry or may involve the use of due-diligence tools that survey specific cultural dimensions of each firm. In the first instance, the coach works with the group in an open dialogue to map the various differences between the companies and facilitates the group to consider how the cultural attributes and management behaviors could affect outcomes. Another way is to use assessment tools to objectively measure differences between the firms. Both approaches offer opportunities for the group to learn about each other and, most importantly, devise systems and structures that help them through the cultural challenges that may exist. As the group proceeds through this inquiry and, in the Consolidate phase, builds the structures of the alliance, collaboration begins to form into a third entity that fits in between the companies, providing value to both and integrating the cultural structures of each.

Organizational Review

Another useful exercise is an organizational review. The group maps the decision-making structure that is used to manage each business: how staff interface with functional areas, and the nature of internal relationships between departments and groups at each company. Reviewing how each organization works allows the teams to discern the potential challenges they may face as they organize the alliance. Although some of this information was shared in **T2**, most of it was commercially focused and not implementation- or operations-centered. At this moment in the process, the goal is to understand in more specific terms how the alliance may be managed and developed. The group will determine the best way to connect their organizations so that they work fluidly together. This could mean devising, in Phase 3, an alliances organizational structure where the operations or marketing teams from the two companies work together. In other instances, there is cross-functional collaboration between different teams from each company, for example marketing from one firm working with operations from the other.

Establishing Roles and Responsibilities

Establishing roles and responsibilities involves mapping all the key activities of the alliance. At this point in time, it is simply a process of distinguishing which company will be leading what functional area and which will be supporting each major activity of the business partnership. Some areas may require greater joint efforts and collaboration. This does not include building the entire governance/collaboration structure, but merely involves focusing on the basics.

Setting Rules of Engagement

Setting the rules of engagement can be applied as an ongoing facilitative intervention that helps the group to become operative at different points in **T3** Create & Consolidate and **T4** Negotiate & Launch. As described (Chapter 6, p. 107), the rules of engagement are social contracts used at the moment when the group is stuck or needs to work through a particular set of challenges. In the innovation session, rules of engagement can come from World Café practice, as well as from the group itself.

To summarize, the Create phase of **T3** begins with the intentionally divergent innovation session. The results of that session are refined by the group in follow-up meetings and work sessions to solidify understanding and consolidate activities. The *Partnership Coach* uses the exercises detailed above, depending on group challenges, to help it work through important elements of the business, as well as help and sustain its path toward greater inquiry, more authenticity and increased relatedness (Figure 29). The figure opposite demonstrates the divergent opening produced by the innovation session and the different activities engaged in as the group works toward consolidation.

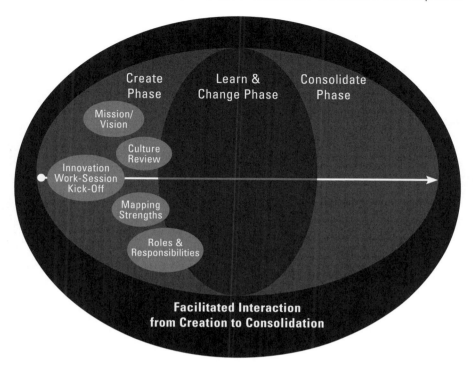

Figure 29 – Map of Territory Three – Create Phase

Phase 2
Learning & Change

There is no road sign or on-ramp that distinguishes when groups enter the Learning & Change Phase of **T3**, the apex of the alliance development process. Progress is discernable from the point of view of the *Partnership Coach* who tracks the group's progress down the inverted cone (pp. 66-70) and across the 5-Territories. According to the *Operative Partnership Methodology*, the group can enter a state of learning at any moment across the territories. However as far as the Learning & Change Phase is concerned, discernable group behavior corresponds to changes in business structure and assumptions that begin to be questioned. In addition, to successfully complete **T3**, the group must develop and sustain the capacity for learning and change so that it may accommodate to each other long enough to reach the consolidation phase. At this point, the group must discern what is relevant, remove what is not and through collaboration finalize the alliance structure (Graph 3). The graph opposite demonstrates the relationship journey the groups must take down the vertical axis as they progress across the horizontal axis toward establishing an alliance. In this respect, the Learning & Change phase, the nexus of both paths, is the bridge to getting there.

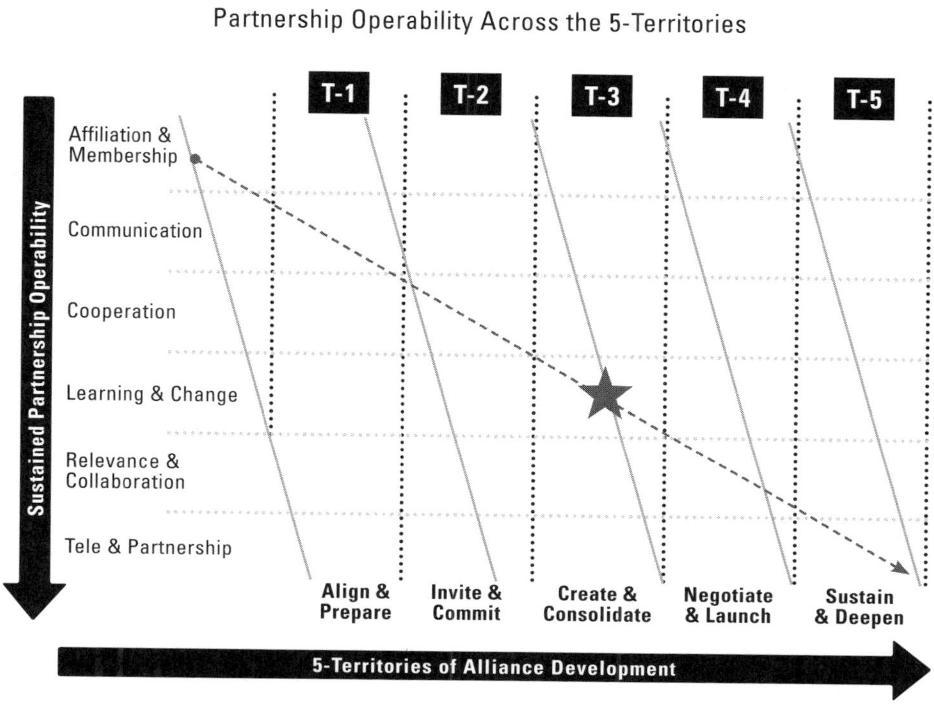

Partnership Operability Across the 5-Territories

Graph 3 – Depth of Partnership Operability Across the 5-Territories

As the group cooperates and begins to enter the ***Learning & Change Phase***, it uncovers deeper challenges that become more and more explicit while tackling more difficult topics. This naturally occurring process midway through **T3** begins with the group reconstructing, reviewing, reframing and deepening its agreements. Learning is change and traversing change requires learning. The group begins to accommodate to each other from an operative point of view. Subjectively, this is a process of the group metabolizing each other's strengths and deficiencies as it begins to enter the task stages in a more sustained fashion.

Additionally, in this phase, the group will begin to generate learning from itself, by reflecting on inputs from research, testing the validity of assumptions, piloting to determine operability and developing practice fields to determine the viability of shared activities. At the same time, group participants will have to socialize decisions taken within each of their respective companies as they design-test and obtain any necessary approvals needed. These activities will place the group in a position where participants need to face together the realities of market conditions and organize themselves based on those conditions, while also adjusting to new opportunities they may discover. Learning and change emerges from these deeper explorations of possible business alternatives and the reflective work between formulating ideas, testing them and including stakeholder inputs. If the teams can traverse this phase they begin to truly collaborate as a group.

As the group begins to establish more productive relationships, patterns of relating will begin to show themselves. These patterns will aid the *Partnership Coach* in supporting group change, which helps solidify the alliance and take it from the beginning to the end of the territory. In working together, the group discovers the limits and possibilities of the partnering companies, slowly arriving at the right place—perhaps not exactly where it might have expected, but where a realistic alliance structure can be built. This comes as the result of the group working together and accommodating to each other, through the commitment made in **T2**.

Practice Fields

An efficient way to promote the learning that is needed in **T3** is through practice fields. These provide valuable information on the group's ability to make decisions and cooperate. They also allow the alliance group to determine to what extent it can begin including new actors. Practice fields may include building a short-lived implementation team to work out a particular contained project that is co-developed by the alliance. This alliance pilot of sorts can be structured around a definite beginning and end. It can also involve a sub-group of the alliance group or a mixed set of new actors and individuals of the original teams. These alliance pilots help build the internal capability to deal with change and at a deeper level provide understanding on how the two organizations will work together. The information obtained may be used to establish the alliance's governance structure in the next phase and help the group devise strategies for working with cultural and organizational differences.

Socializing & Documenting Ongoing Agreements

Oftentimes, change and learning is prompted when each sub-team of the *new alliance group* reports back to its internal stakeholders, socializing the alliance and sharing important information. In those moments, the sub-team returns to the group with feedback that has implications on how the alliance will be formed. This allows the discovery of productive ways to jointly consolidate feedback. In these instances, the group is an integral part of the process of having two large organizations working together. Consequently, participants learn to act both as advocates for each other in their respective organizations as well as members of the alliance group.

At times, the process of socializing and documenting ongoing agreements may involve new participants becoming involved in group work sessions. Since the new entrants create a new group, this signifies another clear moment where there is learning and change. In these instances, it becomes the responsibility of the original group, through some helpful coaching, to assist the new entrants to become introduced to the social norms of the alliance and become part of the partnership. As new entrants enter and leave, the group eventually begins to strengthen its capacities to deal with the changes that occur and, over time, begins to build the unique cultural interactions of a cohesive unit that is expanded through the territory.

Research, Test & Piloting

Learning by doing is the ultimate test of good ideas. It strengthens inter–company relating and allows the group to determine from a realistic point of view what is possible. By this moment, the group will have documented ideas about potential product design elements or service configurations, or other areas of potential partnership they believe will be successful. The group begins to test and tweak by building practical experiences for shared customers, conducting research, rapid prototyping, and employing other methods to test its thinking and strategies.

Documenting Learning

As the groups work through Phase 2, Learning & Change of **T3**, results are documented and information shared with key stakeholders of each company. This information is used as a transition point into the consolidating phase and incorporated into business plans (Figure 30). Learning & Change involves socializing the alliance, researching, testing and piloting so that the group can ground its ideas into a workable partnership and alliance.

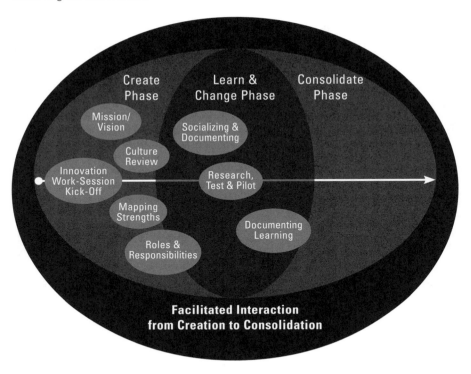

Figure 30 – Map of Territory Three – Learn & Change Phase

Enabling the Emergence of an Interdependent Collaboration

Learning and change is an inevitable part of building an alliance. For the *Partnership Coach* this is not a question of "if" but a question of "when" and "how". He/She supports the group through the difficulties of accommodating to the realities of doing business together, learning from each other and realizing what each company can or cannot accomplish. In a tangible way, the reality of what is actually achievable by each company will be made clear. The group, made by imperfect firms, has defects and deficiencies and yet, through continued commitment, will discover what will work and how to operationalize the collaboration.

Successfully traversing learning and change is made possible by the introduction of specific exercises and interventions that enable the emergence of interdependent collaboration. The group, made up of the invited company and the invitee, does not become an *Operative Group* until it has successfully traversed this middle phase. To pass through the learning and change process, the group needs to build a set of capabilities, know the strengths and weaknesses of its members and build relational capacities to face challenges as an operating unit. Like in the sport of soccer, in each player there must be a representation of the eleven adversaries of their ten companions and also of themself participating in the action of forming an alliance (Tubert-Oklander & Hernández de Tubert, 2004, p.58). For that to happen, groups must traverse states of conflict and struggle when the underlying intentions, fixed ideas and unexplored assumptions emerge. Conflict and struggle are intertwined with change and learning. Groups that struggle and challenge themselves build the internal strength to manage change and build the reflective capabilities to enter the project moment and work their way down the inverted cone.

The following describes facilitative interventions and exercises that support the group in shifting into a positive reinforcing dynamic that supports collaboration. While these can be used in other parts of the partnership process, they are most relevant in the midst of **T3**, where the learning and change process is at its most acute.

Shifting Group Perspective and Focus

Supporting the group to see things from different perspectives helps the group expand its capacities to undertake the collective project of learning together. Perspective taking can come in the form of seeing things from the view of the potential customers, supplier or other third-party points of view. Perspective taking can be as dialed-down as supporting a person with empathic facilitation or as dialed-open as understanding what is happening in larger contexts. These can be market conditions, political challenges the group is facing, as well as environmental and/or geopolitical perspectives that the group must take into account to be successful. It may also take the shape of helping one company understand the perspective of the other and vice versa.

Oftentimes in partnership development, groups can become overly focused on which company will get what, what is the cost, etc. before engaging in joint discovery based on the market opportunities. Although discussing these topics is not unreasonable, often it is the timing that is off. In these moments, rather than working through the details, groups fall prey to wanting to have all the answers before beginning to clarify the alliance fundamentals. In these circumstances, group focus is misdirected and scattered. At other times there is something unresolved; the group may feel as though the same topic is being discussed over and over again. The process of helping the group reframe and shift perspective allows participants to see topics that have been left incomplete and get back on track.

Enabling Shared Inquiry and Joint Decision Making

In addition to perspective taking and focusing, the group's capacity to become operative is directly related to its capability to practice shared inquiry and make decisions together. Decision making does not come from one unique individual but from the shared deliberations and dialogue that the group engages in. Like sailing a ship toward a final destination, the group must orient itself by taking wind, currents and weather into account when making tactical decisions toward a common destination. Decisions are made from moment to moment and charted through time and space. Consequently, the capabily to use inquiry and advocacy effectively helps the group chart the best course forward.

At times, groups may be in a state of communication and cooperation but there are elements in the relating that seem to stifle real learning. At these moments, the field is rife with individuals in the group asking questions that suggest they know the answers. The group may scapegoat someone, disregard their contribution entirely or, conversely, because of that participant's authority, make them into the leader while simultaneously resenting that person. Unproductive inquiry can produce distrust in the field and show the dynamics of control and fear which so often emerge in groups. A method of helping the group resolve these situations is to inquire about the situation and to support participants to take greater ownership of their own opinions and ideas. The act of supporting more effective inquiry can also involve having the group consider what else is missing or what questions would help them find new opportunities or resolve challenges they are experiencing. Learning often arises as a result of questions posed and reflected upon by the group. A good question often helps to ignite new possibilities. Productive inquiry can help the group progress through moments of real change and adaptation to market realities and opportunities. Using techniques from Open Space Technology can be quite helpful in supporting the group entering states of shared productive inquiry and dialogue (Chapter 6, pp. 96-111).

Productive advocacy is as important to group operability as productive inquiry. With only inquiry, the team can fall prey to "analysis paralysis" and fail to agree to an action to move them forward to learn more. Conversely, rapid and ramped advocacy leads to fragmentation and the feeling of being lost and directionless. Productive advocacy involves the group speaking from its point of view and sharing the thinking that leads to decisions. Individuals demonstrating advocacy state their ideas, directions and interpretations openly and invite others to discuss and dialogue together. As such, facilitating effective advocacy is asking people in the group to share their thinking with others. In this regard, facilitation aids in steering a middle road between productive advocacy and good inquiry, so the group can learn, take decisions, reflect and learn again.

Exploring and Surfacing Assumptions, Labels and Judgments

Another helpful approach is supporting the group to explore and surface assumptions, labels and judgments so it can face differences and obstacles openly. One method for doing this is clarifying the language being used. Oftentimes, the group may speak in language that is not clear to everyone. Corporate jargon that stems from one company may be unclear to the other company. At times, it can be used to hide assumptions, labels and judgments. The temptation to pass difficult things off as problems of semantics can become a possible derailer in the change phase. Having a shared language goes a long way to helping the group to be on the same page. From the *Partnership Coach's* point of view, when the group is aligned on language and terminology, this signifies there is agreement. It is the *Partnership Coach's* role to assist in identifying gaps in understanding and help the group agree to specific definitions of key terminology being used; this assists the group to work with competing desires in such a way that it can be surfaced productively.

Another tool that can be used to surface the implicit is the "left-hand" column exercise developed by Rick Ross and Art Kleiner (2008) based on the work of Chris Argyris and Donald Schön (1974). The tool helps surface group assumptions by chronicling what is said in working sessions and surfacing collective thoughts and assumptions behind those actions (Kleiner, Senge, Roberts, Ross, & Smith, 1994, p. 246). The exercise asks the group to write what they are thinking on the left hand of a sheet of paper and what they have shared on the right. As the coach works with the teams, he progressively requests that the left side be shared. Although the tool was conceived for individual work, it can be used at the group level. The method aims not to analyze individual contributions, but rather to go through the conversation sets and inquire into the operating assumptions below. Oftentimes, such assumptions relate to misunderstandings of intentions and expectations that are not fully explored and understood. This process involves working with cognitive assumptions and emotional obstacles that are hindering thinking (Tubert-Oklander & Hernandez de Tubert, 2004, p. 133).

Finally, through facilitative reframing, assumptions can be drawn out by the group and worked through. Reframing can be as simple as asking the group: "In what other ways can you see this particular challenge?"; "What elements of the challenge can be understood in new ways and what alternatives are there in terms of perspectives?" Reframing allows for alternative viewpoints that help the group find new and innovative ways of understanding, shifting participants' perceptions. It is a reflective process that helps the group accommodate to reality and learn from its own interpretations and well as from the environment. Overall, working through the latent dimension raises the group's ability to tackle problems effectively and build the bonds of trust that allow for the alliance to consolidate.

Metaphoric Interventions

Metaphoric interventions support groups in leveraging change and learning together. They can be used in **T3**, as well as in **T4** and even in **T5**, where PR and communications strategy are conceived and the sustaining and deepening structures are developed. The essence of metaphors is for understanding and experiencing one kind of thing in terms of another (Lakoff & Johnson, 1980 p. 5). The use of metaphors allows groups and participants to organize their thinking and concepts, relate them to varied ideas and create living experiences as they communicate, verbally and nonverbally, intra-psychically and intervivos. In this respect, it is through metaphors that groups, societies and cultures emerge (Katz, 2013, p. 15). As a facilitative intervention, "metaphoring" involves engaging in productive and conscious creation of strategic metaphors that help the group reach a deeper and more productive level of shared meaning and understanding. Using metaphors as a facilitative intervention provides valuable insights to the group, helps it surface discontinuities and challenges which it can address together.

Consequently, as groups work through the process of encapsulating the alliance through a metaphor they develop, they conceptualize and create the language and cultural foundations of the alliance. The intervention can be quite powerful in helping the group coalesce and consolidate across cultural differences. This helps to achieve uniformity of purpose and develop emotional links between organizations (Cacciaguidi-Fahy & Cunningham, 2007, p.137).

Examples of metaphors that groups can use include container metaphors, journey, sports, movement, and travel. There are many more that involve real-life experiences. As an emergent co-construction of the group, the metaphor becomes infused with desires, intentions and emotional realities. It becomes the product of cultural group thinking that produces a process of acculturation of ideas and provides the 'conceptual glue' that keeps a system of culture together (Danesi & Perron 1999; Cacciaguidi-Fahy & Cunningham, 2007). Group metaphors act and establish the real foundations of collaboration in a shared linguistic conceptualization of the alliance.

Immunity to Change & Learning

Groups may experience moments of anxiety and conflict that restrict progress and hinder the learning and change process. In these instances, the work of Robert Kegan and Lisa Laskow Lahey is valuable in helping to identify competing commitments that produce immunity to change and learning. Groups have goals and intentions and yet face difficulty in achieving them because of the differing obligations at play. Like dialectic tensions (pp. 37-38), these commitments produce behaviors that run contrary to group goals and operate at an unconscious level.

Kegan and Laskow Lahey (2009) developed a facilitative process to identify these competing commitments in order to overcome them. This involves mapping out commitments and goals, then working with the group to describe what it is doing and not doing with regards to those obligations. Next, they work to ask why there are competing commitments. This helps the teams to illuminate and objectify the contradiction they *are*, and converts these into a contradiction they *have* (Kegan & Laskow Lahey, op. cit., p. 55). In this way, the group objectifies the dilemma it is in by creating distance between itself and what it discovers in this intervention. Once the why is discovered, the group works to identify the "big assumption" that undercurrent the behaviors. Through facilitation, the coach helps the team uncover and objectify the assumptions and its implications so that the group can become operative. This intervention supports the team's capacity for learning and the adaptive change needed to proceed into the *Consolidation Phase*.

Overcoming the Trust Dilemma

The conflict and difficulties that emerge as groups enter the learning and change phase are an opportunity afforded to them to garner its power productively. Constructive conflict allows the group to leverage emotionality and open conversations that help the group find opportunities and resolve problems. When the group experiences conflict as constructive, the need to control and the fear that comes along with letting go falls away. Most importantly, this process builds the relational trust to consolidate the alliance fundamentals.

For example, when the group begins to work through roles and responsibilities it must let go of the need to control important aspects of the alliance and rather let the sides work out certain elements of the partnership independently. In this respect, the dialectic tension between risk/fear and control must be managed by the group. As this happens, members begin to learn and start trusting each other more, testing what they produce, what they say, and learning to count and rely on each other.

In alliance literature there is much written about the importance of trust and what results when there is mistrust: poor alliance performance. Yet, there remains little written on how trust is actually built over the course of establishing alliances. In the literature, "trust" seems to be identified as some inanimate object, rather than conceptualized as a journey that the group must undertake through the process of alliance building. When it is thought of as a state that results from interpersonal connecting, woven through cooperation, communication and support, it can then be co-created. The leverage into trusting partnerships lies in the group creating a path into it, as a collective team supported by interactions enabled through facilitative interventions.

The worst possible derailer is the mistrust that remains undisclosed and unexplored well into the negotiation and into the launching of the alliance. For example, a group produces a business agreement that does not work entirely, yet the group chooses to not address the issue and covertly sabotages the alliance by complaining internally about the unfairness of the deal. These types of transgressions become the seeds that lead to the alliance's eventual failure, and are likely a good reason why 50% of alliances and partnerships fail to reach their intended goals.

A successful Learning and Change phase results in the group consolidating the alliance by determining what is relevant and achievable in the short and medium time frame. Explicitly this involves consolidating the thinking and organizing work-flow in accordance with the new learning. From a relatedness point of view, the group now enters the *Operative Partnership Group* stage as participants begin to collaborate more. In the Consolidation phase, participants demonstrate an ability to sustain a culture of performance, relating with greater ability to have more difficult conversations to solidify agreement.

Phase 3
Consolidate

As groups enter consolidation, ideas are further solidified, work planning is organized, based on the roles and responsibilities articulated, creative actions are identified, and unattainable ideas and opportunities are dismissed or simplified to pave the way forward. The group works to consolidate the activities that form the foundation of furthering the alliance's goals. If the group was able to enter the learning and change phase, it can take that learning further to produce more concrete activities and ideas on how exactly the alliance will function. By this time in the process, the group should be quite adept at engaging in *Action Reflection & Inquiry* as it is starting to build its own culture of relating and working together.

Partnership coaching and facilitation continues to be relevant as the group becomes an *Operative Partnership Group*, helping it sustain greater levels of relatedness mapped down the inverted cone. There are challenges ahead for the group to ground the final elements in **T3** and continue toward **T4**. In the final phase, it clarifies the business model, establishes the financial terms, creates the *Collaboration & Governance Structure* and prepares and executes the *Alliance Term Sheet*—the legal binding agreement that triggers the final contract negotiations and launching activities of **T4**.

After this stage, effective coaching maintains productivity in order to ground the key elements of the alliance. The group must relate in more fundamental ways, being willing and able to express itself more authentically and more deliberately in order to build a workable blueprint for the alliance. In reverse fashion to the Create phase, where the work was purposefully divergent and the facilitation was focused on opening the field of relationship to allow for inquiry and possibility, in the Consolidate phase it is convergent. It involves a narrowing down of potential options, grounding possibilities and solidifying decisions. It is necessary to end **T3** with a term sheet and a realistic blueprint of how the alliance will operate.

Consolidating Findings & Mapping the Future

To do this, the group works to determine what is possible in the near future, perhaps the first two years, and mapping what potential projects can be developed beyond year three. In this way, the group determines what can be implemented for the alliance in the short term, without losing sight of potential business opportunities in the mid-term. It consolidates findings from the piloting activities, research and learning experienced. For example, a product development alliance with a particular retailer may involve kitchen products designed specifically for a set of customers with a white label agreement structure where the store's brand is used. The teams may see the possibility to develop a whole set of other products and services that are related but not possible in the near future. These potential opportunities, rather than getting lost, can be mapped and documented for future implementation. In this respect, the work of consolidating determines what is immediately do-able while creating the collaboration structure to decide and implement potential short-term opportunities.

The Collaboration & Governance Structure

In alliance parlance the term used for describing how an alliance is to be managed is *Alliances Governance Structure*. However, the term *Collaboration & Governance Structure* is more precise for our purposes. Collaboration requires an ongoing group process that includes activities meant to maintain a level of collaborative-relatedness to support the ongoing functioning of the business. Governance refers to the clearly defined rights, privileges and authorities that are afforded to the alliance partners. The *Collaboration & Governance Structure* can be varied and is meant to be a tool to support sustained success for the alliance to function optimally, and for the groups to have clear guidelines in working together. It is not meant to be a substitute for group relating. As a tool, parts of the *Collaboration & Governance Structure* can be refined and optimized over time so that it meets the demands of the market and ensures the ongoing success of the business.

The *Collaboration & Governance Structure* is organized depending on the level of coordination and collaboration necessary for the alliance and its goals. Since there is no best way to develop the structure, many organizations have chosen between a mirror structure, the lone ranger structure, or, alternatively, *a multiple points of contact structure* (De Man, 2014, p. 73).

- In the mirror structure, each organization mirrors the other one. In this case, operations works with operations of the other firm, marketing with marketing, etc. Another term often used is *zippering the alliance*, where each organizational structure mirrors or zippers with the other. This kind of structure is typically used in international alliances where entire organizational structures are almost copied in different parts of the world.

- In the lone ranger structure, also referred to as *alliance-manager* structure, one manager or team is responsible for the entire alliance's success, thus working as the central point of contact with the other firm. This model is used more often in smaller alliances than in larger, more integrated partnerships operating across several firms, an international region or several parts of the company's value chains (De Man, op. cit., p. 74).

- The multiple points of contact model, used in larger alliances, is typically organized in three ways: the specialization type, the joint team type and the peer to peer type, each based on the level of collaboration necessary and the intention behind each.

  o The specialization model occurs when companies need to simply combine different competencies to achieve goals. This type of structure is more commonly used in **Strategic Collaborations** as described in **T2** (pp. 186-187).
  o The joint team model is more appropriate for an **Alliance/Partnership** structure, where there is a greater amount of interweav-

ing of work product and, as such, a greater level of integration. In this respect the groups work jointly where work product is shared.

o In the final structure, the peer-to-peer structure, the work product is separate but here there exists two of everything; each partner working on similar activities to the other, which can be implemented in the **Strategic Collaboration** or the **Alliance/Partnership** structures (De Man, op. cit., p. 74).

In practice, of course, a wide range of structures combine the varied elements described.

Key elements of the governance portion of the structure refer to the documentation of the alliance and demonstrate in black and white terms how it will be managed over time:

Clear, Defined Organizational Structure: when it comes to the daily execution of the alliance activities, the organizational structure needs to be clearly defined and documented. Like any structure that contains reporting lines, the organizational structure defines these communications and responsibilities. The structure helps in the day-to-day management of the relationship, as well as ensuring that the various parts of the organizations productively engage with the other partner during human-resource transitions and other such changes.

Responsibility Assignment Matrixes: this describes the participation of the different roles that are used in completing tasks for the alliance. They can map to specific business processes that the alliance uses to conduct activities or are generally applied in the day-to-day functioning of the alliance. The most typically used structure is Responsible, Accountable, Consulted and Informed (RACI). In this matrix, Responsible refers to the actual person or persons that will achieve the tasks assigned. Accountable refers directly to the person who is answerable and accountable and, oftentimes, is the individual that delegates that task to the one(s) responsible. Consulted is the individual or group whose opinions or expertise is sought for completing the tasks. Informed are the individuals or groups in the organizational structure that are told of the activities and progress of the plan. These can include the executive sponsors or others.

Clearly Defined Decision Rights: depending on the kind of organizational structure and the activities of the partnering firms, there may be a variety of decision rights that will have to be developed. There is no tried-and-true decision rights structure because of the variety of collaboration models available (strategic collaboration, alliance/partnership and JV/equity company) and whatever falls in between. It is important that the decision rights be clearly defined between the companies and while this is often the case, a certain role may be "managed" by one partner or the other. Also, it is important that both provide the other with input on important decisions, particularly key decisions that affect the fundamental functioning of the partnership. For example, consider the case where one partner is fully responsible for running the technology platform behind the service they are bringing into market, while one other holds the decision rights on the day-to-day operations of the platform, making sure the platform is running and processing to standard etc. Both partners have a say when it comes to deciding on a new technology platform or vendor, critical technical upgrades, etc. Important decisions should be joint decisions.

Levels of Engagement & Oversight: different levels of engagement and oversight are often used in larger and international alliances that operate across a geographic region (e.g. Europe, Latin America, Asia etc.). Undoubtedly there will be several levels of oversight and decision rights—not to mention a process for resolving disputes and differences within the partnership at these levels. The following is an example of this kind of structure.

> The first level could involve an *Execution and Implementation Team*. This ensures that plans are being executed, activities accomplished, and metrics attained. It constitutes the group on the front lines of the day-to-day management of the business.

> The second level could be the Business Oversight Team, standing one level up from *Execution and Implementation*. This team is often composed of the local country head and part of the regional team that supports local execution. Either way, the *Business Oversight Team* serves as the governance body in the middle: the team that supports the decision-making that takes

place behind the most important pieces of the business. They do not formally do the day-to-day management, they merely provide oversight. This team is best served if it includes members of each company's executive committee, because it is often tasked with resolving disputes between the implementation teams. This team may meet quarterly or when critical decisions or negotiations are taking place. During each quarterly meeting, it reviews progress and makes key decisions to support steering the alliance in the best possible direction.

The third level is the *Executive Committee*: responsible for managing the key decisions of the alliance such as new product roll-outs, increased or decreased success metrics, termination issues, major alliance investments, major dispute resolution issues, and approval of strategic goals.

Dispute Resolution Process: this allows the working groups and teams to have an understanding on how problems will be handled depending on the RACI structure, and based on different levels of oversight. For the larger disputes, this ties directly into the contract termination provision mentioned in **T4** (p. 238).

Measurement Systems and Dashboards: these are a way to measure the objective business results of the alliance as well as keep a good feel on the pulse of the partnership relationship. Many companies have used the Balanced Score Card (BSC) as a tool to help them maintain a pulse on the alliance. The BSC develops a set of objective and subjective targets; these are measures that relate to the more critical aspects of the alliance. These may involve measures that focus on the strategic goals of the alliance, select a small number of critical measures to monitor, and use both a mix of financial and non-financial data points. In this way, the BSC is meant to take the original vision of the alliance articulated earlier in **T3** (pp. 195-196) and build operational goals behind it. The BSC should link that vision into group and individual performance measures on the collaboration participants in each firm responsible for its success (e.g. executives, partnership managers, alliances teams, etc.).

Oftentimes, alliances establish dashboards to measure the alliance on an ongoing, almost day-to-day basis. Metrics can include both individualized numbers that represent the success of one alliance partner or the other, as well as shared metrics, where shared success is measured. Success here must include metrics pegged not only to alliance goals but to alliance progress (Hughes & Weiss, 2007, p. 4).

Subjective health checks should be included to survey the attitudes and undercurrent of the relationship, as well as the emotions that support the alliance's success. Health checks are particularly effective at catching habits and potential future disruptions, or determining whether the partnership is healthy and operative. In some instances, the alliance team from each company may realize it is hitting all their number metrics, but there is an underlying disagreement between the teams which, if not properly resolved, could derail the alliance in the future.

Key elements of the Collaboration portion of the structure help to maintain the collaboration between the alliances teams by continued learning, connection and relatedness. These additional elements, while implying more work, actually help to further establish and solidify the capability of the alliance to become self-generating and self-correcting.

Annual Planning Cycle: this involves the process where the groups measure and review annual plans, business plans, investments and initiatives, as well as plan and prepare for follow-on activities. These annual planning cycles coincide with the product roadmaps and other opportunities identified in the earlier phases of **T3** (pp. 193-202). There continues to be action-reflection and feedback loops that set in place the annual goals and help to refine activities throughout the years as more is known and shared horizontally and vertically in the alliance.

Ongoing Meetings: especially during the first 180 days of launching activities, there will be more meetings. As the alliance progresses, various oversight groups may meet quarterly or semi-annually to review deliverables and progress on goals. Best practice is to prepare an annual calendar of these meetings to ensure there is effective tie-in to all the operating groups.

Organizational Feedback-Loops: throughout the entire process of establishing the *Collaboration & Governance Structure* there need to be feedback loops that support the overall functioning of different groups so that they continue to learn from each other while they develop plans and execute activities in the marketplace.

Action Reflection Cycles & Operative Group Facilitation: ensuring that practices developed in the earlier territories are continued to maintain the culture of the partnership and ensure ongoing operability.

Alliance Operating Principles: these are documented sets of statements that reflect an accepted tenet or rules of conduct that the alliance is committed to following throughout the collaboration. These principles express how the partners want to work together. They can include statements that form the collective agreements at the individual–group–company level and are used to both reflect its intentions and operationalize the alliance once launched. They can also be used to help perpetuate the alliance culture. Developing the *Alliance Operating Principles* can be done in concert with the *Mission & Vision* work to help solidify the alliance.

Mission & Vision: maintaining documentation and visual representations of the alliance's mission and vision helps public relations efforts, and maintains the spirit of the partnership.

To create the *Collaboration & Governance Structure* it is important to ensure the input of the people who will actually be doing the alliance work, those individuals that will be working together in the day-to-day activities. Best practice is to include the people who have been involved since the first *Partnership Innovation Work Session* and involved along the process. Oftentimes the *Cooperation Structure* is not fully completed in the Consolidate phase of **T3**, but drafted for further review and refinement in **T4**. Still, at this point in the process, the general guidelines and understanding of annual planning, the basic metrics of success, and key elements of the *Collaboration & Governance Structure* are developed and added to the *Alliance Term Sheet*.

There is no better determinate of potential alliance success than ensuring full engagement, where groups address relationship challenges consistently, proactively and productively. This means ensuring that information is being shared, meetings are made and agreements are followed through. Dashboards and management systems help the alliance to address problems and challenges which will invariably arise after launch. Key is the group's continued capacity to maintain its operability of relatedness so as to address challenges together.

Building the Financial Models & Implications

The most emotionally charged part of building the alliance involves determining the answers to the age-old business questions of "what will it cost?", "who will get paid what?", "who will get paid how?" and "what is the financial structure going to be?". This conversation is not entered into blindly, since the group determined the basic structure of its collaboration back in **T2** (Strategic Collaboration, Alliance/Partnership or JV/Equity Relationship, pp. 196-198). Additionally, the inviting firm modeled the basic financials back in **T1**, during *Align & Prepare* (pp. 125-171). In this case, the inviting company determined the kind of relationship it was looking for and had an idea how resources would be shared between the parties. However, things may have changed since then, depending on the results from work sessions and any recent learning.

Although there are a wide variety of potential ways of developing the financial structure of the relationship, when the group gets down to building the financial models, it tends to work in one of three ways:

1. An Open Book Approach, where the group develops the model together in the open
2. A Closed Book Approach is just the opposite; the teams each develop their own financials; and
3. A Shared Approach (each partner will develop and present a shared model, but will also develop a separate model for internal purposes).

When it comes to these three approaches , there is no best practice and, generally speaking, what happens is indicative of each company's business culture and level of comfort with full transparency.

Openness helps everything to be clear, but is not a prerequisite for success and operability. In alliances that involve several players in an ecosystem, the transparent approach is the only way to go, because to build an alliances ecosystem or network, one cannot negotiate the financial terms of every relationship. Yet, all businesses alliances are different. There are fundamentally different types of alliances, with different cultures, in different industries, with diverse organizations (public, private, non-profits), and not all fit perfectly into a mold. Groups have to work through the approach that best fits their corporate culture, what each alliance team can work with and what the group can agree on.

The Open Book Approach: this is probably the easiest to review; the group builds a business model which includes all aspects of the business and establishes the payment structure and profit and loss statements (P&Ls) for each particular piece—the costs and expenses related to the activities in which each company is engaging in or in which the different parts of the ecosystem are involved.

The Closed Book Approach: each team shares only the assumptions that go into each piece of information needed to run their separate business models. This means that each understand the inputs of the shared business in which the companies are engaged. For example, in credit card co-brand alliances, the bank which issues the card will provide the retailer/partner with their projected card sales, expected attrition, etc. so that the retailer can understand and optimize its own loyalty program. The ultimate result is to build a co-brand card program for the most loyal customers. The bank will need not only the spending data of the partner's customer base (this information should have been collected in the QAD in **T2**), but also the numbers of customers in the loyalty program, other spending information, and other pertinent data to build its projections. With these assumed numbers in place, the partners will be able to discuss the actual investments based on their respective roles and responsibilities.

The Shared Approach: this is a model developed together by the partners, but each party still maintains its own model. This occurs when the model for the alliances is part of a larger business, a business in which the alliance is only one part. In this case, the group proceeds much as it would in the Open Book Approach and then adds the extra layer of maintaining an internal model. Yet, at times the Shared Approach can also include sharing just the revenue side of the financial model and not the operational costs side. Each company maintains a cost structure and works to negotiate the revenues. This could be complicated, but it is always possible.

Within the approaches described, there is an additional critical element to consider; the actual financial distribution of revenues and costs. A simple framework of options to consider is listed below. Each of these options, however, comes with different pros and cons that need to be discussed by the group.

1. Money upfront; revenue shared before either party incurs any expenses.

   This occurs mainly when there are clear and distinct roles and when value-added activities can be sequenced and separated in an understandable and measurable way. This allows partners to negotiate a percentage revenue share that is objective, fair, and sensible. This is mostly used in alliances/partnerships and/or strategic collaborations; less so in joint venture companies. The key is that each party is responsible for its own costs and can manage them independently. This creates individual accountability in the project, but can result in disconnect within the partnership if good coordination between the parties is not established.

2. Money in the middle; revenue shared once some agreed-to expenses have been incurred.

   This usually happens when the project is a result of non-sequential activities or actions, when the development is less discrete and there is more integration of work between the companies. As such, certain expenses incurred by each partner are attributed to the revenue, but not all costs. For example, an alliance may incur a great deal of marketing and advertising investment and, based on the branding ownership, all of that may or may not be distributed as a cost to the partnership. Money in the middle will inevitably have costs that are attributed to the revenues and split, but those costs need to be identified and discussed. Of course, it is impossible to have a completely closed-book approach to money in the middle, since information and costs do need to be shared.

3. Money at the end; revenue shared either before taxes are incurred or after, but generally after all costs have been accounted for.

This tends to be used most often in JVs and equity relationships where either a separate entity is created for the alliance, or where there are very large up-front investments made. Through money at the end, all costs related to the partnership are loaded on the P&Ls and then distributed fully either before or after taxes, depending on the business structure. In a JV, the entity pays taxes and then profits are distributed. That is the general norm. However, in an alliance using the money at the end structure, sometimes profits are distributed before taxes. Money at the end could become an audit and administrative nightmare, where both firms have rights to review spending. That is the reason they are mainly used in JV/equity scenarios, where the alliance is more tightly structured as opposed to alliance/partnerships and strategic collaborations.

Preparing Detailed Business Cases

Throughout the process of consolidating the key pieces, many companies use business cases to document all key aspects of the business and obtain the necessary approvals for investments. Often, alliance teams from each firm may develop separate business cases that fit their firm's unique needs. Yet, in certain circumstances, particularly in market- and customer-driven alliances, a single business case often is a better approach. In such alliances, the collaboration is meant to bring new capabilities to shared customers.

In this ideal operational model, the idea is to design the business as if it were being driven by a stand-alone firm. Such a firm is responsible for all the elements of the business in terms of customer value proposition, pricing, customer segments, activities, resources and other partners that help to deliver the product or service to market. The group then works to solidify the elements of the business case split by the roles and responsibilities mapped previously and pulls it all together into a comprehensive plan that is used for approval at both companies. From there, the companies can work through the key elements of the term sheet (Palmer, Visioni, Weiss, Hughes, Kliman, 2009, p. 4).

Drafting the Alliance Term Sheet

The *Alliance Term Sheet* is the blueprint of the alliance that is being formed but it does not lay out all the details. However, it is legally binding on the two companies and is more formal than the *Mutual Commitment Agreement* described in **T2** (pp. 189-190). Additionally, like the *Mutual Commitment Agreement*, it is a gate from **T2** into **T3**. So is the *Alliance Term Sheet* a defining moment when the groups transition from **T3** to **T4**? The key elements of the sheet are those that involve the financial arrangement, the basic governance structure and length of the agreement. Other topics may include how the alliance would be terminated should it fail and under what conditions this would happen. The sheet will also delineate the kind of legal structure that will be used, either a new-co entity or one of a variety of equity arrangements, such as minority equity investments, equity swaps and/or simple contractual agreements. Other elements that may be included are:

- Contract jurisdiction
- Market roll-out prioritization for multi-country relationships
- Customer ownership
- Investments and key metrics of success
- Intellectual property rights
- Exclusivities and non-competition clauses
- Agreement on roles and responsibilities of each firm
- How relationships will be governed generally (partner managers for example)
- Product road-map if there is one
- Some key legal provisions, timeline for final contract negotiations, teams that will be involved in the final negotiations
- Warranty provisions, liability provisions, and other legal aspects that may be added by the legal team

At the end of the process, the *Alliance Term Sheet* needs to make sense from all angles. From both partners' sides, it must have coherence, make objective sense and have balance. Discontinuities that do not make sense and are unnatural can turn into problems later in **T5**, where *Sustaining & Deepening* of the alliance is the focus.

Consequently, there are many different alliances structures that can be created. These include everything from contractual alliances to equity alliances with a variety of investment financial options, balanced through a variety of collaboration and governance structures. Today, contractual alliances are the most popular type. In the 1970s, 90% of alliances were equity alliances, while today, the high-tech sector makes 90% of alliances through contractual agreements. Overall, 75% of other industry alliances are contractual, while the remainder is equity based. Still, equity alliances are on the rise as larger companies partner with smaller promising tech firms (De Man, op cit., p. 71). Oftentimes, firms use a contractual alliance first and then build the equity arrangements necessary to bring the relationship into a JV equity relationship. As a result, teams will establish a wide array of alliance agreements, balancing out differing investment accords with a variety of decision rights. Overall, for the alliance group, this is a process of walking between the various tensions to build a coherent structure that can really endure and ensure the alliance reaches its goals and objectives.

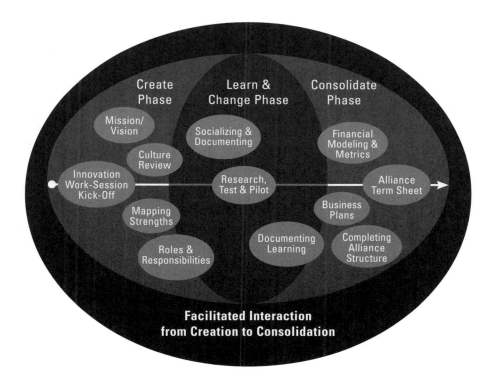

Figure 31 – Map of Territory Three – Consolidate Phase

Enabling the Emergence of Interdependent Collaborative Groups

The Consolidate Phase involves the group working to ground its collaboration by completing the *Alliance Term Sheet* and becoming prepared to enter the contract negotiations and launch of the alliance in **T4** (Figure 31). This final phase involves the groups collaborating on the key business elements needed to consolidate the alliance structure. On the part of the *Partnership Coach*, it involves continued active facilitation and coaching to help the group become operative in the alliance development process.

Supporting the team to arrive at this particular state involves consciously working with the *Operative Partnership Group Methodology* and particularly through the more intense dialectic tensions that the group will encounter. Throughout the process the group has been working through these tensions mapped down the *Inverted Cone*. However, because of the difficulties encountered really in grounding the alliance with governance, decision rights and financials in black and white terms, the level of group effort is heightened. At this stage, it is important for the *Partnership Coach* to take note of two key challenges. The first is assisting the group to not slide backwards. *Action Reflection & Inquiry* continues to stimulate learning while, at the same time, supporting the active documenting of the alliance structure into the *Alliance Term Sheet* – discerning together what is relevant or not. The second more tactical task is to continuously support and help work through the dialectic tensions that the group faces toward the end of **T3**. These tensions are elements of the partnership that must be constantly worked through as a collective group. For the *Partnership Coach*, supporting the group to progress through these specific tensions helps to build the right *Collaboration & Governance Structure* and the most appropriate *Alliance Term Sheet*.

These dialectic tensions are the oppositional forces that the group must face together as it puts concepts in writing. They represent the core challenge the group faces and which the coach helps to tackle.

The Now vs. the Future

Often groups can become fascinated by all the possibilities of the alliance and at certain moments even use the many potential opportunities as a way to not fully commit to grounding the structure. In these instances, it is important to help the group map the future of the alliance and to frame what is relevant in the first years of the alliance and what can be placed into a planning tool or roadmap. This tension, while very acute in the Consolidation Phase because of the need to really determine what is relevant for the *Alliance Term Sheet*, is also noticeable in **T2**.

Full Control vs. Laissez-faire

When building the *Collaboration & Governance Structure*, the group has to work through the dialectic of developing a completely rigid framework that seeks to control everything, or deciding to let the group handle the alliance, without too many rules and regulations. Conversely, in certain respects the group needs to find ways to work through a *Collaboration & Governance Structure* that guides it to build a successful alliance while not closing off the capacity to make the right decisions at the right time. In many respects, the group needs to come to terms with the uncertainties the future may bring while constantly touching base on the shared commitments and opportunities for continued collaboration.

Transparency vs. Opacity

Another clear contradiction that the group will have to traverse occurs during financial modeling. In this respect, the group will have to choose between the open, closed and shared approaches to modeling the financials and decide where to be transparent and where not to be.

Specific vs. Broad

Another tension in the *Consolidation Phase* is building an alliance structure that is specific enough to be appropriate and broad enough to be operative. In preparing the *Alliance Term Sheet* the group needs to determine what is truly critical before entering **T4**, without drafting the entire contractual agreement. The term sheet is a pathway into negotiation, but not a substitute for it. In this respect, the *Alliance Term Sheet* must have the minimum for each team to feel comfortable, with enough clarity to take them into the next territory.

Legally Binding vs. Not Legally Binding but Important

When grounding the structure of the alliance, oftentimes the group will have to work through the tensions of what should be legally binding in the *Alliance Term Sheet* and what should be left for later in the *Alliance Contract*. For example, the *Collaboration & Governance Structure* can be created as legally binding in the *Alliance Term Sheet* or contract, or can simply be referred to as an appendix to the contract. The right mix of power/control with the right amount of relatedness and oversight is the tension represented here.

As the group finds ways to reconcile the various tensions by voicing in more authentic ways its views, ideas and feelings, it begins to build the dynamics of *Trust & Tele* that carry it forward into the **T4**.

Chapter 11
Territory Four:
Negotiate & Launch

One could argue that the alliance group has been negotiating all through the process, yet, from the perspective of the *Partnership and Alliance Framework* this is not the case. Rather, the group has been aligning desires, intentions and commitments based on shared understanding of a potential vision developed in **T2**, creating the vision and consolidating together how it will work in **T3**. Only now does it work through contract negotiations. This relates to the activities of solidifying the alliance contract terms, while simultaneously preparing and working on the pre-launching activities of the alliance. While negotiating the contract, the implementation teams can begin to work together to establish project plans, timelines, and other execution components, while the alliance group negotiates the final terms of the contract.

The group has progressed effectively and there is a small chance of failure to launch. At this moment, it is more a matter of tightening up the loose ends of the contracting. Most of the heavy lifting for the team should have happened in the *Consolidation Phase* of **T3** (pp. 211-227). The dual tracks pre-suppose that one group can focus on hammering out the final contract terms, while working groups can start building the marketing campaign, or writing some preliminary code, or working on other activities to bring the alliance more rapidly to market once the contract is executed. Once the two tracks converge, the alliance is launched.

This dual-track process goes contrary to typical sales relationships, where companies almost never build anything before they finalize negotiations. Here, the companies and the alliance group have built an operative relationship and an alliance structure where a majority of the business has been developed in working sessions. Potential ideas have been worked through; agreements on roles and responsibilities are in place, the financials have been run, etc., with all the important pieces documented in the signed *Alliance Term Sheet*.

Phase one of this chapter explores negotiation theory and its applications to partnership negotiations. At the same time, it offers insights into a new model of negotiations supported by the *Partnership Coach*. Again, throughout this territory, the *Operative Partnership Group Methodology* is employed. Some key elements of the pre-launching phase and some final important activities of the alliance's launch will also be presented (Figure 32). A two-track simultaneous process is used. One track is to finalize negotiations and the other to begin working on launching activities.

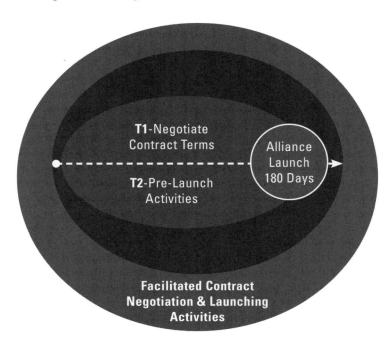

Figure 32 – Map of Territory Four-Dual Track Process

Phase 1
Track One:
Negotiating the Alliances Contract

While there are many books written on negotiations (Patterson, 2011; Fisher, 2011; Ury, 1993; Minton, 2009), few take into account the dynamics of partnerships and alliances, as well as the strategies, standards of practice and approaches needed for their success. General negotiations theory tends to come from a very different and distinct point of view. Perhaps it is better to say that partnering negotiations come with a completely different set of assumptions and foundations and as such require different and distinct ways of engaging and negotiating. General negotiations theory has been split between two different models that frame a set of approaches and tactics which negotiators employ. The theory has also divided the behaviors of negotiators in respect to their activities within each model. While many theorists like to split out negotiations behavior from the models themselves, for our purposes, the models explained here include both behaviors of negotiators and the negotiation approach, structure, tactics and activities used. Because behaviors are a result of individual and group beliefs, preferences, value systems and ways of operating (pp. 72-92), combining both provides insights into how the different models apply to partnership negotiations or otherwise.

The competitive/adversarial model often referred to as a *distributive strategy* can be recognized when negotiators try to maximize what they consider to be scarce resources regardless of the other party. In this sense, they make high opening demands on the counterparty, and use threats and other hard tactics to powerfully bring the counterparty to submission. The problem-solving model is considered an *integrative approach*. Here, the negotiator tries to maximize the possible returns using a common interests approach within a larger context (Murray, 1986, p. 182). The negotiator tries to understand the interests of the other and employs a set of tactics described in Roger Fisher and William Ury's book, *Getting to Yes, Negotiating Agreement Without Giving In* (1981).

While the two models do have some differences, further described in the tables here (Table 14 & 15), they do maintain some important similarities for our purposes. The first is the role of the negotiator. In both instances, the negotiator is the one individual who approaches the negotiation using varying styles. Even though the styles and models are different, the concept of the individual negotiator is common to both. In none of the existing literature is there the conception of a group that is negotiating. Most, if not all of the literature available is centered on two individuals negotiating on behalf of their companies; almost never a group, although most of the time it is groups that are negotiating. A second similarity is that both conceptions of negotiation theory presuppose that talks will take place and then implementation or commitment will occur. In these two instances the idea is that negotiations take place prior to any 'real' work, such as shared research or piloting efforts etc. that take place. While the problem-solving model is more process-driven and the competitive/adversarial model is less so, both are limited conceptually in time and space. Both focus on negotiation before doing and learning. Lastly, in both models the negotiations are normally conducted by individuals who will not be involved in implementing the actual business once the deal is consummated.

Apart from these similarities between the models, there exist some striking differences based on a variety of elements. These differences make the competitive/adversarial model incompatible with partnering and the problem-solving model more compatible to partnering but still inadequate.

	Model 1: Competitive/ Adversarial Model	Model 2: Problem-Solving Model
Basic Belief (forms the basic conception of negotiations)	The world is made up of scarce resources that we each want. The pie is limited and distribution of these resources compels us to compete.	There are problems to resolve. The world is full of opportunities and the pie can be expanded based on the complementarity of the interests we each have. Still a problem exists and we negotiate together to resolve and find common ground.
Time Orientation	There is pressure to close a deal fast. Today's decisions will not affect tomorrow's.	There is some time available for the parties to find common ground. Today's decisions will affect tomorrow's.
Goal	To close the best deal possible, regardless of the consequences to the other party and to do so before commitment.	To close the best deal possible without destroying the relationship and to resolve the problem before commitment is reached.
Power Structure of Negotiation	One party is more powerful than the other in terms of resources/market share etc. One needs the other more.	One party is less powerful or both are equally powerful.
Number of Issues to Negotiate	One or very few.	Several issues.
Relationship Structure	Ongoing business relationship is not needed for the deal to be consummated.	Ongoing business relationship to resolve ongoing problems.

Table 14 – Standard Negotiations Models

The competitive adversarial model operates from the underlying belief that there are scarce resources, while the problem solving model sees a greater degree of cooperation based on varied interests which lie beyond the actual resources being sought after (Table 14). The goals are varied based on the power structure and kind of relationship.

These differences show up as different negotiator behaviors and attitudes are employed in each model (Table 15).

	Negotiator Behaviors & Attitudes of the Competitive/Adversarial Model	Negotiator Behaviors & Attitudes of the Problem Solving Model
Roles Involved	Negotiators doing the negotiation and passing on to the implementation teams.	Negotiators doing the negotiation and passing on to the implementation teams.
Approach	Distributive *Structural & Strategic, Concession* Approach – situational driven.	Integrative *Cooperative* Approach – process and method driven.
Emotional Tone	Fight, Conquer, Out-Smart, Out-Maneuver, Win-Over / Win-Lose – Hard Style.	Find common ground, manipulate other into your point of view, cooperate through accommodation, Win-Win – Soft Style.
Process	We negotiate based on limited knowledge based on positions.	Negotiations based on interests that are disclosed to each other in order to find common ground together.

Tactics & Tools	• Good guy/ bad guy routines	• BATNA – Identify your Best Alternative to a Negotiated Agreement
	• Coercion	
	• Opening Strong	• Separate the people from the problem
	• Salami Tactics	
	• ZOPA (Zone of Agreement)	• Identify the interests of the other party and share yours
	• Making fake concessions	
	• Escalating Demands	• Find alternatives through brainstorming and other means
	• Refusal to Negotiate	
	• Threats & Delay Tactics	• Use objective criteria
	• Passing the buck	

Adapted from Murray, *Understanding Competing Theories of Negotiation* and Fisher & Ury, *Getting to Yes Negotiating Agreement Without Giving In.*

Table 15– Standard Negotiations Models Behaviors and Attitudes

Generally, behaviors and attitudes do not always concord with models and methods. There may be negotiators using tactics from the competitive/adversarial model and the problem-solving model. As a discrete strategy, however, the competitive/adversarial model would probably not survive through the alliance development process. Ultimately, the company invited into the opportunity to partner would either not participate in **T2**, or would reluctantly commit to enter **T3** where it would have to change approach or exit. The proposed *5-Territories of Alliance Development* compels the group to take responsibility to engage, relate and progress down the inverted cone with the help of partnership coaching and, as such, become more transparent in expressing its interests and assumptions.

Alternatively, the problem solving approach provides a small possibility for the alliance to be consummated and perhaps reach a good level of cooperation. However, in **T2**, the group using the problem solving model will have to be willing and able to begin exerting efforts and resources to discover the potential of the partnership. In essence, it must commit to taking action and working together before negotiating all the details.

More often than not, groups operating from the problem solving model will enjoy shifting from a problem mindset into a co-creation way of thinking. The **Co-Create Model** proposed and employed in the alliance development process in negotiating partnerships and alliances is a clearly divergent path from the previous two (Table 16). The **Co-Create Model** is an integrative model like the problem solving one, in which groups work together toward a common purpose, based on the sharing of intentions, etc. Yet this contains some important differences that make room for real partnership development for the *Collaborative Enterprise*.

	Model 2: Problem Solving Model	Model 3: Co-Create Model
Basic Belief (forms the basic conception of negotiations)	There are problems we each want to resolve. The world is full of opportunities and the pie can be expanded based on the complementarity of our interests we each have. Still a problem exists and we negotiate together to resolve and find common ground to problems.	Through our interdependence we can create something that we envision and share. Value is co-created and co-discovered through our interactions.
Time Orientation	There is some time available for the parties to find common ground. Today's decisions will affect tomorrow's.	There is time to produce the alliance, as the journey of collaboration is traversed.
Goal	To close the best possible deal without destroying the relationship to resolve the problem before commitment.	To bring to market something that leverages strengths in a complementary or supplementary way.

Power Structure of Negotiation	One party is less powerful or both are equally powerful.	Regardless of who is more powerful, there is both an opportunity and a contribution that results from our joint efforts.
Number of Issues to Negotiate	Several issues.	Many interdependent opportunities and possibilities where *Circles of Influence* and *Circles of Concern* coincide.
Relationship Structure	There will be an ongoing business relationship to resolve ongoing problems.	Creates a relationship with the capacity for being self-correcting and self-generating.

Table 16– Problem Solving and Co-Create Negotiation Models.

What distinguishes the **Co-Create model** from the problem solving model (Table 16) is the foundational belief that through relationships groups can expand the possibilities for their collaboration beyond problems that may be identified by either partner. Certainly, partnerships can be developed based on the problem solving model. If in **T1** Align & Prepare the focus is to fix a problem identified, however, and if in **T3** there is no time to create innovative ways to solve the problem, many partnership opportunities not identified in **T1** or **T2** could be lost. Additionally, more than 50% of alliances are focused on bringing new products and services to market (De Man, op cit., p. 73) making **the Co-Creation Model of Negotiations** foundational to improving alliances success.

In this respect, the negotiator's behaviors, attitudes and tactics used in the Co-Create Model go beyond those of problem solving (Table 17).

	Negotiator Behaviors & Attitudes in the Problem Solving Model:	Group Behaviors & Attitudes in Co-Create Model:
Roles Involved	Negotiators doing the negotiation and passing onto the implementation teams.	Negotiation is conducted by a group or set of people who have been part of activities from the beginning. The partnership's negotiator supports the journey.
Approach	Integrative *Cooperative* approach – process and method driven.	Integrative *Collaborative* Approach – driven by *Operative Partnership Methodology.*
Emotional Tone	Find common ground, manipulate others into your point of view, cooperate through accommodation, win-win – soft style negotiation.	Reciprocity, coherence, and operability; win-win – authentic Negotiation (hard and soft but not manipulative).
Process	Negotiate based on interests disclosed to each other in order to find common ground together. Commit. Time is limited to negotiating.	Committed to the process of discovery and creation. Negotiation happens once we have learned together how to best collaborate. Time includes negotiation but is preceded by co-creating.

Tactics & Tools	• BATNA – Identify your Best Alternative to a Negotiated Agreement. • Separate the people from the problem. • Identify the interests of the other party and share yours. • Find alternatives through brainstorming and other means. • Use objective criteria.	• Facilitative practices and coaching techniques (Operative Partnerships Methodology). • Dialogic practices. • Focusing on the shared opportunity. • Shared principle-based negotiation. • Group action reflection practice. • Establishing the ongoing structures. • Discerning the principles that continue to form the cultural elements of the alliance. • Authentic engagement. • Reframing differences etc. • Identifying perceptions and attributions. • Identifying reactions and inquiring etc.

Table 17– Behaviors and Attitudes of Problem Solving and Co-Create Negotiations Models

The differences between the problem solving model and the co-create model are evolutionary. Both being integrative models, one essentially stems from the other. In the co-create model, the role of the group as implementers and negotiators is expanded and preferred, from individuals to the group/team – with the support of the *Partnership Coach* to deepen the group's operability.

Additionally, the emotional tone behind problem solving vs. co-creation is distinctly different, and, as such, the process employed equally so. Here the standard of practice shifts from one of a tactical strategic method of negotiating to a methodology of partnership development that evolves over the course of the 5-Territories. In the context of the final negotiation, the standard of practice continues its evolutionary trajectory which began initially within the context of commitment. A commitment made in **T2**, solidified through communication, cooperation and learning in **T3**, is now ripening into contractual terms and group partnership.

In **T4**, the group focus is to consolidate previous ideas, clarify commitments and conversations into a legal document and on-going *Collaboration & Governance Structure*. The standard of practice is of continued co-creation and balance. In the competitive/adversarial model, negotiators can become overly focused on using all kinds of methods to close the deal. The integrative methods of the problem solving approach can be helpful, as long as the focus is not only deal-making. At this point in the process, the focus is on consolidating thinking and keeping in the agreement key principles of balance, reciprocity, transparency, and structure. However, this does not mean that there must be an equal distribution of revenues or costs, but a fair and clear structure based on the teams' capacity to negotiate openly, clearly and authentically. Balance is built into the alliance based on clearly developed decision making and power being equally weighted, with exit clauses that take into account the parties' respective rights. Determining the fundamentals resides on the ability of the teams to find ways that the companies can work together, even though there may be structural differences. What remains shared is the complementarity and/or supplementarity of their goals and objectives for co-creation.

The Final Pieces

Because the *Alliance Term Sheet* has only a partial framework of the final contract there will invariably be some additional final elements to complete and/or other contractual areas to add. These are just a few important ones:

Collaboration & Governance Structure may require a more detailed description of the roles and responsibilities in a RACI Matrix (Responsible, Accountable, Consulted and Informed) or others such as RAPID® (Recommend, Agree, Perform, Input and Decide) registered by Bain & Company (a management consulting firm) which is used to clarify decision roles among other things. For larger alliances these more detailed descriptions and operating manuals of the alliance collaboration structure help reduce any misunderstanding once the alliance is on-line.

Termination Provisions requires a good deal of back and forth by the partners to realize the best structure. At times, the termination structure is coordinated with the contract term. However, there will be negotiation on early termination by either party and how this should be handled. Generally speaking this tends to line up with the dispute resolution provisions and processes.

Intellectual Property Rights are oftentimes one of the most difficult elements to negotiate in alliances where joint development takes place. In these instances, most partnering teams decide between different options. One or either party may have the right of first refusal to purchase the intellectual property from the other; parties may retain certain rights of the property depending on how it was introduced into the alliance, or shared property can be either jointly owned or jointly retired. At the end, there are several options but only so many combinations available to the group.

Customer Ownership Rights are one of the most contested issues in services and some product-related alliances. There are several standards for working through customer ownership, such as who has primary access, who had the customer prior to when the alliance was first developed, etc.

Legal Structure is relevant both in contractual alliances and in JV/equity-based deals. In contractual alliances, of course, understanding and discussing the implications of the companies signing the agreement is important.

There is no optimal structure for negotiating the final pieces of the agreement. While the standards of practice for the negotiation are distinct, in real world applications negotiations teams may resort to less effective competitive/adversarial tactics, or work well through the problem solving approaches. By now, the team should have a culture of collaboration and self-reflection and authentic engagement capabilities that allows it to complete these final pieces of the contract negotiation. With the help of the *Partnership Coach* and the implementation of the co-create model, the teams will work what they may perceive to be the more charged and critical elements of the contract.

Enabling the Negotiations of an Interdependent Partnership Group

As the group enters the negotiations, continuing its process down the Inverted Cone, at times learning and at others consolidating its thinking through collaboration and continued communication, it becomes immersed in an *Operative Partnership Group*. Yet, as mentioned previously (pp. 67-68 & pp. 91-92), the phenomenon of *Tele* can still have an effect on the group. Because *Tele* is based in large part on subjective relational patterns that can be directed unconsciously into the group, facilitation helps illuminate these possible patterns so the group can negotiate effectively.

Negative and positive *Tele* affects how negotiations are conducted, perceived and take place. At times, the subjective telic experiences taint the negotiations and move them in directions that, from the group's perspective, seem appropriate and reasonable, but oftentimes are not really productive. Groups may believe that they are negotiating the foundations of the "deal structure" when they are really acting out their intersubjective telic experience. Many times in these situations, the subjective is projected onto what is being perceived as the objective structure of the negotiation. Negative *Tele* can play out as rigid negotiation positions without clear articulation of "why," which can be expressed in ways that do not seem concordant to the issue at hand. Tactics can be perceived as hard-styled, when in fact they are a reenactment of previous unsatisfactory experiences. However, when groups work together through their positive *Tele*, it facilitates their focus on tasks. Helping the group work through the negative *Tele* that emerges supports positive change toward a successful negotiated outcome. In this sense, the smallest give from one side can move the negotiations in a positive direction. Unbeknown to the group, this is a direct result of telic resonance experienced within the team doing the negotiation, demonstrated by the continued progression down partnership operability and forward into **T4** (Graph 4).

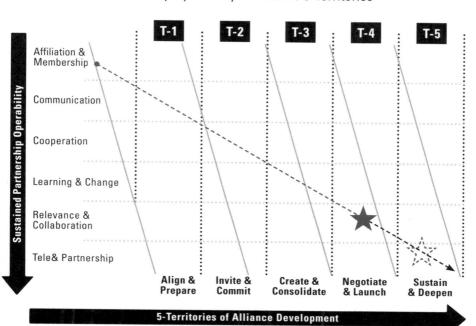

Partnership Operability Across the 5-Territories

Graph 4 – Sustain Progression of Operability toward Telic Experiences

Consequently, when thoughts and interactions operate on a subconscious level they tend to be subject to habits of mind based on more immature patterns. It is better for groups to become explicitly aware of their relationships if they are to negotiate effectively and rise to a level of a more consciously interacting community. As the *Partnership Coach* facilitates group work through the negotiated elements of **T4**, he may use a variety of methods to bring the group into awareness of its telic functioning. Sometimes this involves directly and other times indirectly supporting the group work with the telic elements that are hindering progress.

Identifying & Naming Perceptions & Attributions is a facilitative approach to help the group to see instances where attributions are being placed on comments or ideas. These attributions carry within them the telic experiences of the group. The *Partnership Coach* names and identifies the attributions, either spoken or inferred through prosody or tone, which the team elaborates and responds to.

Identifying Reactions and Inquiring is a correlate of the previous process and involves noticing and calling out the reactions of the group to understand better what is going on. This is not necessarily to identify attributions but helping to raise awareness of what is occurring in the relational field.

Shifting Group Roles. Since Tele has been identified as a role-dependent phenomenon, there are ways in which the coach can help the teams shift roles in the negotiations. This is not to change the formal authority of who has the power to negotiate on behalf of the company, but to work with the team to find alternative approaches to arrive at common ground. Shifting the roles of negotiating and working through hypothetical alternatives helps the group shift when negative *Tele* is operating in the relational field.

Individualized Personal Reflection as Part of Action Reflection Inquiry. While in business negotiations it is difficult to explicitly discuss how negative Tele is affecting the group. Oftentimes, group participants' reflections on how others affect them help to open a collective insight into ways in which unproductive inter-subjective challenges are emerging and hindering the goals.

These are just some examples of the coach's work strategies during the actual negotiations. Others include working with negotiating principles, of which reciprocity, sharing your thinking and transparency are quite helpful, to name a few. Other exercises the coach implements are *Action Reflection & Inquiry* strategies and the *Operative Partnerships Methodology* used throughout the process.

The coach's interventions, tools and methodology promote an alliance that makes sense and has coherence, from a structural perspective and relational point of view. Ultimately, positive Tele will shine through the system of relating between the two companies, which will enable the alliance to grow and prosper once launched.

Phase 1
Track Two:
Pre-Launching Phase

In addition to the final negotiations while the contract is being finalized, other groups work on the pre-launch activities to prepare their companies internally. Success in alliances comes as a result of well executed business plans that incorporate strategies to manage the cultural contradictions and possible challenges that stem from inter-company transition to implementation. As such, effective transitions into implementation occur when the actual launching activities are preceded by a well thought out pre-launch phase. This includes two critical components of activity. The first involves ensuring that all the tools, processes, dashboards, etc., are developed and in place. The second is the strategy and approach of solidifying and expanding the culture of collaboration into the wider parts of each organization, essentially expanding the field of relationship. This is a process of harmonization of the two cultures into structures, policies and practices that support a formalized and unique organization founded on value creation supported by shared cultural alignment and coordination. This includes creating a PR campaign, communications tools and other strategies of getting the word out to ensure that when the launch occurs, it conveys inwardly to each company and into the marketplace the spirit, commitment and promises of the alliance group.

Designing the Alliance Launching Platform

Designing the right platform to launch the alliance involves a group process of discerning the overriding cultural elements that have been developed over the course of the journey and making them into a real set of practices and rituals that give the culture of collaboration form. Helpful tools include the *Alliance Operating Principles*, the way that the alliance is governed, managed and measured, the way meetings are held, and facilitated, agendas prepared, and other such factors.

In many respects, the group working on both sides of each company (or set of companies, as the case may be), is now part of a new "company"—this new group of people who have worked together consistently through the alliance's development have shared metrics of success, ensuring that the promises they have made are followed through effectively over time. They are the entrepreneurs of the alliance, who collaborate together toward the common objectives and visions that were once only an intention in the beginning phases of the alliance process and are now an integral part of the alliance itself. This new "company of people" has boundaries, rules of engagement, and metrics of success—and a new culture of collaboration and partnership. It is up to them to maintain group operability by solidifying engagement protocols.

The platform developed to launch the alliance is a tool and an approach by which the field of relationship is expanded into larger circles of influence within the companies, the marketplace and even with stakeholders and shareholders. Over time the launching platform is solidified and put in place operationally and culturally in Sustain & Deepen phases of **T5**.

Alliance launching platforms are as varied as alliances themselves and contain the following key elements:

Reflecting on the Narrative

The narrative that encapsulates the partnership goes back to the initial invitation presentation held in **T2**, through to the innovation work session in the beginning of **T3** and up until the present. The narrative includes presentations made and specific contextual opportunities and challenges overcome by the group. Also included are the potential opportunities identified, the *Alliance Operating Principles*, and the vision and mission of the alliance. Reflecting on the narrative helps the group establish the PR platform to be used internally within each company and externally in the marketplace. The narrative will contextualize what has happened, and the challenges that have brought the alliance to life.

The narrative that emerges from reflecting on the experiences of the group is used to stimulate and engage the respective organizations. This reflection process helps the group to put into words the potential and the promises the alliance has committed to as it prepares to launch. The promises are unique to this new company of people and reflect the value that the alliance is creating. Executives can talk about their expectations and aspirations for the alliance as a way to establish the cultural glue that helps the companies to launch and, over time, sustain and deepen their collaboration.

Reflecting on the Challenges

Certain challenges the group has faced are a direct reflection of the cultural nuances of the companies, as well as the different methods that they use for decision making and management. Building a platform that helps to address these challenges involves establishing ways in which both firms can learn from and continuously understand and contextualize each other's differences, both organizational and cultural. The platform should contain processes that allow the companies to maintain a certain level of understanding for new employees that work in the alliance, as well as help extended parts of each organization to work together. Building a platform where people are consistently introduced and educated into the alliance's structure and language keeps it alive.

A Final Strategic Metaphor

Throughout the process metaphors have been used to help the group coalesce around a particular topic or understand the varying dynamics and complexities of an issue. Some metaphors have been created by the group in times of disagreement, others have been referred to and used over several meetings and in this sense have remained more alive and more pertinent to the group. At the point in the process, it is about choosing one metaphor that conveys the fundamental essence of both organizations' strategic intent, core values, key principles and heart (Cacciaguidi-Fahy & Cunningham, 2007, pp.137-144). The use of strategic metaphors supports differing cultures and company

values system in coming together through a set of cognitive construc-
tions that act not only as a way to deliver the spirit of the alliance (the
narrative) from the original group's conception, but also as a way to
bring both companies even closer together.

The launching platform will include a variety of tools that, depending on the
size and complexity of the alliance, will be used to support the launch and
continue well into the Sustain & Deepen activities in **T5**.

The launching platform may include:

> **Alliance Charter**: a document that encapsulates the alliance goals,
> mission and vision, how it will operate and who is involved. In certain
> respects, it is a key document used in larger organizations to lend
> credibility and structure to the collaboration.
>
> **PR and Media Campaign (Internal and External)**: this is established
> based on the narrative and metaphorical elements of the collabora-
> tion. It may include alliance logos and other collateral.
>
> **Visuals and Materials** are used as part of the launching campaign
> both internally in the companies and on an ongoing basis. These can
> include video, presentations, etc.
>
> **An ongoing alliance program** may involve cross-cultural training,
> consisting of conferences, lunches, training videos, job sharing and
> other activities.
>
> **Share sites and other technical collaboration tools** may be used to
> assist in the working together across business units, etc.
>
> **Annual planning templates and materials**, manuals and other tools
> can help to sustain, manage and deepen the alliance and partnership.
>
> **The Actual Launch Plan** includes venue, invitees, presentations, etc.
>
> **Action-Feedback and Oversight Loops** are set in place between im-
> plementation teams, stakeholders and others.

Phase 2
Finale:
Launching the Alliance
– the first 180 days

At this point, the contract has been executed and the alliance is being launched both internally within each company and in the marketplace. Some companies may choose to launch internally first, depending on the kind of collaboration that is being executed: operational, market driven, research, etc. Launching the alliance involves ensuring a smooth shift into implementation, setting in motion the alliance platform, and most importantly ensuring a higher degree of implementation, measuring, reflection and learning between management and working groups.

As such, these initial learning cycles are about focusing on the questions: "What have we learned so far and are the plans that we have developed and put in place actually working? If not, what do we need to change and optimize?" In this respect, the stakeholders and teams should be overly vigilant on execution goals and measurement systems, discerning together what may require tweaking. This higher degree of shepherding ensures that the structures developed concord with the realities of each company's differences and any shifts or unexpected happenings in the marketplace. This process is again a kind of dialectic the groups must manage, letting the business evolve naturally and, further still, focusing on what is initially working.

The *Partnership Coach* continues to help the groups maintain continuity in their respective roles and manage the challenges of real-time and real-life implementation. However, the role of the partnerships coach may also be slowly reduced depending on whether the person was an internal support or an external consultant. If the role of the *Partnership Coach* is an internal role, that person may continue supporting the alliance consistently into Sustain & Deepen. If it is an external consulting role, the person may come in inter-mittently to help support implementation challenges here as well as in **T5**, depending on what the groups are working on.

Chapter 12
Territory Five:
Sustain & Deepen

The hallmark of a successful alliance is that it endures over time. It does so by meeting the alliance's initial strategic goals, executing on projects originally mapped in **T3** and generating new opportunities not fully seen nor identified previously.

The alliance is sustained by the continued efforts of the companies to engage in a variety of activities. They work through the implementation of the collaboration governance policies and practices that operationalize the alliance. This ensures that there continues to be executive support, and that performance is measured and reviewed on an ongoing basis. Over time the successful partnership will help each company to expand its capacities and capabilities and to identify new opportunities for collaboration outside the current stage of development. As the alliance produces results, the *Collaborative Enterprise* begins to expand its *Circles of Concern* and *Circles of Influence* to build networks of collaboration, perhaps growing from *Firm-Centric* to *Post-Modern*, or *Post-Modern* to *Emergent-Enterprise*, or from *Emergent-Enterprise* to the next new stage, creating more value for shareholders and stakeholders.

Collaborative Leadership continues to be fostered at the group level through the *Operative Partnership Methodology* supporting the transition from *Sustain* to *Deepen* through productive activities and implementation of strategies guided by facilitative intervention (Figure 33). The result is a self-sustaining and self-generating partnership and alliance operating as a new living entity in between the firms. It is founded on the collaboration of individuals, groups and companies building value together, embedded as part of a larger ecosystem of business actors. It is through their continued strategic needs and relationship practices that they continue to generate value for both companies, and expand into new enriching opportunities for their continued growth.

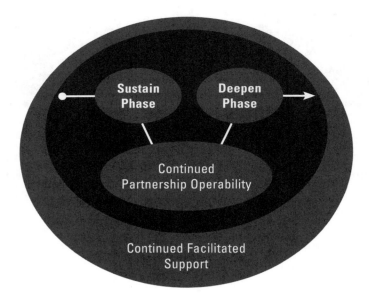

Figure 33 – Territory Five Sustain & Deepen

Phase 1
Sustain Phase

For alliances to be successful after launching they have to enter the **Sustain Phase** where the alliance is made operational and set on course toward meeting its strategic objectives. In this respect, the launching platform is solidified to include the ongoing collaboration structure. The PR campaign continues to keep the alliance top of mind in the market and in each company and the cultural and learning programs maintain continuity. Important to the Sustain Phase is ensuring that there remains a level of stability in terms of the people who manage the alliance and the kind of talent that is recruited when alliance managers or others transition out of the partnership. Consistency of alliance management contributes positively to stability and sustainability. At a minimum, the people who began the journey through the territories should form part of an oversight team and, in the best case, be part of the implementation teams that ensure success.

When alliance talent transitions out, recruiting the right managers into the alliance is invaluable. One way to do this is to have joint human-resource planning to ensure there is bench strength prior to transitions. Additionally, both companies should cooperate in hiring talent to work in the alliance. Training alliances staff across both companies for new and current groups on the capacities and capabilities for alliance making is also an important way of sustaining excellence. Finally, developing a program for getting new talent on board helps to maintain the alliance's cultural continuity.

Additionally, as the alliance becomes more operational, groups will continue to work through dialectic tensions "of striking a balance between two seemingly contradictory themes: collaboration and competition" (Das & Teng, 1997, p. 9). From one perspective, the alliance is meant to maintain a collaborative structure where the companies work together to meet strategic objectives. In this respect the teams and companies have developed a sustaining system that includes a *Collaboration & Governance Structure*, shared business plans, ways to measure and methods for working well together in a consistent fashion. Yet, at times, groups and even companies may "engage in opportunistic behavior to take advantage of the [other] partner" (Das & Teng, op. cit., p. 10). This brings pressure on the alliance groups to work on two aspects of their collaboration. The first relates to the need of the groups to continue to address their relationship challenges by engaging in facilitated conversations that continue to build the capacities for operability and authenticity. When there is so much uncertainly and so much complexity in today's business environment, the continued process of working through group challenges toward common goals and objectives remains important. The work of enabling collaboration as an ongoing process continues to be important for sustaining the alliances success. The second aspect is the consistent championing of the collaborative venture inside each company. This involves ensuring that important internal stakeholders continue to be committed to and engaged in the alliance's success.

It is up to the alliance groups to help their organizations move closer to the *Collaborative Enterprise*. The dialectic tension between collaboration and competition requires that groups continue to create the capacity and capability to productively direct competitive forces while remaining collaborative to support the alliance's development. As such, the competitive forces should help the alliance to focus its efforts on expanding its capabilities, mining opportunities and learning through collaboration to execute accordingly. Competitive focus should be pointed outward toward the marketplace where the alliance must remain competitive. To do so, the alliance must consistently refine and clarify shared goals and the joint strategic reasons for its existence. In this respect, the spirit of collaboration is used as an inward pointing force that engages groups to operationalize and meet the challenges of a competitive marketplace. Conversely, if competitiveness is directed inward toward the partnership and the groups, the alliance can turn in on itself and implode. To sustain itself over time, the alliance works with these contradictions.

Concurrent with maintaining balance between collaboration and competition, sustaining the alliance also requires that coherence between the *Circles of Influence* and the *Circles of Concern* of each partnering firm be maintained. As such, the alliance becomes a functioning whole when the Circles of Influence (customer services, operations, sales and marketing within each company) and Circles of Concern (the strategies and goals of each) come together. In this respect, the alliance is sustained objectively by its structure, what it can truly influence and subjectively with what it truly believes to be important and relevant. This tension is one that both companies consistently work through together to sustain their activities.

Continued Collaborative Leadership Engagement

Collaborative Leadership continues to be a group activity that emerges only when a group comes together to work through shared interests and intentions. This is as pertinent now in **T5** as it was when the groups entered into the initial conversations in **T2**. In this respect, **T5** is not an end but simply a continuation of a collaborative business relationship that will sustain itself as the groups continue working together through their relatedness. A great majority of alliances fail due to issues of trust, communication and culture. To avoid this, groups need to productively sustain the alliance by the continued use of the *Operative Partnership Methodology* and the concurrent applications of exercises, tools and strategies. In this way, from their continued relatedness, groups operationalize around challenges they face between the dialectic tensions they will continue to encounter in the future.

Consequently, this involves the work of the alliance group to successfully sustaining a culture of its own. This is accomplished by following the continued rituals of interaction, inquiry, reflection and facilitation that support groups to work through the various moments of interaction (task, pre-task and project). Maintaining the field of relationship between groups and companies by constantly applying various types of meeting, and working to constantly solidify interactions, will over time build the next level of collaboration.

Flexibility, Decision-Making & Operating Structure

Structurally speaking, ensuring that the alliance maintains a level of flexibility and decision-making authority outside of the parent companies leads the groups to work together in more productive ways. They must find innovative methods to grow their business and meet the strategic goals of the alliance. This flexibility pertains to the alliance's ability to shift and change its operating structure to meet market needs. This exists not at the contract level, but in the ability to shift tasks, focus and productivity areas, leading to improved productivity and excellence. From an operating structure perspective, the alliance directs resources to the most productive activities while maintaining strategic direction.

Transitioning

For alliances that meet their strategic goals and find that the market has shifted too far for their collaboration to continue, the transition into a respectful termination is not a failure, but rather a natural progression of a successful collaboration. For the alliance that sees continued possibilities, the aim is to deepen relatedness and build the capabilities that enable growth into new business opportunities. Alliances succeed through relatedness that enables groups to find and develop opportunities to deepen their strategic collaboration. Also, through their relatedness they can mine the opportunities that the marketplace affords them, which they identify and even create together. Regardless of whether the alliance results in a respectful completion or transitions into a deepening of potential, both are a result of *Collaborative Leadership* and the capacities for authentic relationship.

Phase 2
Deepen Phase

After completing a full circle in the *sustain phase*, the next transition of alliance engagement is deepening and expanding its capabilities. Deepening of the relationship between the companies who began the journey and now includes the subsequent deepening of the strategic partnership between the two companies. Not all alliances enter the deepen phase of collaboration. Some transition into a different type of alliance such as a JV/equity relationship or remain as strategic collaborations or alliances/partnerships with newly discovered opportunities for growth.

For the companies that do enter this phase, an opportunity is ignited to take the alliance to a new level of creativity as it spirals outward once again to create new opportunities. In this respect, the alliance enters new territories of collaboration. It can begin to identify and execute on new-found opportunities or even start to engage with new potential alliance partners to build a network of collaboration. In either case, this alliance of individuals, groups and companies has built a level of relationship that provides a foundation for even more possibility, grounded in strategic market opportunities that lie ahead. Here, commitment to the alliance is deeper, palpable both in cultural continuity and structural performance.

This next level of deepening the alliances is contextualized and grounded by a rebirth of the alliance through another journey across the territories. This begins in the Align & Prepare Territory, where new strategic realities are faced by the alliance and perhaps even potential new alliance partners are identified. Here the alliance is operating as a new entity of collaboration looking for opportunities to grow. The alliance will then proceed across to **T2** reaffirming commitment to expanding, or working with new alliance partners. They will then continue forward working in **T3** through Create & Consolidate and again negotiating and launching, formalizing and contextualizing the new expanded opportunities. In other cases, the alliance may proceed directly into **T3**, reigniting its potential by engaging in continued innovation. It may test new ideas and opportunities that are then consolidated and negotiated once again in **T4**. This continued journey for the alliance is in essence a continued expansion and growth across new *Circles of Influence* and *Circles of Concern* of each firm, deepening commitment toward growth through continued collaboration. New challenges ahead may ensue and along with them new opportunities that the alliance is now more prepared to confront.

Each company that enters the alliance may want to continue expanding its alliance capabilities into other areas across its value chain. Each independently may want to deepen its capability to develop more partnerships in other areas and continue again through the Align & Prepare Territory, establishing an alliance business unit and taking a portfolio approach to alliance making. It may grow from a *Firm-Centric Company* into an *Emergent Enterprise*. In this respect, the company slowly becomes a *Collaborative Enterprise* that builds new opportunities across a whole network of alliance partners and engages in continued reflective practices to work through the challenges of business collaboration.

Section Four
Final Reflection, Coherence

Coherence

co·her·ence

kōˈhi(ə)rəns

noun: **coherence**; plural noun: **coherences**

The quality or state of cohering: as

    1. Systematic or logical connection or consistency

    2. The quality of forming a unified whole.

    3. Integration of diverse elements, relationships, or values

The state of *Coherence* reached by the partnership is reflective of the interlocking capabilities of each company to collaborate based on their interdependence and relatedness. As alliances and partnerships are developed, companies begin to grow their organizations from *Firm-Centric*, to the *Post-Modern Corporation* to the *Emergent Enterprise*. Each level reflects a state of internal corporate coherence of partnership capability between departments and teams. A hologram, when broken into pieces, has the same image contained within each. This mirrors the capacity to build collaborative business partnerships. The ability is embedded across all areas of a company's functioning. Companies that establish this capability internally can build the capability externally, enabling *collaborative leadership* and *collaborative advantage* to be continuously developed. As companies work to create the third entity that resides between the two partnering firms, they support each other's growth into new levels of operating. When a *Post-Modern Corporation* works with a *Firm-Centric Company* they both learn and develop their capacities for inter-organizational collaboration. These experiences extend through the alliances teams of each firm and into the groups that come together to form the partnership, operationalize and maintain it. Over time, if both firms continue to develop the capacity to collaborate they help each of their organizations to grow, seize on new opportunities and build new businesses across their interdependent value and supply chains, extending their *Circles of Concern* and *Circles of Influence*.

Coherence becomes both an optimal stage of functioning and also an unending process interwoven by the individuals, groups and companies that form through alliances and partnerships. As such, the process of collaborating becomes an emergent spiraling and living process of human relationship that establishes the structures that underlie it. Working through the 5-Territories, groups and their companies experience a rhythm of ebbs and flows, extending outward down the territories as they learn and return to reformulate and accommodate. This ebb and flow is part of a circularity embedded in *Coherence* which occurs both along the territories and from meeting to meeting as groups come together to work. It is woven together through the *check-in* and *check-out* practices of the group, the roles that members take on over time and the patterning out of conversations across the *pre-task*, *task* and *project phases*. Over the course of the process, there are conversational threads of questions and opportunities which arise in one meeting and are later resolved and developed in future interactions. Weaving these conversations, important concepts are reformulated, shaped and polished, redirected and solidified in the moments of group cohesion and productivity.

Spiraled Circularity is the prominent pattern generated and experienced by individuals, groups and organizations as they work together to create alliances and partnerships. The circle comes back around every time a topic is revisited or relational space experienced. In such cases, there is an opportunity for a deepening of relationship where upward spiraled movement is possible. Over the course of the process, the group operationalizes around a set of agreed-upon structures, both subjective and objective, that establish a self-correcting and self-sustaining *Strategic Alliance and Partnership*.

When business relationships reach a state of *Coherence*, either as a *Strategic Alliance and Partnership* or as an *Operative Group* there exists balance in structure, in group functioning and relatedness. The operating structures make sense and have a level of integration, which leverages the interdependence of the companies, people and teams involved. There exists a level of consistency of action, continuity, integrity, and solidarity of relating that conforms and conjoins to become a productive united whole. The contracts that form the alliance make sense, are balanced and integrated based on the important human relationships that form into a meaningful structure. The roles and responsibilities are congruent with each company's core strengths and capabilities. When a networked alliance structure including many actors is created, policies, processes, value-generation and sharing are agreed, understandable, transparent and equitable.

As a sustained whole, the alliance is launched to meet its goals and intentions. After some time, it expands outward again to include new opportunities and projects beyond what was originally conceived. The companies again enter ebb and flow states by learning what is working and reformulating alliances into their organizational visions, growing and extending collaborative capabilities further outward.

The sine qua non qualities needed are the desire of groups and organizations to take on this journey, as well as the *courage* to engage in a way that preserves individual needs and corporate interests, while collaborating and making space for the potential of *Strategic Alliances and Partnerships*. The promise of collaboration resides in our collective capacities to challenge ourselves to reach greater states of *Coherence* as interdependent actors in a global system of relatedness.

GLOSSARY

Alliances-CROS is a reflective process of adaptation to the real word and the real world goals tested by the alliance group and supported through facilitation. This involves testing within each organization the kind of alliance that would work as well as testing product and services being contemplated together and aligning concepts for the eventual partnership relationship and alliances structure.

Alliance Development Process is the process made up of five territories that groups and companies must undergo to develop a strategic alliance.

Alliance Operating Principles are the set of agreements made by the alliance teams that express the fundamental precepts of what and how groups relate together (e.g. transparency, fairness, directness) after they have launched the alliance.

Check-In is the process used to begin every meeting in which the group expresses goals and desires for the session. It is a practice used to frame the field of relationship being built throughout the partner process.

Check-Out is the process used to end every meeting in which the group expresses what was accomplished and how it feels about its work. The practice is used to frame the field of relationship being built throughout the partner process.

Circles of Concern refers to the intentions and interests of organizations that guide strategic decisions.

Circles of Influence refers to operating elements where companies invest their resources.

Circles of Influence and Circles of Concern comprise the place where companies focus intentions their resources.

Collaborative Advantage is a competitive differentiator that allows companies and organizations to outperform the competition through the collaborative leadership capabilities they develop internally and the Strategic Alliances and Partnerships they enter into.

Collaborative Enterprise is an organization that has a particular capacity to garner the collective capacities of teams to partner and create together both internally and externally.

Collaborative Leadership is leadership that happens only at the group level. It is the capacity and capability of groups to collaborate as whole entities and concrete units of collective intention, emotion and action, as distinguished from individual-centered leadership.

Emergent Enterprise is a company or group of companies that operate through open ecosystems of value creation where they compete on platforms of inputs and outputs (e.g. Google, Facebook and other technology firms).

Field of Relationship is the atmosphere, temporal space and place where groups meet to develop alliances and partnerships.

Group-CROS refers to the shared conceptual, referential, operative schema produced by the group, enabled by coaching and facilitation, which the group uses to become operative.

Leadership Summation Fallacy is simply a misconception that suggests that individual leadership is added together in some fashion to create group leadership. This conception incorrectly assumes that for Collaborative Leadership to emerge it only requires that individuals work on themselves and not as a group. Nothing could be further from the truth; Collaborative Leadership is a group activity that emerges singularly at the group level when individuals are working together.

Firm-Centric Company is a company that contains most of its value-creating activities inside its walls and builds alliances and partnerships in the most conservative areas of its business.

Operative Partnership Methodology is the combined set of methods, practices, strategies and tools that are used by the *Partnership Coach* to support groups to become operative in their tasks.

Patterns of Relationship are the third-person inter-subjective, emotional and communication patterns of the group that are discernable by the *Partnership Coach*. These can include the social roles that people take, the tone of their communication, jokes and all repeated interactions that occur in the Field of Relationship.

Partnership and Alliance Framework is the framework developed in this book that incorporates the *Operative Partnership Methodology* and the *5-Territories of Alliance Development*.

Partnership Coaching and Facilitation involves the conscious application of methodologies, practices, strategies and tools used to enable the emergence of Collaborative Leadership in groups.

Partnership Process is the subjective process down the inverted cone that groups undertake to become a collective operative group.

Post-Modern Corporation is a company that has extended its partnerships and alliances into more strategic business areas than the firm-centric company, leveraging the power of others to gain collaborative advantage.

Partnership Field of Relationship is the field of relationship established by the *Partnership Coach* which supports the group in operationalizing and allows for new groups to enter and participate in alliance making. It is a place where connection, authentic emotions and diverse points of view are allowed to happen.

Patterns of Relationship are the interactions discernable by the coach of how the group is relating within itself. These patterns can include emotional patterns, roles that individuals take repeatedly, the tonality of the group and other aspects that show up during partnership development.

Pre-task Phase, Task Phase and Project Phase refer to the possible phases discerned by Enrique Pichon-Rivière that groups may progress through when they meet to work together on a task.

Principles of Engagement are rules groups agree to follow to help them accomplish their tasks. These principles can change from meeting to meeting and are not imposed on the group, but are rather agreed to jointly by the *Partnership Coach* and the group.

Operating/Engagement Principles consist of a facilitative intervention where the coach helps the teams establish certain principles for a particular meeting or work activity. They can be distinguished from Alliance Operating Principles which are guidelines meant to be sustained once the alliance is launched.

Operative Group is the term that refers to a technique and methodology employed on the entire phenomenon of life in groups regardless of the domain of activity e.g. business, government or social services. The Operative Group technique and methodology comes from the work of Enrique Pichon-Rivière.

Operative Partnership Group is a group that progresses down the inverted cone and arrives at a state of true partnership. It can then function at optimal levels on the tasks set. The group is made up of individuals from other teams, which work for other companies and/or groups of companies. Groups distinguished from teams are made up of individuals or teams from different companies who form a partnership.

Operative Partnership Methodology is the methodology employed by the *Partnerships Coach* to help teams of all types and classes work productively together as a group.

Small Group is a set of 3 to 20 individuals from different teams or different companies who come together to form a partnership and through their relating and progressing of the explicit and implicit challenges work together on joint tasks.

Team is comprised of members of the same company or members of the same department who work consistently together. Teams are distinguished from groups and are made up of individuals who work for the same company.

Tele is the emotional disposition that participants have toward each other and in relationship to the work they are engaged in.

^{V}**MEMEs** are the gene equivalents of value systems expressed through individuals and groups.

BIBLIOGRAPHY
& ADDITIONAL
REFERENCES

Adamson, G. (n.d.). *El ECRO de Enrique Pichon Rivère.* Retrieved August 18, 2013, from Escuela de Psicología Social del Sur Web site: http://www.psicosocialdelsur.com.ar/alumnos_textos_contenido.asp?idtexto=4

Adamson, G. (n.d.). *Reflexiones acerca del grupo operativo.* Retrieved August, 18, 2013, from Escuela de Psicología Social del Sur Web site: http://www.psicosocialdelsur.com.ar/contenido.asp?idtexto=16

Adler, P., Heckscher, C., & Prusak, L. (2011). Building a collaborative enterprise. *Harvard Business Review, July–August,* 95–101.

Alfredson, T., & Cungu, A. (2008). Negotiation theory and practice: A review of the literature. *EASYPol Module 179.* Retrieved October 22, 2013, from http://www.fao.org/docs/up/easypol/550/4-5_negotiation_background_paper_179en.pdf

Argyris, C. (1995). Action science and organizational learning. *Journal of Managerial Psychology 10*(6), 20–26.

Argyris, C. (1991).Teaching smart people how to learn. *Harvard Business Review, May–June,* 99–109.

Argyris, C., & Schön, D. A. (1989). Participatory action research and action science compared. *American Behavioral Scientist, 32*(5), 612–623.

Austin, James. (2003). Strategic alliances managing the collaboration portfolio. *Stanford Innovation Review 1*(2), 48–55.

Autopoiesis. (n.d.). In *Wikipedia*. Retrieved September 27, 2013, from http://en.wikipedia.org/wiki/Autopoiesis

Balanced scorecard. (n.d.). In *Wikipedia*. Retrieved July 14, 2014, from http://en.wikipedia.org/wiki/Balanced_scorecard

Baranger, M., & Baranger, W. (2009). *The work of confluence: Listening and interpreting in the psychoanalytic field*. London: Karnac.

Barret, F. J., & Cooperrider, D. L. (1990). Generative metaphor intervention: A new approach for working with systems divided by conflict and caught in defensive perception. *The Journal of Applied Behavioral Science, 26*(2), 219–239.

Barsi, E. (n.d.). *Nociones primarias de psicología social*. Retrieved January 2, 2014, from Escuela Virtual de Psicología Social Web site: https://psicologiasocialparaguay.files.wordpress.com/2012/06/nociones_primarias_de_psicologia_social.pdf

Beck, D. E., & Cowan, C. C. (1996). *Spiral dynamics: Mastering values, leadership, and change*. Malden: Blackwell Publishing.

Berger, P. L., & Luckmann, T. (2001). *La construcción social de la realidad*. Buenos Aires: Amorrortu.

Bernal Z., H. A. (n.d.). *Sobre la teoría del vínculo en Enrique Pichón Rivière: Una sistematización del texto Teoría del vínculo de Pichón*. Retrieved September 20, 2014, from Fundación Universitaria Luis Amigó Web Site: http://www.funlam.edu.co/uploads/facultadpsicologia/578481.pdf

Bion, W.R. (1961). *Experiences in groups and other papers*. New York: Routledge.

Blatner, A. (2009). TELE: The dynamics of rapport. Retrieved July 12, 2014, from http://www.blatner.com/adam/pdntbk/tele.htm

Bleeke, J., & Ernst, D. (2013). The way to win in cross-border alliances. *Harvard Business Review, 11*(1), 2–10.

Bleger, J. (2011). *Psicología de la conducta* (2nd ed.). Buenos Aires: Paidós.

Bojer, M., Knuth, M., Magner, C., McKay, E., & Roehl, H. (2006). *Mapping dialogue*. Johannesburg: Pioneers of Change Associates.

Borda, Fals, Orlando. (2013). Action research in the convergence of disciplines. *International Journal of Action Research, 9*(2), 155–167.

Boulding, K. E. (1965). *The meaning of the twentieth century*. New York: Harper Colophon Books.

Braun, W. (2002). *The system archetypes.* Retrieved May 7, 2013, from University at Albany Web site: /faculty/gpr/PAD724/724WebArticles/sys_archetypes.pdf

Brown, J., Isaacs, D., & The World Café Community. (2005). *The World Café: Shaping our futures through conversations that matter.* San Francisco: Berrett-Koehler.

Bruce Tuckman. (n.d.). In *Wikipedia.* Retrieved January 2, 2014, from http://en.wikipedia.org/wiki/Bruce_Tuckman

Cacciaguidi-Fahy, S., & Cunnincham, J. (2007) The use of strategic metaphors in intercultural business communication. *Managing Global Transitions, 5*(2), 133–155.

Cambio. (n.d.). In *Diccionario de psicología social.* Retrieved April 8, 2013, from http://www.academia.edu/6406643/DICCIONARIO_DE_PSICOLOG%C3%8DA_SOCIAL_PICHON_RIVIERE.

Cartwright, D. (1979). Contemporary social psychology in historical perspective. *Social Psychology Quarterly, 42*(1), 82–92.

Clare W. Graves. (n.d.). In *Wikipedia.* Retrieved March 25, 2014, from http://en.wikipedia.org/wiki/Clare_W._Graves.

Collins, J. C., & Porras, J. I. (1996). Building your company's vision [Electronic version]. *Harvard Business Review: On Point, 9*(1), 64–78.

Colvin, G. (2006, June 12). Why dreams teams fail [Electronic version]. *FORTUNE Magazine,* 1–5.

Connors, J. V., & Caple, R. B.(2005). A review of group systems theory. *Journal for Specialists in Group Work, 30*(2), 93–110.

Corrigan, C. (2014, March 14). Open Space Technology. Retrived from http://www.chriscorrigan.com/openspace/whatisos.html.

Cufuade, J. (2005). The art of facilitative leadership: Maximizing others' contribution. *The Systems Thinker, 15*(10), 2–5.

Das, T.K., & Teng, B. (1997). Sustaining strategic alliances: Options and guidelines. *Journal of General Management, 22*(4), 49–64.

Dawlabani, S. E. (Speaker). (2014). Review of MEMEnomics: The next generation economic system (Audio Interview). *The Daily Evolver.* Accessed March 25, 2014, from http://www.dailyevolver.com/2014/01/review-of-memenomics-the-next-generation-economic-system/.

Dawlabani, S.E. (2013). *Memenomics: The next generation economic system.* New York: Select Books.

Dawlabani, S.E. (2013, June 9). The psychological DNA of capitalism. *The Huffington Post.* Retrieved from March 25, 2014, from http://www.huffingtonpost.com/said-elias-dawlabani/the-psychosocial-dna-of-capitalism_b_3882188.html

Debold, E. (2005). The business of saving the world. *What is enlightenment?*, *28*(3), 60–98.

Del Cueto, A. M. (2012). *Grupos, instituciones y comunidades: coordinación e intervención* (3rd ed.). Buenos Aires: Lugar Editorial.

Deloitte. (2012). *Corporate development 2012 leveraging the power of relationships in M&A*. USA: Author.

De Man, A. (2013). *Alliances: An executive guide to designing successful strategic partnerships*. Cornwall: Wiley.

De Man, A., Duysters, G., Krijnen, A., & Luvison, D. (2012). *The fourth state of alliance management study*. Presented at the ASAP Global Alliance, Las Vegas, NV.

De Man, A., Duysters, G., Krijnen, A., & Luvison, D. (2009). *The third state of alliance management study*. ASAP. Retrieved May 19, 2009, from http://www.duysters.com/Downloads%20managerial/ASAP%20survey.pdf.

Dialectical materialism. (n.d.). In *Wikipedia*. Retrieved February 9, 2014, from http://en.wikipedia.org/wiki/Dialectical_materialism

Dictionary.com. (2014). Retrieved from http://dictionary.reference.com/

Duysters, G., de Man, A., Luvison, D., & Krijnen, A. (2013). The state of alliance management: Past, present, future. ASAP.

Dyer, J. H., Kale, P., & Singh, H. (2001). How to make strategic alliances work. *MIT Sloan Management Review, 42*(4), 37–43.

Edmondson, A. C. (2012, April 26). Teamwork on the fly. *Harvard Business Review*. Retrieved April 15, 2014, from https://hbr.org/2012/04/teamwork-on-the-fly.html

Elmuti, D., & Kathawala, Y. (2001). An overview of strategic alliances. *Management Decision 39*(3), 205–217.

Enrique Pichon-Rivière. (n.d.). In *Wikipedia*. Retrieved January 2, 2014, from http://en.wikipedia.org/wiki/Enrique_Pichon-Rivi%C3%A8re

Ertel, D. (2004). Getting past yes: Negotiating as if implementation mattered. *Harvard Business Review, 82*, 60–68.

Feller, A., Shunk, D., & Callerman, T. (2006). Value chains verses supply chains. *BPTrends, March*, 1–7.

Ferraz Meyer, L. F. (2006). The commons dilemma revisited: Toward an integral approach. Retrieved April 6, 2014, from http://www.tede.ufv.br/tedesimplificado/tde_arquivos/5/TDE-2009-05-21T075914Z-1615/Publico/texto%20completo.PDF

Fisher, R., & Ury, W. (1983). *Getting to yes.* New York: The Penguin Group.

Flaherty, J. (2010). *Coaching: Evoking excellence in others* (3rd ed.) Burlington: Butterworth-Heinemann.

Fox, J. (2008). *The essential Moreno: Writings on psychodrama, group method, and spontaneity by J.L. Moreno, M.D.* New Paltz: Tusitala, Print.

Franzoi, S. L. (2007). History of social psychology. In R. Baumeister & K. Vohs (Eds.), *Encyclopedia of social psychology* (pp. 431–439). Thousand Oaks, CA: Sage.

Friedman, B., & Neuman Allen, K. (2011). Systems theory. In J. Brandell (Ed.), *Theory and practice of clinical social work* (pp. 3–19). New York: The Free Press.

Fuhs, Clint. (2013). In favor of translation: Researching perspectival growth in organizational leaders. Retrieved December 15, 2013, from https://foundation.metaintegral.org/sites/default/files/Fuhs_ITC2013.pdf

Garvin, D. A., & Roberto, M. A. (2001). What you don't know about making decisions. *Harvard Business Review, 9*(1), 108–116.

Goldman, D. (2004). What makes a leader? *Harvard Business Review, January.* Retrieved July 30, 2006, from https://hbr.org/2004/01/what-makes-a-leader

Graves, C. W. (1974). Human nature prepares for a momentous leap. *The Futurist, 8*(2), 72–87.

Graves, C. W. (2005). *The never ending quest: A treatise on an emergent cyclical conception of adult behavioral systems and their development.* Santa Barbara: ECLET.

Griffin, E. (2003). *A first look at communication theory.* New York: McGraw-Hill.

Grinberg, L., Sor, D., & Tabak de Bianchedi, E. (1977). *Introduction to the work of Bion.* New York: Jason Aronson.

Group dynamics. (n.d.). In *Wikipedia.* Retrieved January 1, 2014, from http://en.wikipedia.org/wiki/Group_dynamics

Group psychotherapy. (n.d.). In *Wikipedia.* Retrieved January 1, 2014, from http://en.wikipedia.org/wiki/Group_psychotherapy

Hackman, J. R. (2011, June 7). *Six common misconceptions about teamwork.* Harvard Business Review Blog Network. Retrieved January 2, 2014, from https://hbr.org/2011/06/six-common-misperceptions-abou/

Hackman, J. R. (2009, May). Why teams don't work. *Harvard Business Review, 87,* 99–105

Hallowell, R. (2009). Humberto Maturana and Francisco Verela's contribution to media ecology: Autopoiesis, the Santiago School of Cognition, and enactive cognitive science. *Media Ecology Association,* 10, 143–158.

Hamilton, Craig. (2004). Come together: The mystery of collective intelligence. *What Is Enlightenment?,* 25(5), 58–79.

Hardin, D., & Rigby, D. (2009). *Winning in turbulence: Pursue game-changing m&a and partnership.* Boston: Harvard Business Press.

Hardin, G. (1968) The tragedy of the commons: The population problem has no technical solution; it requires a fundamental extension in morality. *SCIENCE, 162*(9), 1243–1248.

Herasymowych, M., & Senko, H. (2004). "Positive" systems archetypes. *The Systems Thinker, 15*(5), 6–8.

Herman, N. G., Cary, J. M., & Kennedy, J. E. (2001). *Legal counseling and negotiating: A practical approach.* New York: Matthew Bender & Co.

Heron, J., & Reason, P. (1999). *The practice of co-operative inquiry: Research with rather than on people.* Sage Publications.

Hill, L., & Anteby, M. J. (2006). *Analyzing work groups: Case study.* Boston. Harvard Business Publishing.

History. (n.d.). *University of Michigan: Research Center for Group Dynamics.* Retrieved February 1, 2014, from http://www.rcgd.isr.umich.edu/history/

Hopper, E., & Weinberg, H. (2011). *The social unconscious in persons, groups, and societies.* London: Karnac Books Ltd.

Hughes, J., & Weiss, J. (2007). Simple rules for making alliances work. *Harvard Business Review, 11*(1), 1–9.

IBM Institute for Business Value. (2012). Leading through connections: Highlights of the global chief executive officer study. Retrieved May 12, 2013, from http://www-01.ibm.com/common/ssi/cgi-bin/ssialias?subtype=XB&infotype=PM&appname=GBSE_GB_TI_USEN&htmlfid=GBE03535USEN&attachment=GBE03535USEN.PDF#loaded.

IMAP. (2012). *Global Pharma & Biotech M&A Report.* Switzerland: Author.

Iñón, C. (1997).Vectores del cono invertido. *Scribd.* Retrieved December 4, 2013, from http://www.scribd.com/doc/7105834/Vectores-Del-Cono-Invertido#scribd

Isaacs, W. (1999). *Dialogue and the art of thinking together: A pioneer approach to communicating in business and in life.* New York: Doubleday.

Jacob L. Moreno. (n.d.). In *Wikipedia.* Retrieved January 2, 2014, from http://en.wikipedia.org/wiki/Jacob_L._Moreno

Jasiner, G. (2011). *Coordinando grupos: Una lógica para los pequeños grupos.* Buenos Aires: Lugar Editorial.

Jung, C. G. (1969). *On the Nature of the Psyche* (Vol. 8). Princeton: Princeton-Bollingen.

Kahane, A. (2012). *Transformative scenario planning: Working together to change the future.* San Francisco: Berrett-Koeher Publishers.

Kahneman, D. (2011). *Thinking fast and slow.* New York: Farrar, Staus and Giroux.

Kale, P., & Singh, H. (2009). Managing strategic alliances: What do we know now, and where do we go from here? *Academy of Management Perspectives, 23*(3), 45–62.

Kania, J., & Kramer, M. (2013). Embracing emergence: How collective impact addresses complexity. *Stanford Social Innovation Review, 21*(1), 1–7.

Kaplan, R. S., Norton, D. P., & Rugelsjoen, B. (2013). Managing alliances with the balanced scorecard. *Harvard Business Review, 1*(1), 1-9.

Katz, M. S. (2013). *Metaphor and fields: Common ground, common language and the future of psychoanalysis.* New York: Routeledge.

Kaufman, R., & Watkins, R. (2000). Getting serious about results and payoffs: We are what we say, do and deliver. *Performance Improvement, 4*(1), 1–16.

Kegan, R., & Laskow Lahey, L. (2009). *Immunity to change: How to overcome it and unlock the potential in yorself and your organization.* Boston: Harvard Business Press.

Kegan, R., & Laskow Lahey, L. (2001). The real reason people won't change. *Harvard Business Review: On Point, 11*(1), 85–93.

Kira, M., & M. van Eijnatten, F. (2008). Socially sustainable work organizations: A chaordic systems approach. *Systems Research and Behavioral Science, 25*(9), 743–756.

Klein, R. (2009). *El trabajo grupal: cuando pensar es hacer.* Buenos Aires: Lugar Editorial.

Kleindorfer, P. R., Wind, Y., & Gunther, R. E. (2009). *The network challenge: Strategy, profit, and risk in an interlinked world.* Upper Saddle River: Prentice Hall Publishing.

Kleiner, A. (2008). *The age of heretics: A history of the radical thinkers who reinvented corporate management* (2nd ed.). San Francisco: Jossey-Bass.

Kolb, D. A. (1984). *Experiential Learning*. Englewood Cliffs, NJ: Prentice Hall, Inc.

Kożuch, B. (2009). The culture of collaboration: Theoretical aspects. *Journal of Intercultural Management, 1*(2), 17–29.

KPMG. (2012). *Why strategic alliances are now in fashion*. Germany: Yuk, Kwan, Pam.

Kramer, M. R. (2011). Crating shared value. *Harvard Business Review, 1*(1), 2–17.

Kudelka, P. (2013). Consciousness and "levels of existence". (Thesis, University of Vienna. Ann Arbor: ProQuest/UMI, 2013). *Publication No. 0500551*.

Kurt Lewin: Groups, Experiential Learning and Action Research. (2001). *In The Encyclopedia of Informal Education* (1st ed.). Retrieved June 27, 2014, from http://infed.org/mobi/kurt-lewin-groups-experiential-learning-and-action-research/.

Kurt Lewin. (n.d.). In *Wikipedia*. Retrieved January 1, 2014, from http://en.wikipedia.org/wiki/Kurt_Lewin

La Piana, D. (2010, Spring). Merging wisely. *Stanford Innovation Review, 8*(2), 28–55.

Lakoff, G., & Johnson, M. (1980). *Metaphors we live by*. Chicago: The University of Chicago Press.

Laszlo, A., & Krippner, S. (1998). Systems theories: Their origins, foundations and development. *Elsevier Science, 3*(1), 47–74.

Learning organization. (n.d.). In *Wikipedia*. Retrieved January 2, 2014, from http://en.wikipedia.org/wiki/Learning_organization

Leibner, J., & Mader, G. (2012). Strategic commitment: Creating the organizational environment that turns apathy, compliance and defiance into exceptional performance. (White paper). Retrieved July 15, 2014, from http://strategiccommitment.com/wp/wp-content/uploads/2012/02/StrategicCommitment-whitepaper.pdf

Lewin, K. (1997). *Resolving social conflicts: Field theory in social science*. Washington: American Psychological Association.

Lewin, K. (1948). *Resolving social conflicts*. New York: Harper & Brothers.

Lewin, K. (1947). Frontiers in group dynamics: concept, method and reality in social science; social equilibria and social change. *Human Relations, 1,* 143–153.

Lewis, J. D. (1999). *Trusted partners: How companies build mutual trust and win together*. New York: The Free Press.

Lewis, J. D. (1990). *Partnerships for profit: Structuring and managing strategic alliances*. New York: The Free Press.

Lewis, T., Amini, F., & Lannon, R. (2001). *A general theory of love.* New York: Vintage Books.

Listado de las Teorías de la Organización. (n.d.). Retreived February 12, 2014, from http://www.scribd.com/doc/159635717/teoria-de-las-organizaciones#scribd

Littlejohn, S. W., & Foss, K. A. (2011). *Theories of human communication.* Long Grove: Waveland Press.

Lowen, A. (1994). *Bioenergetics.* New York: The Penguin Group.

Maggio, L. (2012). Espiral dialéctica: concepto central como ontología relacional en la teoría de Pichón Rivere. *KAIROS, 16*(29), 1–7.

Maglo, D. (2002). Kierkegaard and Foulkes: The advantages of group therapy in treatment of despair ('… a sickness of the spirit, of the self …'). *The Group-Analytic Society, 35*(10), 27–42.

Mañanero Brito, R., & Villamil Uñarte, R. (2004). Reflexiones sobre la practica grupal. *TRAMAS, 21,* 99–121.

Marshall, E. M. (1995). The collaborative marketplace. *American Management Association, 20–26.*

Martínez, C. R. (2010). *Psicología social en las organizaciones: estrategias tácticas y técnicas para el cambio organizacional.* Buenos Aires: Lugar Editorial.

Maturana, H. R. (2008). Emociones y lenguage en educacion y politica. Retrieved March 14, 2014, from Course Extract Systems Theory Online Web site: http://turismotactico.org/proyecto_pologaraia/wp-content/uploads/2008/01/emociones.pdf

Maturana, H. R. (1988). Reality: The search for objectivity or the quest for a compelling argument. *The Irish Journal, 9*(1), 25–82.

Maturana, H. R., & Varela, F. J. (1980). *Autopoiesis and cognition: The realization of the living.* Dordrecht: Reidel Publishing.

Maturana, H. R., & Verden-Zoller, G. (1996). Biology of love. In G. Opp & F. Peterander (Eds.), *Focus Heilpadagogik.* Germany: Ernst Reinhardt.

Mawson, C. (2011). *Bion today.* New York: Routledge.

McCain, R. A. Cooperative games and cooperative organizations. *Journal of Socio-Economics, 37*(6), 2155–2167.

McCauley, C. D., Drath, W. H., Palus, C. J., M.G. O'Connor, P., & Baker, B. A. (2006). The use of constructive-developmental theory to advance the understanding of leadership. *The Leadership Quarterly,* 634–653.

McKee, R. (2003). Storytelling that moves people: A conversation with screenwriting coach Robert McKee. *Harvard Business Review, 81*(6), 51–55.

McRae, M. B., & Short, E. L. (2010). *Racial and cultural dynamics in group and organizational life.* Sage Publications, Inc.

Meadows, D. H. (2008). *Thinking in systems, a primer.* White River Junction: Chelsea Green.

Meadows, D. (1999). *Leverage points: Places to intervene in a system.* Hartland, VT: The Sustainability Institute.

Menkel-Meadow, C. (2009). Chronicling the complexion of negotiation theory and practice. *Georgetown Law Faculty Publications, 10*(1), 415–429.

Montgomery, C. (2002). Role of dynamic group therapy in psychiatry. *Journal of Continuing Professional Development, 8*(1), 34–41.

M. Scott Peck. (n.d.). In *Wikipedia.* Retrieved January 2, 2014, from http://en.wikipedia.org/wiki/M._Scott_Peck

Murray, J. S. (1986). Understanding competing theories of negotiation. *Negotiation Journal, 4*(1), 179–186.

Mustieles Muñoz, D. (1993). Intervención grupal con adolescentes de un barrio marginal argentino. *Asociación de Psicoterapia Analítica Grupal,* 257–280.

National Training Laboratories. (n.d.). In *Wikipedia.* Retrieved January 2, 2014, from http://en.wikipedia.org/wiki/National_Training_Laboratories

Neal, C., Neal, P., & Wold, C. (2011). *The art of convening: Authentic engagement in meetings, gatherings, and conversations.* San Francisco: Berrett-Koehler Publishers.

Neumann, J. (n.d.). Kurt Lewin- Field Theory Rule. *The Tavistock Institute.* Retreived March 23, 2014, from http://www.tavinstitute.org/

Object relations theory. (n.d.). In *Wikipedia.* Retrieved November 16, 2014, from http://en.wikipedia.org/wiki/Object_relations_theory

Ohmae, Kenichi. (1982). *The mind of the strategist: The art of japanese business.* New York: McGraw-Hill.

Orgaz, M., & Ferreyra, N. (2013). Una experiencia de intervención organizacional en el "vector comunicación". *Escuela de Psicología Grupal y Análisis Institucional.* Retrieved from February 27, 2013, from http://www.psicologiagrupal.cl/escuela/index.php?option=com_content&view=article&id=228:una-experiencia-de-intervencion-organizacional-en-el-vector-comunicacion&catid=43:articulos&Itemid=69.

Owen, Harrison. (1997). *Open space technology: A user's guide* (2nd ed.). San Francisco: Berrett-Koehler Publishers.

Pain, R., Whitman, G., & Milledge, D. (2010). *Participatory action research toolkit: An introduction to using par as an approach to learning, research and action.* Durham, UK: Durham University.

Palmer, N., Visioni, L., & Weiss, J., Hughes, J., Kliman, S. (2009). Right from the start: The seven virtues of a successful alliance launch. *Vantage Partners.* Retrieved December, 13, 2010, from http://vantagepartners.com/researchandpublications/viewpublications.aspx?id=1699.

Partnership. (n.d.). In *Wikipedia.* Retrieved September 25, 2013, from http://en.wikipedia.org/wiki/Partnership

Pentland, A. (2012). The new science of building great teams. *Harvard Business Review, 61–70.*

Persall, J., & Bill, T. (1995). Entry Name. Def. Number. *The Oxford English Reference Dictionary* (2nd ed.).

Pichón-Riviere, E. (2011). *El proceso grupal: del psicoanálisis a la psicología social* (2nd ed.). Buenos Aires: Nueva Visión.

Pichón Riviere, E. *Problema institucional.* Retrieved September, 14, 2013, from Escuela de Psicologia Social del Sur Web site: http://www.psicosocialdelsur.com.ar/contenido.asp?idtexto=34

Poole, M. S., Hollingshead, A. B., McGrath, J. E., Moreland, R. L., & Rohrbaugh, J. (2004). Interdisciplinary perspectives on small groups. *Small Group Research. Spec. issue of Small Group Research, 35*(1), 3–16.

Porter, M. E. (2012, May 1). Creating shared value: *The path forward.* FSG Shared Valued Leadership Summit, Harvard Business School. Boston, MA. Retrieved October 1, 2013, from http://www.fsg.org/Portals/0/Uploads/Documents/2012_Summit_Porter_Keynote.pdf

Porter, M. E. (1997). How competitive forces shape strategy. *Harvard Business Review, 7*(1), 2–10.

Porter, M. E. (1996). What is strategy? *Harvard Business Review, 11*(1), 60–78.

Porter, M. E., & Kramer, M.R. (2011). Creating shared value: How to reinvent capitalism and unleash a wave of innovation and growth. *Harvard Business Review, 1*(1), 2–17.

Porter, M. E., Hills, G., Pfitzer, M., Patscheke, S., Hawkins, E. (n.d.). Measuring shared value: How to unlock value by linking social and business results. *FSG.* Retrieved October, 1 2013, from http://www.fsg.org/Portals/0/Uploads/Documents/PDF/Measuring_Shared_Value.pdf

Positive interdependence. (n.d.). In *Wikipedia*. Retrieved May 9, 2014, from http://en.wikipedia.org/wiki/Positive_interdependence

Prinsloo, Maretha. (2012, June). Consciousness models in action: Comparisons. *Integral Leadership Review*. Retrieved March 24, 2014, from http://integralleadershipreview.com/tag/maretha-prinsloo/

Psychodrama. (n.d.). In *Wikipedia*. Retrieved June 3, 2014, from http://en.wikipedia.org/wiki/Psychodrama

Raelin, J. (2006). Does action learning promote collaborative leadership? *Academy of Management Learning & Education, 5*(2), 158–168.

Reason, P., & Bradbury, H. (2008). *The SAGE handbook of action research* (2nd ed.) London: Sage Publications.

Reason, P. (1999). Integrating action and reflection through co-operative inquiry. *Management Learning, 30,* 207–225.

Restrepo Ruiz, F. (2005, June). Reflexiones en torno al concepto de tarea en el grupo opeartivo. *Poiésis, 9.* Retreived August 20, 2013, from Fundación Universitaria Luis Amigó Web Site: http://www.funlam.edu.co/revistas/index.php/poiesis/article/view/483/458

Riechmann, J. (2010). *La habitación de pascal.* Madrid: Catarata.

Ries, E. (2011). *The lean startup: How today's entrepreneurs use continuous innovation to create radically successful business.* New York: Crown Business.

Ritterstein, P. (2008). *Aprendizaje y vínculo: una mirada sobre el aprendizaje: Enrique Pichón Rivere y Paulo Freire.* Retrieved October 24, 2013, from Universidad de Buenos Aires Web site: http://www.catedras.fsoc.uba.ar/ferraros/BD/pr%20aprendizaje%20y%20vinculo.pdf

Roemischer, J. (2002). The never-ending upward quest. *What Is Enlightenment?, 22*(3), 4–24.

Rooke, D., & Torbert, W. R. (2005). Seven transformations of leadership. *Harvard Business Review, 4*(1), 1–12.

Rowe, M. (2002). *Negotiation: Theory and practice.* Retrieved July 17, 2014, from MIT: http://ocw.mit.edu/courses/sloan-school-of-management/15-667-negotiation-and-conflict-management-spring-2001/study-materials/negotiation101.pdf

Rubenstein, H. (1996). Rev the death of competition: Leadership and strategy in the age of business ecosystems. *Harper Business.* Retrieved September 3, 2012, from http://www.herbrubenstein.com/articles/THE-DEATH-OF-COMPETITION.pdf.

Salvino, M. J. (2012). Partners in high performance. *Outlook 2*(1), 2–9.

Salvo Spinatelli, J. (2007). Psicología social: Enrique Pichón Rivere. Retrieved August 20, 2013, from Universidad de la República Web site: http://www.psico.edu.uy/sites/default/files/cursos/int-teorias_enrique.pdf

Schein, E. H. (1999). *Process consultation revisited: Building the helping relationship.* Reading: Addison-Wesley.

Schein, E. H. (1995). Kurt Lewin's change theory in the field and in the classroom: Notes toward a model of managed learning. *Systems Practice 3821,* 1–33.

Schelling, T. C. (1980). *The strategy of conflict* (2nd ed.) Cambridge: The Harvard Business Press.

Schvarstein, L. (1992). *Relaciones entre lo manifiesto y lo latente. Psicología social de las organizaciones.* Buenos Aires: Paidos.

SD in action: Myths and metaphors. (n.d.). *Spiral dynamics.* Retreived October 6, 2013, from [LINK].

Seagal, S., & Horne, D. (1997). *Human dynamics: A new framework for understanding people and realizing the potential in our organizations.* Waltham: Pegasus Communications.

Senge, P. M. (2006). *The fifth discipline: The art & practice of the learning organization* (2nd ed.). New York: Doubleday.

Senge, P. M., Kleiner, A., Roberts, C., Ross, R. B., & Smith, B. J. (1994). *The fifth discipline fieldbook: Strategies and tools for building a learning organization.* New York: Doubleday.

Shaphiro, D. L. (2010, October). Relational identity theory: A systematic approach for transforming the emotional dimension of conflict. *American Psychologist,* 634–645.

S.H. Foulkes. (n.d.). In *Wikipedia.* Retrieved January 4, 2014, from http://en.wikipedia.org/wiki/S._H._Foulkes

Slobodnik, A., & Wile, K. (1999). Taking the teeth out of team traps. *The Systems Thinker, 10*(9), 1–5.

Social group. (n.d.). In *Wikipedia.* Retrieved from January 2, 2014, from http://en.wikipedia.org/wiki/Social_group

Social trap. (n.d.). In *Wikipedia.* Retrieved from Septem ber 25, 2013, from http://en.wikipedia.org/wiki/Social_trap

Stacey, M., & Torbert, B. (2013, June). *Action inquiry: Transforming leadership in the midst of action.* Lecture presented at the ALIA Summer Institute, Halifax, Nova Scotia. Lecture notes retrieved June 24, 2014, from http://aliainstitute.org/blog/track/action-inquiry-transforming-leadership-in-the-midst-of-action/

Steinhilber, S. (2008). *Strategic alliances: Three ways to make them work.* Boston: The Harvard Business Press.

Strachey, J. (1967). *Sigmund Freud: Group psychology and the analysis of the ego.* London: The Hogarth Press.

Strategic partnerships: The real deal? (2009). PricewaterhouseCoopers. Retrieved March, 25, 2013, from http://www.pwc.co.uk/en_UK/uk/assets/pdf/strategic-partnerships-the-real-deal.pdf

Swann Jr., W. B., & Bosson, J. K. (2008). Identity negotiation: A theory of self and social interaction. In O. John R. Robins, & L. Pervin (Eds.) *Handbook of personality: Theory and research,* 3rd ed. (pp. 448–471). New York: Guilford Press.

Tajfel, H. (1981). *Human groups and social categories: Studies in social psychology.* Cambridge: CUP Archive.

The Boston Consulting Group. (2005). *The role of alliances in corporate strategy.* United States: Author

Thomson, A. M., & Perry, J. L. (2006). Collaboration processes: Inside the black box. *Public Administration Review. December Special Issue*

Tironi, Ernesto. Humberto Maturana: Emociones y Lenguaje en Educación y Política. *Curso de Teoria de Sistemas. n.p. n.d.* Seminar.

Todeva, E., & Knoke, D. (2005). Strategic alliances & models of collaboration. *Management Decision, 43*(1), 123–148.

Torbert, W. and Associates. (2004). *Action inquiry: The secret of timely and transforming leadership.* San Francisco: Berrett-Koehler.

Trigant Burrow. (n.d.). In *Wikipedia.* Retrieved January 2, 2014, from http://en.wikipedia.org/wiki/Trigant_Burrow

Tubert-Oklander, J. & Hernández de Tubert, R. (2004). *Operative groups: The Latin-American approach to group analysis.* London: Jessica Kingsley Publishers.

Tubert-Oklander, J. (2014). *The one and the many: Relational psychoanalysis and group analysis.* London: Karnac Books Ltd.

Tubert-Oklander, J. (2013). *Theory of psychoanalytical practice: A relational process approach.* London: Karnac Books Ltd. Print.

Tuckman, B. W. (2001). Developmental sequence in small groups. *Group Development. Spec. issue of Psychological Bulletin, 63*(6), 66–79.

Unilever. (2013). *Annual report and accounts.* United Kingdom. London: Author.

Unilever Foundation. (2013). *Building better lives for a sustainable future.* United Kingdom. London: Author.

Urch, V., & Wolff, S. B. (2001). Building the emotional intelligence of groups. *Harvard Business Review 3*(1), 81–90.

Value system. (n.d.). In *Wikipedia.* Retrieved March 25, 2014, from http://en.wikipedia.org/wiki/Value_system

Vanpoucke, E., & Vereecke, A. (2009). *The predictive value of behavioral characteristics on the success of strategic alliances.* Belgium: Vlerick Leuven Gent Mangement School.

Von Bertalanffy, L. (1968). *Organismic psychology and systems theory.* Barre: The Barre Publishing Company.

Von Bertalanffy, L. (1968). *General system theory: Foundations, development, applications.* New York: George Braziller.

Wahyuni, S. (2003). *Strategic alliances development: A study on alliances between competing firms.* The Netherlands: Labyrint Publications.

Weick, K. E. (1976). Educational organizations as loosely coupled systems. *Administrative Science Quarterly, 21*(1), 1–19.

Weick, K. E. (1969). Information systems approach to organizations. In E. Griffin (Ed.), *A First Look at Communication* (pp. 278–288). New York: McGraw-Hill Retreived August 30, 2013 from http://www.afirstlook.com/docs/infosystems.pdf

Wilber, K. (2000). *A brief history of everything* (2nd ed.). Boston: Shambhala.

Wilber, K. (2000) *Integral psychology: Consciousness, spirit, psychology, therapy.* Boston: Shambhala.

Wilfred Bion. (n.d.). In *Wikipedia.* Retrieved from January 2, 2014, from http://en.wikipedia.org/wiki/Wilfred_Bion

Williams Woolley, A., & Caruso, H. M. (2008). Harnessing the power of emergent interdependence to promote diverse team collaboration. In Eduardo Salas (Ed.), *Diversity and groups (research on managing groups and teams)* (pp. 245–266). Oxford: Emerald Group Publishing Limited.

Wundt, W. *The history of social psychology.* Unpublished manuscript. Retrieved January 4, 2013, from http://highered.mheducation.com/sites/dl/free/0073370592/640244/The_History_of_Social_Psychology.doc

Yontef, G. (2002). The relational attitude in gestalt theory and practice. *International Gestalt Journal 25*(1), 15–34.

1 http://en.wikipedia.org/wiki/Selling. *Wikipedia,* 25 Sept. 2013.

2 http://www.oed.com/. *Oxford English Dictionary,* 25 Sept. 2013.

4 http://www.oed.com/. *Oxford English Dictionary,* 25 Sept. 2013.

INTRODUCTION TO MARTIN ECHAVARRIA

Martin Echavarria has focused his professional career on collaboration, the nexus where individuals and small groups come together to work productively. From building strategic alliances and partnerships across industries, culture, and geographies, to coaching executives and their teams to collaborate effectively, Martin has successfully combined alliance development know-how with collaborative-leadership methodologies.

He has over 15 years' experience of enabling strategic collaborations between global companies. He earned a Master's Degree in International Management from Thunderbird School of Global Management, a Bachelor's Degree in Business and Political Science from Emory University, and studied strategic alliances at the Wharton School, Integral Coaching at New Ventures West and Leadership for Collective Intelligence at Dialogos.

He has dedicated himself to the identification and creation of alliances through his consulting company, Coherence (www.coherence360.com) and has also built a successful executive leadership coaching career. Committed to collaboration, Martin has worked in alliance development and coaching with Verizon, Hewlett-Packard, American Express, MasterCard, Scotiabank, PriceSmart, Digicel, Orange Telecom, Bunge, Tam Airlines, Continental Airlines and many others.